MY FATHER'S WARS

"My father was born into war," begins this remarkable saga in Alisse Waterston's intimate ethnography, a story that is also twentieth-century social history. This is an anthropologist's vivid account of her father's journey across continents, countries, cultures, languages, generations—and wars. It is a daughter's moving portrait of a charming, funny, wounded, and difficult man, his relationships with those he loved, and his most sacred of beliefs. And it is a scholar's reflection on the dramatic forces of history, the experience of exile and immigration, the legacies of culture, and the enduring power of memory. This book is for Anthropology and Sociology courses in qualitative methods, ethnography, violence, migration, and ethnicity.

Alisse Waterston is Professor, Department of Anthropology at John Jay College of Criminal Justice, City University of New York. She is Editor of *Open Anthropology*, the public journal of the American Anthropological Association and President-elect, American Anthropological Association. Professor Waterston is author of two ethnographies on urban poverty in the US (*Love, Sorrow and Rage: Destitute Women in a Manhattan Residence* and *Street Addicts in the Political Economy*), and of the edited volumes *An Anthropology of War: Views from the Frontline* and *Anthropology off the Shelf: Anthropologists on Writing* (co-edited with Maria D. Vesperi). Alisse Waterston is a Soros International Scholar affiliated with Tbilisi State University in Gender Studies, and serves on the Executive Board, American Anthropological Association.

Innovative Ethnographies

Editor: Phillip Vannini

The purpose of this series is to use the new digital technology to capture a richer, more multidimensional view of social life than was otherwise done in the classic, print tradition of ethnography, while maintaining the traditional strengths of classic, ethnographic analysis.

MY FATHER'S WARS

MIGRATION, MEMORY, AND THE VIOLENCE OF A CENTURY

ALISSE WATERSTON

Routledge
Taylor & Francis Group

NEW YORK AND LONDON

First published 2014
by Routledge
711 Third Avenue, New York, NY 10017

Simultaneously published in the UK
by Routledge
2 Park Square, Milton Park, Abingdon, Oxon OX14 4RN

Routledge is an imprint of the Taylor & Francis Group,
an informa business

Library of Congress Cataloging-in-Publication Data

Waterston, Alisse, 1951- author.
My father's wars : migration, memory, and the violence of a century /
Alisse Waterston.
    p. cm. — (Innovative Ethnographies)
    Includes bibliographical references and index.
1. Waterston, Michael, 1913-2006.   2. Jews, Polish—
United Stated—Biography.   3. Jews, Polish—Cuba—
Biography.   4. Jedwabne (Poland)—Biography.   5. Jews—Cuba—
Biography.   6. Jews—United States—Biography.   I. Title.
    E184.37.W38A3 2014
    943.8'3604092—dc23
    2013006503

ISBN: 978-0-415-85917-2 (hbk)
ISBN: 978-0-415-85918-9 (pbk)
ISBN: 978-0-203-79874-4 (ebk)

Typeset in Mrs Eaves
by Apex CoVantage, LLC

Printed and bound in the United States of America by Edwards Brothers Malloy

To my husband
Howard Horowitz
with all my love
The best is yet to be

. . . the life we live is never the one we write, but the written life, two-dimensional and never fully true, is the only one that can be preserved.

John Matteson, *The Lives of Margaret Fuller*

We shall not cease from exploration
And the end of all our exploring
Will be to arrive where we started
And know the place for the first time
T.S. Eliot, *Little Gidding*

www.myfatherswars.com

Readers of the electronic version of books in this series will be able to make use of hyperlinks embedded throughout the text. Readers of the traditional, print-based version of books in this series can access the same web pages by referring to the URLs and directions noted in footnotes. Hyperlinks can be activated by clicking on the words preceding the following symbols:

📷 indicates a *photograph*;

🌐 indicates an interactive Google *map*/Google Earth link;

🔗 indicates an external *web link*;

📹 indicates a *video*;

🎵 indicates music or another type of *audio* file;

🖼 indicates a bonus *multimodal essay*;

💬 indicates an interactive *dialogue* platform such as a blog;

📐 indicates additional information such as a bonus text-based *essay*;

⊞ indicates drawings, sketches, graphics, or other *visual art* displays.

CONTENTS

ACKNOWLEDGMENTS

With the publication of this book, I come to the close of a decade plus-long project that has been guided, nurtured, and supported by many people from different parts of my life. The pieces of this endeavor have finally come together, an effort that has sometimes been very difficult and very painful, and at other times extraordinarily rewarding and pleasurable. Though the words don't adequately capture the truth of the statement, the fact is I could not have accomplished this project without the sustenance I have been so lucky to receive from family, friends, colleagues, and the institutions with which I have been affiliated.

I am deeply grateful to my parents, the heart of this project. Beyond the tribute to my father and my mother on the pages of this book, I thank them for providing me the sense and sensibility to appreciate the displaced, dispossessed, and marginalized, and to push myself towards deeper understanding of the social forces implicated in human suffering. I know my father's experiences of displacement and disenfranchisement have directed me to study outsiders. I know my mother's belief in the principle of inclusiveness—her commitment to union, association, integration, connection—has directed me to pursue "justice, justice," a word written twice. She taught me a form of Judaism that asks, "Why is the word justice written two times?" And she taught me a form of Judaism that responds, "To teach us that we must practice justice at all times, whether it be for our profit or for our loss, and towards all men, Jew and non-Jew alike." By means of this message, my mother left me with hope for a future disarmed from all hostility. So much of contemporary political discourse centers on fear and loathing, words that lead to even more violence, destruction, and death. I hope this book can become part of a different conversation, one focused on empathy, understanding, and reconciliation—what my mother would call "all-embracing love."

My colleagues, students, and administrators at John Jay College of Criminal Justice, City University of New York, deserve acknowledgment for providing me collegial support over the years of this project. A special thank you goes to Ric Curtis, the most wonderful department chair who always finds a way to support my work, and to John Matteson, Suzanne Oboler, Barbara Price, Robert Riggs, Ed Snajdr, and Shonna Trinch for their friendship, their early reading and suggestions, and their ongoing encouragement. I appreciate the kind generosity of President Jeremy Travis, Provost Jane Bowers, and Dean Anne Lopes of John Jay College. I am very grateful to have received the honor and financial support of the Mellon Faculty Fellowship at the Graduate Center, City University of New York, Committee for the Study of Religion (2011), the PSC-CUNY Research Award (2005–2006 and 2007–2008), and the John Jay College Research Assistance Award (2005–2006). I also extend many thanks to Richard Grinker (editor, *Anthropological Quarterly*) and Virginia Dominguez (past editor, *American Ethnologist*) who provided important support for this project by publishing its early iterations. I also acknowledge Bryan Turner and Anthem Press who published a chapter based on my "Poland narratives" in *War and Peace: Essays on Religion, Violence, and Space*.

It has been very gratifying to work with Phillip Vannini, editor of the Routledge Series on Innovative Ethnographies, graphic designer Kate O'Rourke, my editor Samantha Barbaro, production editor Emma Elder, editorial assistant Margaret Moore, copyeditor Neil Dowden, and cover designer Tom Hussey at Routledge. I thank them for their enthusiastic support and the careful attention they have given the book. I also extend special thanks to my research assistant Sebastian Chrostowski who also served as my Polish-language translator.

I extend my heartfelt thanks to the entire "Danielski" family from Łomża and Jedwabne in Poland, and Greenpoint, Brooklyn in New York, for so warmly welcoming me into their lives, for their generosity of spirit, and for providing me important information and insight.

I wish to express my warmest gratitude to family, friends, and colleagues, many of whom were readers who helped me assess what I had written—what I might revise, and what I might trust in and keep. I thank Maria-Luisa Achino-Loeb, Patricia Antoniello, Lee Baker, Avi Bornstein, Arachu Castro, Shuki Cohen, Paul Farmer, Blair Ford, Gelya Frank, Carol Greenhouse, Faye Harrison, Samuel Heilman, Jack Jacobs, Victoria Klein, Nancy K. Miller, Leith Mullings, Carolyn Nordstrom, Neni Panourgiá, Caroline Reitz, Oona Schmid, Abby Stein, Terri Teleen, Stephen Tolkin, and Maria D. Vesperi. I acknowledge the extraordinary support of my reviewers: Tim Black, Case Western Reserve; Joan Cassell, Washington University, St. Louis; Mary Patrice Erdmans, Case Western

Reserve; and Fran Mascia-Lees, Rutgers University. I especially want to thank Barbara Rylko-Bauer, my fellow traveler in the new territory we call intimate ethnography.

My amazing family has supported me on all levels and at every stage of this project. I thank my sister Linda and her son Andres for their interest in this project, and am very grateful to my sister Jessica for the constancy of her support. To David, a wonderful cinematographer, photographer, and brother, I extend many thanks for his enthusiasm and his assistance. To Adrienne, my sister who is also my confidante, I thank her for the unwavering confidence she has shown in the project, the book, and in me. Her daughter, Micaela Louise, named for our parents, is our family's cherished one and delight. I am deeply grateful to my dearest friend Claudia Brandt Arioli, who has been with me from the beginning. I also appreciate the support of Beth Zuckerman, Roberta Horowitz, Zelia Ferreira, Helen Oxenberg, Elaine Horowitz, and Sidney Horowitz who also helped me with Yiddish translations.

I am grateful to my beautiful daughter Leah for her love and our special bond. I thank her for her patience and deep understanding as she grew up alongside the development of this project and book. My son Matthew gives me a special kind of sustenance, as true now as when I wrote those same words two decades ago in my first book. I thank him for his love and his friendship, and for the care he has shown to this project, including reading and commenting on multiple versions of the manuscript. Matthew's company, BZ Worldwide, created the companion website (www.myfatherswars.com). I am grateful to him and Berry Blanton for the extraordinary result.

My husband Howard gets my love and appreciation, though he deserves a medal for bearing with this project and with me. I haven't made it easy, and am beyond grateful for his unfailing support. I thank him for so willingly participating in the ritual I invented: each night I read aloud to him what I had written that day. He listened and read, discussed every idea, and offered honest critique and enthusiastic praise. Howie and I share a common understanding of what is amiss in the world, conceptions and sensibilities that sustain us. For his belief in me, and for his perceptiveness and perspective, I dedicate this book to him.

Credits

PROLOGUE

Why remember, to what end, and in what way? . . . The task is not only to remember but to remember strenuously—to explode, decode, and deepen the terrain of memory. What is at stake is not only the past but the present.

Eva Hoffman, *Shtetl* (1997: 13–14)

This is a story that is also a history. It is the story of my father's travels across continents, countries, cultures, languages, generations, and wars. It is a daughter's account of a Jewish father whose life was shaped, framed, and torn apart by the upheavals of the twentieth century. It is an anthropologist's narrative constructed from other people's stories. It is a portrait of a charming, funny, wounded, and difficult man, his relationships with those he loved, and his most sacred of beliefs. And it is a reflection on the forces of history, the power of memory, and the meanings people attach to events, things, words, and others.

My Father's Wars is an intimate ethnography, a term I developed with my friend and colleague Barbara Rylko-Bauer. "Intimate ethnography" captures my approach to this project: I came to my father as a daughter who is a cultural anthropologist. The two roles were inseparable: I am a daughter who chronicled a family narrative, and I am an anthropologist who contextualized the story.[1] Intimate ethnography brings together the dualities, liberating the daughter to enter a deeply private and interior place as an ethnographer.

The dual, daughter–anthropologist role makes it difficult to place this book in an established genre. It is not just my father's biography, not just his narrated memoir; it is not about the anthropologist, not about the daughter; nor is it only about cultural frameworks or national histories or the violence that wreaked havoc during my father's lifetime. It is about all these things at once. Thus the term "intimate ethnography" for it captures the approach I used in this project.

I can't say I have one reason for pursuing this difficult, often painful project, and for writing this book. Like my father's life, his perception of it and his narrative, my motivations are layered and complicated involving who I am as an anthropologist and as a daughter. I am at a point in my life where the urge to reflect on personal history is quite strong. Who was this man with whom I had such difficulty? It took years before I would realize how my father's story shaped my sensibility, and to recognize that his sorrows became my sorrows, his losses my motivation to understand them.[2] And now, at the close of this project, I feel I do have a fuller understanding of this complicated, and in many ways, ordinary man.

Yet I came to this project not just as a daughter but also as an anthropologist seeking to understand how various forms of violence are implicated in individual stories. My central assumption is that twentieth-century political and structural violence explains as much as it is something to be explained. It is commonplace to consider personal identity, interpersonal relationships, and why people do what they do in psychological terms. It is also common to understand social identity and social relations in cultural terms. Yet it is rare that political and structural violence are explored for their roles in shaping the course and quality of human lives.

In this book, I start with the personal for clues to the broader history that is also implicated in the damage, illuminating the factors at play in multiple forms of oppression and conflict. Either–or categories are replaced with multiplicities so that brutality and humaneness, dehumanization and compassion, pathos and humor, displacement and adaptation, and memory and identity permeate at once, revealing tensions between narrative and history that is as true in life as they are in this book. The task has been to unravel some of the complex processes and dynamics of a history marked by violence, and consider the consequences of that history for an ordinary, unfamous man, and by implication, any person in any place thus affected.

I center my own father as subject of this anthropological work. My approach does not conform to disciplinary convention nor does the voice and structure of this book conform to academic or popular narrative style. My goal is not to scrutinize or stretch the methodological boundaries of scholarly or narrative traditions. Instead, I hope to draw readers into a compelling account of one man's movements across a violent century, illuminating along the way the specific ideological and systemic forces implicated in his story that have resonance for contemporary social conditions and dynamics. My father's story highlights the ways in which we are all participant–observers of such violence. The current condition of our world, marked as it is by the shadows of war and genocidal violence, of ethnic conflict, nationalist fervor, and everyday violence, adds urgency to my task.

There is a schism between what scholars produce in academic settings and what gets read outside it. For example, anthropologists know a lot about how social categories are produced, how difference is constructed and can be turned into ideological infection. They know a lot about the macro dynamics of power, past and present, how it works to infiltrate, shape, and manage human lives, and how violence gets normalized. Somehow these analyses get lost in translation when scholars try to share them with audiences beyond the academy. Because I accept Hoffman's premise that the present as much as the past is at stake, I have been guided by a sense of urgency to produce this hybrid work, bridging story and scholarship by means of this intimate ethnography.

I have long struggled to link individual stories to larger histories, to make tangible with words those points of connection between the self and the world that often seem so difficult to grasp. James Baldwin can declare, "people are trapped in history and history is trapped in them," a beautiful dialectic that may resonate as true, but the question remains: how to effectively reveal it? This was my narrative challenge.

I have chosen to tell a story, writing in the third-person omniscient, past tense, privileging the primacy of my father's experience. To a large degree, my narrative is based on his rendition of his life history; his actual words, and the texture, syntax, and sensation of his voice are woven into the description. I lay out the specific features of my father's biography, from birth to death, in segments by time, place, culture, social category (gender, religion), politics and political events (including war and revolution), relationships to larger social groups (ethnic, nation, race, religion, land, labor, work) and broad as well as local historical events. There is mood, feel, aura, flavor, sensibility, image, character, moments, all captured in the story part of the book. There are aspects to the story that are plain facts ("Mendel was born in Jedwabne, Poland"). There are other aspects that reveal cultural truths ("he was born around Purim time"), and still others that offer hints of something deeper, not apparent on the surface ("My father's *shtetle*"). Each of these aspects appears throughout the book.

There is also the first-person voice of the daughter–anthropologist who brings in her experiences with her father, and additional information, facts, figures, events, as well as cultural and political analysis, edging out from the personal to the larger history, all of it to contextualize the main story. The focus is not on one historical moment. Instead, several major historical events over the course of a long transnational history are traced.

The structure of the book is actually quite straightforward: every chapter has two main subsections. The first section is devoted to the story, my narrative of my father's narrative, informed also by others' narratives, evidence, and information.

The second section of each chapter gives voice to the daughter–anthropologist who fills in some gaps in the story and fleshes it out with larger history.

Whereas biographies of key actors in history lend themselves to a single narrative voice, for an ethnographic subject, the connection between a life and larger events is indirect and nonlinear. In my father's case, he had limited awareness of the happenings outside his control that shaped his own course as well as those whose lives did or might have intersected with his. The two-part structure I use in this book reflects how my father thought about and experienced his life— separate and apart from the complexities of the larger historical context of which he was a part. It's not that he was oblivious to the events, but he was unaware of their structural and systemic roots. This idea is captured in a stanza from Bertolt Brecht's poem "On Violence":

> The headlong stream is termed violent
> But the river bed hemming it in is
> Termed violent by no one.[3]

Like most, my father only saw the headlong stream; the violence of the river bed remained imperceptible.

Still, my father was a "subject who remembered."[4] My depiction shows him as I knew him—with his strengths and his vulnerabilities, his flaws and his virtues, his insights and his ignorance, neither all-good nor all-bad, just real. It shows his individuality and his humanity even as I discover in him traces of collective memory and locate his place in society and history. It is the very aspect of balancing these dimensions that represents the strength of intimate ethnography, a method that allows me to humanize and historicize one man's internal battles amidst the wars of the world.

I

The *Shtetl* Jedwabne

My father was born into war.

"In those days, in that part of the world, the Germans were good to the Jews, much better than the Russians," my father Mendel would say. My father, born Menachem Mendel Wasersztejn, told me all about it, as much as he could remember. Well, he told me as much as he could recite, having heard many of the stories himself when he was just a little boy.

Mendel was born in a little town, the *shtetl* Jedwabne. He arrived just at the start of the spring season when the northeast of Poland is still biting cold. Jedwabne lies in the Podlasie Voivodship 🌐, not far from Łomża and Białystok, where a spring snow can freeze your toes in an instant, and the icy wind can give you the chill of death drafting through the cracks of old wooden houses.[1]

Mendeleh was a beautiful baby born on March 3, 1913 on the eve of World War I. We're not all that certain of the exact date, and there is no birth certificate. "It was around Purim time," Mendel asserted, sure at least that much, perhaps not too long before the famous synagogue burned to the ground.[2] Years later his American family would even be confused about the year: was it 1913 or 1914 their father was born?

But we're certain the baby was beautiful. The Wasersztejns were known for their beauty, especially their light, bright blue eyes that stood out as a special trait, different from the rest whose own eyes were dark and looked deep. Mendeleh got those blue eyes and that Wasersztejn shape of the head—exactly round at the back sloping gracefully to the neck; the frontal and parietal bones forming a perfect triangle, giving a lift to the forehead and a lovely frame for the face.

While Mendel told me these stories, I studied the shape of his old head and the thin tufts of white hair that covered his crown. I'd been probing for details about his early life, to get beyond the pat narrative he had recited for so long. "They called me Mendeleh," he said. I knew that already, and that he was the youngest of seven children, once baby Moishe had died. "My mother was Priwa," he said. "Sometimes they called her Riva, but she was Priwa, you know, Priwa," he repeated, impatient that I wanted to know why she was sometimes called Riva. I asked if he remembered Moishe. Of course he remembered Moishe. This question didn't seem to annoy him. Instead, his eyes softened with a memory, not of the boy but of the terrible day he died.

Mendel arrived home from *Cheder* to find his mother cradling the dead child, the second of her babies she would bury.[3] Four-year old Moishe had been sick, perhaps with pneumonia. "He probably walked without shoes," my father wept, recounting the memory eighty years later.[4] His voice became high pitched, groping for the words to describe what was now in his mind's eye. I could see the question took him back, and it was a painful, poignant moment. "Daddy, are you alright?" I asked, putting my hand on his thin arm, the skin blotched from too many decades in the sun. He ignored me, and went on about Moishe.

"He was so beautiful. Blond, blue eyes. The neighbors were grabbing him passing by, grabbing to kiss him. The doctor was called from Wizna, but he couldn't help. The bankas were applied, the cups to draw out the cold, even the strongest kind, but it was no use. Right away Moishe was buried."

Moishe was buried not far from the house near the open field where the children would play. Though he was just a small child, a marker was eventually placed, one among the headstones laid out in a circular pattern that was the Jewish cemetery of Jedwabne.

By then, the war had done its damage in Jedwabne, and some among the Wasersztejns were figuring a way out. The story starts earlier, though, in this little Polish town of Christian and Jew, and of this family.

Decades before I thought this was a project, I asked my father to write for me his hometown and the cities near it, place names I heard him speak of many times but could not keep registered in my consciousness, so far were his roots from my experience. I've kept it all these years, a slip of paper tucked in an old jewelry box.

It's just a torn, tiny piece of paper, a fragment, this side of which has three words, written by my father in his own hand.[5] Now when I look at that remnant, I'm a heartbroken daughter, familiar with the long, bony fingers that held the green-colored pencil that scrawled those words. Now when I look at that remnant, I'm an anthropologist who went looking for documentation, clues, and evidence to flesh out a story I know has significance beyond my father's individual life or my own sentiments. Throughout these pages, I will stay close to yet go beyond these three words written in my father's hand.

Łomża, Białystock, and Yedwabne—where my narrative of my father's narrative begins.

Yedwabne, where Yitzhak Izaak Wasersztejn, an asthmatic, took notice of Priwa's brothers. Mendel recalled, "They were big! tall! Like a different race!" Izaak watched as one of them, a Kromberg, came upon a scene, a public disturbance between a belligerent drunk and the town guard caught in a rough standoff. Priwa's brother stepped in, scooped up the misfit, and planted him square in the wagon. End of case. Impressed, Izaak went after the brother, looking to wed into *that* family, to father boys with that *power*.

He did. Both born in the mid-1870s, Priwa and Izaak married, and their first-born arrived just before the turn of the century, the couple each barely twenty years old.

Both their families were from Jedwabne, Jews whose ancestors may have migrated the thirty miles from Tykocin, an important center of Jewish learning, law, and trade. Mendel believed the Kromberg side is rooted in nobility, outside of Poland.

"The name of Kromberg is blue blood. Blue blood. From a special race," he'd insist often and vigorously, the veins in his neck like a stance, tight and pulsating.

Izaak was so much in love with Priwa though she didn't want to know about love, or about him. But her parents had died amidst the troubles of their century, and Jedwabne was not a big place. Izaak would bring gifts to Priwa's brothers "so they should put a good word in for him," Mendel explained.

Finally she accepted. But that was it. She didn't love Izaak, her son reported. "She didn't look for lovers! She married and that was it. She had her children, sacrificing for them. She was a good wife, cooking, and raising the children."

Jedwabne is just a little town, a *shtetle* as Mendel called it, with a population of 2,000, maybe 3,000 people counting the townsfolk and surrounding farmers altogether. It has seen its fair share—some might say *more* than its fair share—of spilt blood and weary tears. The carnages of the modern centuries wound their way onto the streets of Jedwabne. But it looks peaceful. Flat fields and open pastures surround it, not far from the Narew River and not too, too far from the primeval forest.

Market square was the center of town. With the church on its north side and the synagogue just down the street from it on the southwest corner, the square would come alive on Wednesdays when farmers came to buy and trade. The horses and wagons were full.

"You had to squeeze yourself to get through the crowds," Mendel recalled. "Here come the Polacks from the villages, coming with their horses, with their wagons! They occupied the whole place."

The air hung heavy, a mix of herring and horses, stale urine, and sweets from the baker's oven at the far end of the square. The school was back behind the synagogue over by Łomżyńska Street. Classes started early in the morning but by 10 o'clock the children ran free for a fifteen-minute break. On market day, it was impossible for Mendel, a small boy of 7, 8, 9 years old to wriggle through the people, the horses and wagons, the barrels and baskets, to get home, eat, and back to school on time.

Mendel lived on Cmentarna, just off Przestrzelska Street. On Cmentarna, walk a hundred steps from the elaborate Christian cemetery and you come to a wall. Take another thirty steps and you get to Mendel's house, nowadays made of brick, back then of barn wood. Behind the majestic, double-steepled St. Jacob's Church just over the way from Mendel's house was a huge field where he and his friends would play. There were lots of trees making cool shade from the unbearable heat of long summer days.

Homes and shops lined the dusty streets, some nicer than others, some selling better goods than others. The farmers lived in the countryside, and the Jews and some Christians lived in town.

"But Jedwabne was mostly Jewish," Mendel affirmed. "All the stores were Jewish. Mostly Jewish people had stores—butchers, several shoemakers, one lady with a collection of fabrics she sold by the yard. There were tailors and made-to-order shops."

Before the war, the Wasersztejns were comfortable. They even had a Polish maid to help Priwa with the children. They had a house and a barn, a horse and a wagon. They had a cow for milk, and about an acre of land to grow potatoes. They didn't starve. More than that, Izaak bought and sold wheat.

Then the war came. World War I. It was springtime when the troops and their heavy weapons arrived. The snow was melting, flooding the pastures and making mud everywhere. Military vehicles got stuck in Jedwabne. The Russians and

Germans began to fight right there, their wheels glued to the softening earth. It was horrifying.

Jedwabne was on fire. Mendeleh, barely past a toddler, his sisters, brothers, and mother hid in the basement, huddled all night long against the catastrophe going on outside. They heard the noise of war: bullets, explosions, moaning, death.

Morning came, and the family ventured from their hideout. Przestrzelska Street was filled with dead soldiers. Some soldiers were alive, lying on the street, moaning still and dying.

Mendel was terrified, hiding in the cellar like that. Being in the cellar. Hearing the guns. The shooting. When the others went to look at the dead people, Mendel didn't even take a quick peek. He was too afraid.

"My whole life I was frightened," Mendel said, reflecting on these, his early years, starting with the terror of the first five. "It's why I was a nervous wreck, a nervous wreck all the time," he explained.

One day, not so very long after his time in the cellar, Mendel was on the street not too far from home. Suddenly a pack of soldiers began to run, shooting their weapons into the air. Mendel ran home, screaming to his mother: "*Mame*, is there going to be another war? Killing more people? More shooting at the buildings?" Turns out it wasn't war that time but a celebration because, as Mendel put it, "the Polish got liberated."

Just after war's end, Priwa made her Mendeleh a little jacket, with golden buttons down the front. Mendel put it on and walked out to the street. He knew soldiers and policemen were blanketing the town, but didn't know why. Right at the corner stood a single soldier, waiting. He's going to shoot me, thought the 5-year-old, shoot me for my golden buttons! Mendel spun quickly around, heading fast back home, screaming at his mother: "Why did you put these golden buttons? I don't want them! Take them away!"

"I was frightened of soldiers, of the killing," Mendel said. "I was frightened since I was born."

Back during the war, during that terrible night seared in Mendel's core self, his father Izaak hadn't been in the cellar with the rest of the family. Word was the Russian soldiers were on the lookout for Jewish men, those suspected to be spies for the Germans. Mendel's father went ahead to the nearby village of Wizna before the armies would arrive. As Jedwabne burned—for the terror did not last just one night—people fled, everybody running, hysterical and cold. Later, Izaak was desperate to find his wife and all seven of his children. He stood atop a hill of snow near Wizna, searching. Meantime, Priwa struggled through the mud, urging her children on: "*Yankalee, Yankalee!*" she cried to a son whose boots had been swallowed by the muck. 'Go get them, go, go get your boots, you're going to get frozen," she screamed at her boy, a youngster no older than ten.

Izaak watched as the stream of refugees headed towards Wizna, eight long miles from Jedwabne. Yankl glimpsed his father on the hill, crying out: "Did you see my wife? Did you see my children?" And then they came into view. Izaak saw them, counting them one by one: "Yankl! Priwa! Mendeleh! Where is this one?"

"Here he is!"
"Where's the other one?"
"Heeerrre!"

A baker in Wizna took them in to warm up the children, their clothes wet, their small bodies shivering in the cold. All the children were alive. And Chajcia Waserstejn, their kind, beautiful aunt, she survived too.

Not everyone was so lucky. There was a heavyset woman. She couldn't go on in the cold march from Jedwabne to Wizna. Her husband was there but he had to leave her, and she froze to death. And then there was the little girl so frightened by the shooting she moved to hide herself between her mother and another woman. At that moment, a bullet came flying by, killing the child.

That family too ran to Wizna. The father put the dead child in a sack, carrying it so to bury her later.

Chajcia had a close call amidst the chaos and confusion of the war. In Wizna, Izaak had managed to secure a horse and wagon to take them west towards Łomża. Everyone packed into the wagon—Priwa, the children, and Chajcia with her small children. Izaak wasn't used to the new horse, and the horse wasn't used to the loud sounds of the military vehicles on the road. Though Izaak covered the horse's ears and eyes, the noise was too terrible. Startled, the horse became wild, leaping up off the ground and tossing the wagon and its passengers onto the ground. The German foot soldiers came by to see the commotion. At first, the family wasn't afraid. After all, these were the Germans, Mendel explained, "not the Russians, not the Polacks." One time, Izaak had even let German soldiers into the house when they came knocking at the door, begging to sleep on the floor. But on this road, the German soldiers stopped and got a look at Chajcia, the beauty. Then they wanted to take her away, to have her for themselves. What with the children wailing and the adults pleading, they finally, finally let her go.

The family's troubled journey was not yet over. The things that happened, one after the other, are compressed but not a blur. The bedraggled group made it to Łomża, and found a place to sleep, on straw in a barn. But then the sickness came. It was typhus, the deadly disease of World War I. Mendel's big brother Motl became delirious, climbing the walls with a fever that spiked beyond bearable. Chajcia, who was so devoted to the family, sought out help. There was a Kromberg family in Łomża, the wife of Abram Hirsh Kromberg, Priwa's brother who was becoming a Polish war hero and would be murdered in Jedwabne some time later. Chajcia begged the well-dressed widow: "Come! Help them! They're dying!" The woman and her five daughters followed Chajcia to the barn, peering at the sick family through a window.

Mendel still seemed shocked with what came next, even after all the years long past. "Do you know what they did?" he asked not wanting an answer. "They walked away. They didn't want to get sick."

With nowhere else to turn, Chajcia in despair made her way to the great synagogue in Łomża, defying curfew and pulling open the holy arks. "Help them!" she screamed, "Help them God!"

It was a miracle they all survived. Even so, after the war Izaak had nothing. No money, no house, no food. The family returned to Jedwabne. Everything was burned. The horses and the cows were still on the chains, burnt to death.

Mendeleh remembered the hollow feeling of starvation, and crying to his mother, "I'm hungry, give me something to eat." He winced imagining how his mother suffered his pleas. Mendel shook his head, recalling the aftermath of war. "We were helpless, the poorest of the poor," he said. "Oh, how we survived hunger and sickness. It's a long story how we survived."

Sunrise, Sunset

"When I die," my father told me in 2003, "I don't want any religion or rabbis. Nobody should cry. Just take me to the grave and have someone play *Sunrise, Sunset*, and that's it." He was serious about those requests—no crying and play *Sunrise, Sunset* —as if there would be a dry eye among those of us who would remain to mourn him. As if we would not all be sobbing as his plain pine box got lowered deep into the ground while we heard the sentimental tune and those famous lyrics:

Is this the little girl I carried?
Is this the little boy at play?
I don't remember growing older,
When did they?[6]

The request was not surprising. My father didn't like a show of tears, and I only saw him cry when he was an old man. "What do you have to cry about?" I recall him barking at me with irritation the times he found me a despondent teenager weeping into her pillow. Years later when he recounted certain stories from his past, he *would* cry—sometimes softly with quiet tears, other times a single sob, or, if the memory was particularly raw, a full outpouring of grief.

It was also not surprising that my father made reference to *Fiddler on the Roof*, the American musical. My father completely related to the themes, images, truths, and mythologies of *Fiddler*, the 1964 musical and later the feature film (1971).[7] He had his family view *Fiddler* so we might know of his past and get a taste of his struggles. He had his employees view the film—some more than once—so they might appreciate him and the Jewish people, their beautiful "traditions," and the suffering they have endured for so long. In those moments, my father *was* Tevye, the one "cloaked in nostalgia" as Jewish Studies scholar Seth Wolitz describes him, "the quintessential Eastern European Jewish folk type defending 'tradition' to his peers yet privately questioning God's ways."[8]

The *shtetl* in *Fiddler* is laden with certain stereotypes that resonated with my father at convenient times, and he could call up its mythic aspects to make a point. When under siege by wife or daughters, for example, my father would recall the *shtetl* where husbands were *always* respected and fathers were *always* obeyed. In times like that, my father would slip into mythology and use it to contest the polluting forces of the modern world.

My father, like the various literary and theatrical versions of Tevye, was full of contradictions. Yes, he slipped into mythology at convenient times and invoked generalized images of the Old World. Yet his depictions of his own *shtetl* were often nuanced and precise.

When my father talked about his *shtetle*, his little village Jedwabne, those stories always began with the horrific terror of war. He spoke of specific war—World War I—not as backdrop but as state of being for his young life. War shaped his first perceptions—dead bodies and ruined houses. My father would repeat the same story—the war story—over and over again. The repetition is not captured in the sequential narrative I have constructed from his words, but reiteration is an important part of the story. It underlines the shock he experienced and the fear that would always haunt him. Telling the story over and over again highlights the destructive trauma that is caused by war—war in his time, war before his time, and war at any time, in any place.

By other accounts too, World War I took a huge toll on Jedwabne and its Jewish inhabitants. Stories in the town's history and memorial book (*Sefer Jedwabne* 🔎) affirm Mendel's memory of displacement and destruction.[9] In one entry, the author writes, "When the First World War broke out in 5674 (1914), the Russians expelled all the Jews from Yedwabne, and together with their Rabbi they became refugees."[10] Another reports sober statistics:

> In the year 1910 Yedwabne had 2,929 inhabitants. As a result of the First World War Yedwabne suffered more property losses than any other city in the vicinity of Białystok. Seventy-two percent of the houses were totally destroyed. By 1916 the number of inhabitants decreased to seven hundred. After rebuilding the city in 1921, there were 113 houses and 1,222 inhabitants.[11]

In his depiction of those early years, my father offered a few hints of the troubled history and social group dynamics that *preceded* his birth and that war. He knew that his grandparents, Priwa's mother and father, had died amidst the troubles of *their* century, and that Priwa was born in 1876. He repeatedly described her family as "different" from the other Jews in town, making specific reference to their physical traits. He indicated something significant about the geographic location of Jedwabne to the countries that surrounded it. And he made reference to the nature of the social relationships between key groups: "in those days, in that part of the world, the Germans were good to the Jews, much better than the Russians."

It is very difficult to make sense of these hints. I realize as an anthropologist the need to go back in time to understand how they clue into a larger and longer set of circumstances that ultimately shaped my father's life course. The personal remnants of that part of my family's past are gone, though the larger history could be reconstructed from archives and books. Thus the project led me to those sources, allowing me to understand when and why Jews began settling in the land that became Poland.

I learned it started one thousand years ago when the world was in great motion.[12]

It was the eve of the second millennium when human collectivities defined by culture, language, religion, occupation, networks, and power met and moved across lands and settled in new places. Global migration is not a uniquely contemporary phenomenon; the migrations of medieval times were also of the "global" type across seven civilizations, when "merchants, intellectuals, and religious thinkers interacted, as did the little people along the trade routes spanning the globe and in the vast cultural borderlands in which civilizations overlapped."[13] As people interacted, they also intermixed, making for ever-changing cultural forms in the context of historical events, shifting circumstances, socio-political and economic conditions, and circuits of people, goods, and beliefs. Nothing was static.

Norman Davies begins his famous history of Poland in this period. It was the tenth century when a traveler journeyed from the south, a merchant from the Umayyad Caliphate that had expanded its dominion to Al-Andalus. The traveler kept a diary, offering commentary and description of his voyages north. One place he described was a province that in the future would become known as Poland. Only fragments remain of the travelogue written by Ibrahim ibn Ya'qub who some say was a Jew but who we know traversed thousands of kilometers to arrive in "the land of the Slavs . . . [a place that] produces an abundance of food, meat, honey, and fish."[14]

Ibn Ya'qub was part of the global migratory process of his times, a visitor with the Khalif of Cordoba. Ya'qub's dispassionate observations of that northern land include mention of King Mieszko I, a convert to Christianity who ruled the Polanie, "the people of the open fields."[15] There they dwelt, cradled between the Odra and Vistula rivers, where the food and meat and honey and fish were abundant.

The specific trajectory of the Jewish migration to Polanie is uncertain. By the twelfth century, Jewish settlement extended from Byzantium to the Iberian Peninsula, from southern Slavic territories to Western Europe. Historians believe the Crusades led Jews from the west to Poland; others suggest Jews arrived upon the fall of the Khazar Empire in the east. It is known that in the century following ibn Ya'qub's visit, Jews found permanent settlement in parts of Polanie where they were traders, could own land, and served in the royal mint.

Those features—the group's relationship to land, labor, and power—are central to understanding the fate and fortune of Jewish life in Poland since that time. Over the next several centuries and during the reign of two kingdoms (Piast and Jagiellonian), Jewish settlements flourished in cities, towns, and villages across Poland. Jews were made use of by the ruling class as merchants, bankers, intermediaries in exchange relationships, and long-distance traders who had global connections. In turn, Jews were granted legal protections, given relative political autonomy, and were provided freedom of religion and commerce, codified in the Statute of Kalisz in 1264.

In Poland's feudal system, Jews were consigned to a particular social location and function. The tributary mode of production prevailed in Poland between the fourteenth and eighteenth centuries when the ruling elite shared power with regional overlords to exact tribute from peasant producers. The landed nobility (*szlachta*), some with their own armies, controlled surplus-producing peasants and used Jewish go-betweens to gather tribute (the *arenda* system). It was during this period that hostility towards Jews emerged. Not surprisingly, the (Jewish) tax and rent collector was not a popular figure among the peasants. The nobility remained anonymous and protected while the Jewish estate stewards took the hit from peasants who resented the Jews and, as Eva Hoffman notes, considered them their direct exploiters.[16] The roots of resentment were structural and political-economic, even if antipathy was expressed or understood in cultural or religious terms.

The burgher class was particularly hostile to the Jews, their sentiments enlarging as competition between the two merchants estates increased (Jewish merchants and burghers). Poland was also undergoing other transformations that affected dynamics between various social groups: the Catholic Church grew in influence over the Polish domain starting in the fifteenth century; the Polish kingdom joined forces with the Grand Duchy of Lithuania to form a Commonwealth in the sixteenth century; and the political and economic crises of multiple wars took its toll, especially during the seventeenth century.

Over much of this period, Poland could be characterized as culturally and religiously diverse. The Jewish population saw growth in number and wealth, and steady improvement in its wellbeing. Jews institutionalized a system of localized self-government called the *kahal* (the Jewish Commune) and developed a Poland-wide political-juridical body, *Va`ad Arba Aratzot* (the Council of Four Lands). These rights could only be granted by royal decree and patronage; in turn, the Jewish Commune assessed and collected royal taxes.

By the seventeenth century when the Polish monarchical state was at the height of power, wealth, and prestige in Eastern Europe, it was also situated on a series of fracture zones—"lines of instability that radiate out from specific and discernible crises"—instabilities that are political and economic.[17] The Chmielnicki revolt in the mid-seventeenth century reflected one such fracture zone, a series of violent uprisings that began in 1648 against Polish imperial expansion into the Ukraine and against exploitation of peasants by Polish nobles and their intermediaries, the Jews. Conflicts within the ruling elite, between king and nobility, signaled another fracture zone while the Kingdom of Poland was situated on the fracture zone of competing, expansionist and warring empires— Swedish, Ottoman, Russian, Austrian, British, French, and Danish. In addition to the Chmielnicki revolt, seventeenth-century Poland was at war with Russia, Sweden, and the Ottoman Empire. By the end of the century, Poland was in shambles, its population decimated, its political infrastructure shaken, the kingdom made ripe to be "swallowed up" by three empires in the century to follow.[18]

Still another fracture zone, not disconnected from those already mentioned, was economic, involving trade networks, mercantile wealth, and peasant labor in the tributary mode.[19] The Vistula River provided the main artery for international trade goods, especially grain and lumber. While the grain trade flourished, peasant life remained difficult. Expansion of the grain trade put enormous pressure on rural labor: "In order to meet the demand," Davies argues, "the noble landowners exacted more work and harsher conditions from their peasants," pointing to the social dynamics that would also play into domestic tensions.[20] In their capacity as traders, merchants, and middlemen in urban and rural economies, Jews stood on the fracture zones, their social, political, and economic fates tied to the larger quakes of the times.

It cannot be said that anti-Jewish sentiment was uniform across these centuries or among the social groups (estates) that comprised the Polish social order. The Church, one among the powerful Polish estates, was rooted in Roman Catholic liturgy, teachings, and propaganda, including anti-Jewish belief and rhetoric that resonated or held sway only at particular moments. For example, the Church lent its ideological support to the burghers, supporting their interests against Jewish competitors.

With the crises of the seventeenth century, not least of which were war and economic contraction, the volume of anti-Jewish rhetoric got louder and the persecution of Protestants also increased. Hoffman notes Poland became xenophobic, "less hospitable to differences of all kinds," and the number of Jews accused of and executed for ritual murder rose.[21]

Bigotry always has a history and a context, and is intimately tied to power interests. In periods of political and economic crisis, scapegoating, that maneuver of deflection, will rear its head. Conflicts between Christians and Jews were exacerbated in the mid-seventeenth to early eighteenth centuries coinciding with war, epidemics, and economic crises. That's the pattern.

This was the troubled and troubling state of affairs in Poland at the dawn of the eighteenth century when upheaval cast upon upheaval. The world was in transition, entering a new mode of production whereby monetary wealth could buy labor power, shifting social relations of production from the tributary mode. Western Europe would enter this mode sooner than Eastern Europe but the early significance to the east was in the competitive relationships with the expanding empires in its midst. In particular, the Russian Empire, its eye on the Ottomans, would exert great influence on changing the course of Polish history. By the end of the eighteenth century, the *kahal* would be dismantled, and Hasidism, a new Jewish movement, would emerge, in part as response to the destruction of Jewish religious and political infrastructures. By century's end, Poland would be partitioned: Russia, Austria, and Prussia (1772); Russia and Prussia (1793); Russia, Prussia, and Austria (1795), a political "vivisection" that would inspire passions in the coming age of nationalist ideology and movement—passions my father would encounter.

From the standpoint of our own time, certain social facts and truths seem eternal—as if they have always been and always will be, even in the face of evidence that refutes such a view. The so-called *Volksgeist* or "spirit" that "lives" behind the modern nation-state gives particular nations a quality of timelessness.[22] The nation-state may be new (its "founding" celebrated with annual festivities, etc.) but the "nation" as a people with ancient collective roots, a common origin and fate, and that has permanence is often accepted as truth, though it seems a great leap of faith to believe it. The plain fact is that the nation-state emerged at the end of the eighteenth century with nationalist ideology flourishing thereafter.[23]

The process of nation building involves a choice—to pull from a set of cultural understandings and symbols and make them potent. It is in this way that "a people," and memories of their "tradition" is an invention, negotiated by leaders. Ultimately, ideas about the group can become sacred belief, and the nation of which they are a part can become a fetish. In Poland, certain cultural symbols informed Polish identity as a nation. Specific tropes were invoked, including those developed by nineteenth-century Romantic writers and composers. For example, Adam Mickiewicz, author of *Pan Tadeusz*, the Polish national epic, developed a character that would become the iconic Polish folk hero. The mazurkas and polonaises 🔲 by Frédéric François Chopin, himself a national icon, *became* quintessentially Polish.[24] For Christians in Poland, the Jew became a potent symbol of what Poland would not be.

In the Polish case, the nationalist narrative did not simply march along in a smooth, linear path to become a cohesive story of a homogeneous ethnic, racial, and religious entity with deep roots in the land of open fields. Like many of its counterparts in the European states that surrounded it, Poland in the nineteenth century was engaged in revolt against foreign (dynastic) rule, and in developing and applying ideas about the nation that saw stirrings in the prior century.

The place of Jews in Polish society and ultimately in the Polish conception of itself as a nation was a subject of debate and disagreement that included Jewish voices: at certain points and among certain political sectors, Jews were and wanted to be considered integral to the Polish nation while at other points and among other political and intellectual leaders, they wanted to be and were considered a "nation within a nation."[25]

The flame of ethnic nationalism in Poland grew ever more intense with each defeat against the forces of partition. With the last of these defeats in 1864, nationalist rhetoric increasingly took on an antisemitic tone until it was integrated into the formal political sphere. "Anti-Jewish tropes became a powerful emotive tool for nation building," Joanna Michlic explains. She offers a succinct description of this relatively recent process:

> The concept of the Jew as the harmful alien other constituted one of the major aspects of the thinking among significant segments of conservative and Catholic elites. They transferred it to the level of modern national politics, and in this new form they took it back to society. Without that transfer the concept of the Jew as a national threat could not have become so powerful, potent, and long-lived . . . They used it as a tool in raising national cohesiveness among ethnic Poles of different social classes with conflicting social and economic interests.[26]

Those "conflicting social and economic interests" were shaped by the new world order in which declining and nascent imperial forces would contract or expand on the battlefields of modern warfare. In this new world order, states would become configured on geo-political maps and with their own romantic ideas of the nation.

World War I was billed as the "war to end all wars," seductive rhetoric we now know was empty. What it did do was reconfigure the modern map, and set the stage for the violence to come in the decades that followed. Old empires gave way to new struggles, and new nations got constructed from above. Poland became an independent republic in 1918, and in a world marked by violent upheaval, displacement, disruption, and scarcity, ordinary Poles—now more clearly imagined in homogeneous ethnic, racial and religious terms—found comfort in the idea of *their* community, *their* nation.

Digging into this history illuminates the hints my father offered. Priwa's mother and father, my great-grandparents, died amidst social turmoil: violent uprisings against imperial occupation, the rise of *ethnic* nationalism and systemic antisemitism. My father's insistence that the Krombergs, with their blue eyes and blond hair, were different, "of a *special* race," not merely of Jewish "stock," is a chilling indicator of how race works and of the complexity of racism. Considering

the vast global migrations since the eleventh century and the multiple opportunities for human interactions across groups in that part of the world, it would be
silly to imagine there are definable, traceable *biological* groups—the "blue bloods,"
say, or the "Jews."

My father was probably correct—there was "mixing" along the way in the
thousand-year interaction between empires, tribes, traders, farmers, warriors,
and rulers. But he could not see how the concept of race naturalizes what are
socially constituted groups, where phenotype gets placed on a hierarchy of superior and inferior, signaling status. My father just adopted the racialized messages
and standards of his time where blue eyes, blond hair, and light skin signaled—
and justified—royalty, and the dark-eyed Jew was of a lesser breed.

Jedwabne, in northeastern Poland, was situated amid the battling empires
just at the time Priwa began to have babies. The Russian Empire, losing ground,
struggled to maintain its hold in the face of internal revolt and external threats—
the Ottomans from the south, expansionist Germany from the west. And when the
Great War came, it was fought on multiple fronts. On the frozen Eastern Front
was Jedwabne, a town so small its World War I battles would be forgotten by
history.

Aftermaths

I stood over the sink washing dishes by hand, the way my father had taught me: rinse the dishes clean, then fill up the sink with soapy water and let them soak, taking them up one at a time to scrub, front and back. Drain the sink, then rinse each dish one by one, front and back again, and place on the drain to dry. The warm water and rhythm of the movements helped clear my mind. There was something my father said that stuck with me. He had never before revealed it, mentioning it almost in passing. I had been pushing and probing for details, for things I had not heard before. There it was! A little jewel of information: before World War I, the Wasersztejns were "comfortable" enough to have had a servant—a Polish maid for a Jewish family in Jedwabne.

It was the probing and pushing that brought out the tidbit, but I was unable to learn any more from him about his father's livelihood or his family's status before the war. After all, that was also before my father's time. He was born *into* the war when hardship, hunger, fear, and hostility were his palpable reality. He knew the taste of starvation, the smell of soldier blood, the sound of the battlefield, the sight of trauma. He knew about the aftermaths of war. He took what he knew and put them into words, into anecdotes I could comprehend.

After the war, Izaak struggled to make a living. He was at a loss, not knowing what to do. He traded what he could, although at first there was nothing at all to trade. He'd take his wagon, get something from a farmer and sell in town. Izaak's oldest, Chaim, would go with him. Eventually they would buy horses and they'd buy cows, and resell them. That's how Izaak made a living after the war. There was great devastation in Jedwabne, although some people made out better than others.

"Those whose home didn't burn down," Mendel pointed out, "at least they had that."

The Wasersztejn house was destroyed so Izaak and his sons built a new one with wood from what remained of the stable. There were two low-ceilinged rooms for nine people. It was a simple dwelling, the kitchen with a stove, and in the center of the room, a chimney to warm up the house. They pulled water from the well several hundred yards away, and for toilets, there were the bushes back behind the house. Walking into the house you would have seen the stove first. There was a bench with many uses: by day it held the buckets of well water, by evening it served for sitting at the dinner table, by night it became a bed for two of the boys.

Mendel's four brothers and sister Fagel slept in the kitchen, drawing warmth from the fire. Mendel slept in the second room on a bed of straw in a sack with his father while Priwa curled up with her daughter Sarah. It was crude living, with conditions much deteriorated from what they had been before the war.

Izaak was a fine-looking yet ordinary man. He wasn't particularly brilliant and had a respectful, distant relationship with his religion. He went to synagogue, Mendel recalled, but only because "the community, you are supposed to go to temple every day." During the week, Izaak prayed in the house but on Sabbath and especially Yom Kippur, he would take his *tallis*, the prayer shawl, to the synagogue.

Mostly Izaak worked, looking to make a living for his family. He didn't talk much to his wife or the children but showed his devotion by working. "He sacrificed and suffered for us," Mendel said, making special mention of that point.

And the children were devoted to him too, especially Chaim, the eldest who stood by his father's side even after the others had moved on. Right after the war, Chaim's leg began to ache, a horrible, throbbing pain. His mother laid leaves on the leg, but it did not improve. Izaak took him to Łomża, a larger, nearby town. A doctor prescribed some medication but it didn't help. Izaak took him to the next town. That didn't help either. Then Izaak took him to Warsaw. He actually *carried* him to Warsaw, Mendel claimed, for Izaak had no money to travel any other way. Chaim remembered that, remembered how his father carried him over his shoulder, and remembered his devotion, the sacrifice and love. The doctor in Warsaw could do nothing. "Go to Königsberg, in Prussia," the doctor in Warsaw advised. "He's a specialist in bones. Königsberg is a big city in Prussia. They are sure to help Chaim's leg there." So the father and son trekked north from Warsaw. "My father takes him," Mendel claimed. "He actually carried him to Königsberg."

They got to Königsberg and the doctor walked in. He said, "It's too late, too late."

"Why?" implored Izaak.

"Tell him to raise his hand," the doctor directed Izaak.

"Chaim, raise your hand!" the father commanded the son.

"I cannot. I cannot do it," the boy responded in a weak whisper.

"You know what that means?" the doctor declared. "Gangrene! He has gangrene all over his body! You hear?"

Izaak began to weep. "The only thing we can do is cut off his leg," the doctor explained. Izaak shook his head, not able to imagine life for Chaim with one leg. One leg, how could he live with one leg? the father thought, and then made up his mind. "No. No. I don't let you cut his leg off. If you cannot save him, let him die."

The doctor took pity on Izaak, and maybe on Chaim too, the handsome, weakened young man. There was one other option they could try, though there were no promises, and the outcome would not likely be good. The doctor took a scalpel and made a long opening in Chaim's chest. With the first cut, rotten pus found release, spraying the doctor. And that was it. Chaim lived. Yes, his leg was never quite right after that and he walked with a limp. But he lived.

Mendel got excited at the thought of the miracle. He exclaimed, "Can you imagine? Chaim lived to ninety!"

After the war, other things changed in Jedwabne. A new public school was opened. Up to then, Mendel had only gone to *Cheder* where he learned how to read, to debate, and to pray in Hebrew. The *melamed* (teacher), would give the students something to read, a story let's say, with a dilemma to be considered from many angles. Two boys—maybe Mendel and his friend Moshe Hurwicz— would be sent to read the story and discuss the case. For instance, someone lends his horse to a neighbor. The horse dies. The owner accuses the neighbor, "You killed him." The one who borrowed it says, "No, the horse was sick before you lent him to me." What is the truth? Students had to deliberate, investigate, and decide who is responsible for the dead horse. "Besides how to pray, these are the things we would learn in *Cheder*," Mendel explained.

Mendel went to *Cheder* like the other boys until the public school opened. Most Jewish children still went to *Cheder*, preferring it to the other one. Not Mendel. He wanted to go to the public school. He did, and it was his choice. His parents had nothing to do with his decision. "I wanted to go ahead," Mendel recalled, "I wanted to learn. It's like saying you're going to the university! I wanted to move to a different grade. In *Cheder*, you don't go to grades."

Not that public school was so easy for a Jewish boy in the postwar years. "Mostly the Jewish boys stuck together and the Christian boys stuck together," Mendel said. Two divided people.

It was in public school Mendel learned Polish because at home they spoke Yiddish and in *Cheder* they learned in Hebrew. He became the family expert of the language of the majority. Priwa and Izaak didn't know much Polish, speaking a few words, enough to get by.

Mendel had one Polish friend. "He was friendly with me and I was friendly with him," Mendel described the relationship. His father sold sausages and the boy was very round. Priwa almost seethed with envy when she saw her son with this boy. "Look at him! He's so fat and so healthy," she would exclaim, "and my Mendeleh, my Mendelee so skinny!" But Mendel's Christian friend died before he turned twenty having contracted trichinosis, rumor had it, eating all those sausages.

Mendel said something was wrong in Jedwabne. "Jews were separate and that was wrong." He felt it was wrong the way the children at school sometimes didn't treat the Jewish kids right. Sometimes in the street, the Polish kids would shout at them: "Dirty Jew." "Truth is," Mendel said, "the Jewish children would run away," afraid to answer back the tough Christian boys.

"The Polacks were very antisemitic," Mendel repeated with disdain. He told about the priest's mother, a story that showed how mean they really were, how much hatred they had for the Jew. One time, Mendel and his group of Jewish friends were eating peanuts.

The priest's mother passed by and said in a loud voice, "Why are you eating that stuff? Why don't you get kielbasa?"

Of course, the Jewish boys didn't eat kielbasa. Mendel explained, "It was sausage! Pork! The boys didn't dare answer her but they thought to themselves, 'Can you imagine the nerve that she said that? That she said we should get a piece of kielbasa!'"

Mendel said the teachers in the public schools were teaching the children songs against the Jews. "The teachers were all antisemitic," he repeated, except for the one or two Jewish teachers who taught there too. The Polish teachers would announce that for Passover, the Jews had to kill a Christian child to make the *matzah*.[1] Mendel said the priest in church told them to hate Jews. Everyone knew the priest said that because it was a small town. "The Polacks would come from the farms to go to church and part of the ceremony was to talk about the Jews," Mendel recalled. Afterward, they would go out from church and throw stones at the Jewish homes. Mendel remembered that. How they threw stones at him, threw stones at his house.

Mendel said the rabbi would spit on the ground each time he walked by the church. He let them know he detested them too.

That's how it was between the Jews and the Christians in Jedwabne after the war. Except on Wednesdays, market day. Then it was about business, "a business situation," Mendel noted. "Jews and Polish people were friendly to each other when they came to trade and to buy in the Jewish stores. And when the Polish people came, the first thing they wanted was herring!"

All the fighting, all the wars made it worse for the Jews, Mendel explained. Jedwabne, so near Russia, so near Lithuania and so near Germany–Prussia, was trapped in the middle of the problems. One day it belonged to Poland, one day to Russia, one day to Germany. "They needed someone to blame," he said. "Any of them. When they needed to blame, that's when they persecuted the Jews."

Mendel was beginning to have dreams. Going to the public school was one step, but he wanted more. He would work hard and win a scholarship to the gymnasium, the famous, top private school in Białystok, the Druskin Gymnasium .[2]

He thought maybe some day he could get to America. His mother's brother Yitzhak had left Poland for New York in 1902. He sent letters from there, and sometimes clothes too, things they no longer needed in that rich, fancy country. From America to Poland to Mendel's house. It was like gold, these clothes for his sisters and his mother. He thought his uncle Yitzhak Kromberg was God.

Mendel had a dream because Poland was so poor. He didn't want to be stuck in this place. He wanted to *progress*. He had an idea that America was great, "an open place where you have rights." The Golden Land, that's how he thought of it. "In Hebrew, they teach about Gan Eden," he said, the heavenly garden. He wanted to dream. Dreaming, America was heaven. *Gan Eden*.

Priwa had a dream too. Seeing all those dead soldiers lying dead and dying on Przestrzelska Street, Priwa made up her mind. After World War I, when Poland became an independent nation, she knew they would begin drafting sons like hers. But Priwa would not see her sons fall for the Polish army.

She wrote to her brother in America, the one who sent clothes and reports of the Golden Land from Carroll Street in Brooklyn. From her brother she wanted the necessary papers to get Motl out of Poland before the army could get him. She wasn't worried about Chaim. The army didn't want him with his bad leg, lame and limp. But Motl was a different case. And after him, they would want Yankl, then Josef, then Mendel.

"Just at that time, the United States closed up," Mendel noted. There would be no more immigration to America.

Delicate Memories

It was early August 2001. I was preparing my first trip to Poland, and to Jedwabne , a place I could imagine only in mythic terms.[3] By the summer of 2001, my project was already underway and I had been preserving my father's tales on tape for several years.

This time, my father was visiting my home, and I prepared his breakfast the way he expected it, served graciously and with a certain elegant formality. Up early, he had showered and shaved before making his way to the kitchen. I was anxious to get the conversation going, to get information about Poland that might be useful for my trip. We were quiet at the kitchen table; it was time for eating, not for interviewing.

My father pushed away from the table, clearing the food between his teeth with a suck and a click of the tongue, the sign that breakfast was over. I cleared the dishes and brought him outdoors to the back porch. We could talk there. I turned on the recorder, though worried the noise of the neighborhood would drown out the recorded voices. I brought out a pad and pen just in case.

My father recounted stories I had heard all my life. "The Polish were very anti-semitic," Mendel repeated that day, not just as recollection but also as warning to a Jewish daughter about to visit Poland for the first time. He was still nurturing me on the idea of Polish antisemitism, imbued as a natural, fundamental, and timeless feature of the Polish spirit. He backed his statements with anecdotes, his kind of proof: the songs ridiculing and demonizing the Jews, derogatory comments by Christian teachers and schoolboys, all the nasty rumors; even the bells of the church 🔗, he claimed, rang out hatred for the Jews.[4]

I tried masking my impatience but a few low sighs of frustration escaped, most likely giving me away. I tried getting beyond this theme, beyond the impasse. "Do you remember any Polish words?" I asked. He did, and wrote them down for me. "'*Pan*' is Mr., and '*po*' is for." We laughed as I struggled to pronounce thank you—*dziekuje*—jane-koo-yeh. Then he wrote, "*Muj ojciec se rodgil w Jedwabne Mendel Vasersztejn*," and told me it meant, "My father was born in Jedwabne, Mendel Vasersztejn."

He also drew for me from memory a map of Jedwabne, a place he had last seen seventy years earlier. He prepared me with vivid and compelling images, with names of streets and the exact location of the family home, hovel that it was.

The map 🔗 was accurate.[5] I walked down the streets of Jedwabne, matching my father's drawing of his *shtetl* to the real thing. "Here's the church! There's the plaza with the marketplace! Oh! That's where the synagogue used to be, and the rabbi's house." Following my father's specific directions, I walked the precise number of steps from the wall of the Christian cemetery to the spot where his old wooden home once stood. The house I saw was made of brick.

On that first pilgrimage to Jedwabne 🔗, I felt a terrible unease.[6] I recoiled from the townsfolk, reaching out to no one. I looked suspiciously at the huddle of old women chatting on a stoop. I took special notice of the old men, some

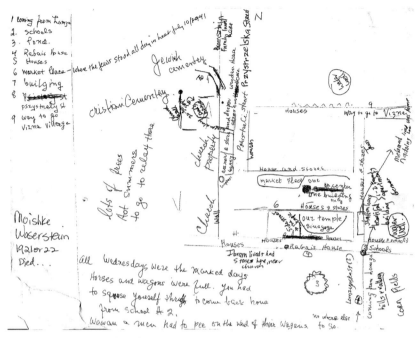

My father's map of Jedwabne (2001)

walking on the street and others grouped on a corner, who peered back at me with equal suspicion. Wasn't it antisemitism I saw in their glower?

This was not like me—the person or the anthropologist—and I was acutely aware of the unfamiliar sensation. I didn't know how or when, but I knew at some point I would need to confront these strange and conflicting emotions.

The whole project was confusing. How would I—the daughter–anthropologist—be able to discern truth from fiction in my father's tales? Of course his stories reflect his perceptions of his experiences and of those around him, but does it matter if his very perception was refashioned by the march of history that came after his own experience of particular times and places? My father had a store of stories that he repeated, following the same narrative structure, with the same intonations and rhythms. He rarely strayed from the script. Does that make those stories more true, or less so? And to complicate it further, did my father's rendition of his own past *become* true and then have consequences for what came next in his life and those close to him? In what ways did my father, by means of the stories he told himself and others "make and remake the world" shaping what would happen to him afterward?[7]

One challenge for me has been to disentangle "truth" from "mythology" in my father's tales, and in my own rendition of the story. My task has also been to recognize what was "true" for my father, and to understand why it was so. What did his words and actions reveal about his character and psychology? What do his words reveal about the cultural and political narratives of the world that were already in place across the chapters of his life?

I think of the "*shtetl*" as a good example, a case study through which to explore these issues. The word *shtetl* is itself evocative. Just to say "my father's *shtetl*" calls to mind a set of characteristics and frozen images: He is Jewish, and so am I; the setting is quaint and eastern European—maybe in Poland, maybe in Russia; his past life was authentically Jewish—his life permeated with religious ritual and the round of the Jewish calendar; the community was homogeneous, populated by pious Jews, poor Jews, "backward" Jews. It is a place that once was, but remains now only in romantic memories and tawny photographs. The idea of it can make the unsentimental weep, and the sentimental nostalgic for what they never knew. Each time I write, "my father's *shtetl*," I invoke the mythological even as it is a true statement. Of course, my father was not innocent in this regard; at the same time, he provided enough detail and vivid description to propel me towards a fuller appreciation of his hometown 🔗.[8]

I also recognize as an anthropologist there is a bigger story behind the making of the mythical *shtetl*.[9] It does not simply emerge from the imaginations of individuals. Once again, I would turn to political-economic and cultural history to fill in the gaps of my personal story.

I learned from these histories there are identifiable sources for the romanticization and mythologization of the *shtetl*, especially as it has been "remembered" by diasporic Jews.[10] The sources include Yiddish literature (*Haskalah* dramas, *maskilic* satire, short stories, and novels), 1200 memorial books of Polish Jewry (*yizkor-bikhers*), some folklore and ethnographic texts (notably, *Life is with People*), the photographs of Roman Vishniac, and, again, the Broadway musical and Hollywood movie *Fiddler on the Roof*.

Barbara Kirshenblatt-Gimblett offers an important observation on the influence of the Yiddish literary tradition, which includes the works of Sholom Aleichem: "So detailed, if ideologically charged, are their accounts of a way of life they repudiated that later readers would confuse the ethnographic burlesque with ethnography proper. They would mistake biting satire for faithful description."[11] She reminds us, as does Seth Wolitz in his "The Americanization of Tevye," that Jewish cultural history is always tied to contemporaneous ideology.[12]

Kirshenblatt-Gimblett analyzes the texts implicated in the making of the *shtetl* as it has come to be imagined: "Bleak pictures of Jewish life, with a strong emphasis on Jewish insularity and persecution, served the reformist objectives of the Jewish Enlightenment and Emancipation movements in the nineteenth century and Zionism in the twentieth century."[13]

Mythical images may have cultural and political resonance, but they are not historically accurate, even if some aspects are truthful. The word *shtetl* means little town, the Yiddish diminutive of *shtot* (town or city). The *shtetl* was one of several settlement forms in Poland that included smaller and larger cities, towns and villages, and within each of these forms, there were multiple types (market towns, urban centers, port cities, resorts). Antony Polonsky considers the indiscriminate conflation of this diversity into the archetype "*shtetl*" to be thoroughly misleading, a practice of the romanticists who erased important, historically constituted distinctions.[14]

My father often referred to Jedwabne as his *shtetle*, the diminutive of a diminutive. In this he was accurate, describing the place of his birth that had been decimated by World War I, losing a large proportion of its population. By his account, Jedwabne was a market town in which Jews comprised the largest proportion of the population but not exclusively so. There were Christians in Jedwabne too. The vast majority were peasant farmers in the countryside but there were some who lived in town, owned shops, living and working side-by-side with Jews. The Catholic farmers worshiped in the town church with fellow congregants who lived in Jedwabne proper.

My father's Jedwabne does not seem frozen in time or homogeneous. Mendel described living in abject poverty, and attributed it to the destructive forces of war. His father, the trader, filled an occupational niche carved out before his time, when many Jews served as brokers, merchants, and middlemen for royalty and nobility, though the period from the partitions to the lead up to World War I saw enormous economic and political change. Industrialization drew more Jews to urban centers; nationalist movements (Polish and Jewish) prompted still other Jews to emigrate. Writing about consequences to the rural economy with the transition to capitalist production in the post-partition period, Kirshenblatt-Gimblett explains the fate of Jews like my grandfather:

> Although the estate system almost disappeared with the impoverishment of the nobility and the emancipation of the serfs, the Jewish presence in their old rural occupations persisted to some degree . . . Jews even took up some new occupations in the countryside. Agrarian reforms instituted in the independent republics after World War I left little place for Jews in the impoverished rural economy. After their emancipation, peasants farmed the land and, though the peasants were largely self-sufficient, Jews still provided many needed services and products.[15]

The round of daily life in Jedwabne may have been limited, but it was not hermetically sealed, immune from outside influences. In my father's anecdotes and between the lines of his narrative, we hear the comings and goings in Jedwabne:

soldiers from afar, nearby towns and cities (Łomża, Białystok), large cities at great distance (Warsaw, Königsberg, Brooklyn), and the aspirations of a young boy and a worried mother. My father's aspirations—to *progress*, for secular education, a willingness to learn the language of the new nation—did not emerge from one boy's unique, individually formed mind. They reflect basic principles of *Haskalah*, the Jewish Enlightenment, a complex, multi-faceted, nineteenth-century revolutionary movement. As the materialist underpinnings of their lives gave way to the forces of structural and political violence, Izaak, Priwa, and Mendel found hope in the modernist promises of Enlightenment.

For Izaak, *Haskalah* likely affected whom he would marry. The early *maskilim* (proponents of *Haskalah*) made romantic love and bourgeois marriage a central feature of their revolutionary program, paving the way for Izaak's life course.[16] Izaak *chose* Priwa as his wife. Before *Haskalah*, each would likely have been betrothed early in their adolescence and by arrangement. *Haskalah*, like other ideological movements of the time, was the purview of men, and romantic love was a male prerogative. By my father's reckoning, Izaak *loved* her, but the feeling was not reciprocal. "She didn't love him," my father stated, and added, "she wasn't looking for lovers," as if to defend the double standard. Marriage, children, and the status of wife were enough for her, my father assumed, leaving the privileges of patriarchy intact in the face of modernization.

In still another way, my father's depiction of Jedwabne defies the *shtetl* stereotype. Izaak was not particularly Orthodox, though he did his part, enough to qualify his membership in a community of Jews. We don't imagine Izaak heavy with whiskers and prayer, bowing in devotion to God like a Vishniac photograph, though we could just picture the town rabbi, bent and bearded as he spat on the ground of the double-steepled church.

Izaak, and my father after him, was neither religious nor secular. Izaak was both, as was his son, and these aspects of their selves were inseparable. They participated in the rituals of food and prayer, a "natural" part of their lives. They *believed*: sometimes in God, sometimes not, sometimes in "tradition," sometimes not. In my father's case, he always *believed* in the idea of the Jewish "people" and their unique, horrific plight. Also, in telling his stories, my father invoked religiously imbued metaphors (God, paradise, Eden), words that flowed effortlessly in his descriptions of quotidian life. His memories became like a dance, partnering the sacred with the secular, old cultural forms and new that together formed authentic emotion. In the early 1990s, my father wrote:

> I just listened to the Fidler on the Roof recording of Sabbath prayer song, May God bless you and keep you, etc. It brought me back memories from a long time ago in our schtetl in Poland when before going to sinagogue for Kol Nidrai services, right after dinner, my mother and father lined us up

between them stretchet their arms over our heads to bless us for a good year. It was so solemn, almost frightening and at the same time asuring . . .

The music may not have been authentically Old World Jewish, but it *became* real, signaling his experience and becoming a true reflection of his remembered life: "One season following another, laden with happiness and tears."

Clearly, my father was not immune to idealization. For example, amongst my father's papers I found this exalted description of his hometown and his family:

How different it was in our shtetle in Poland when we were children. ~~Hardly any~~ no formal education only learned Hebrew to pray and to follow rules from generation to generation ~~that~~ God is the sublime who gave us life health and happiness, ~~and be~~ To be thankful to Him ~~with~~ and praise Him Mother and Father ~~and~~ are the next in category always ~~never allow~~ loving them never allow your mind ~~to angry with them~~ to think otherwise because it is a sin.

He wrote this at a point late in life when he was filled with anger and bitterness. His words and imagery, invoking the holy, seem an exaggeration. I think of it as an act of substitution, mourning a disappointing present by idealizing a lost personal past.

In my father's romanticized version of his past, people more than place are remembered as virtuous, and in hallowed terms. Mendel reserves special adulation for Izaak, who he portrays in extra-human terms. The father literally and lovingly carried an ailing son, already of teen age, across the lands of Polanie. "Then Izaak took Chaim to Warsaw. He actually *carried* him to Warsaw," my father claimed, describing a journey from Jedwabne to Warsaw of over 100 miles. The heroic journey does not end there. Unable to help his dying son in Warsaw, the father takes his son—"actually carries him"—to Königsberg (now Kaliningrad), a trek of more than 200 miles. As in any epic, the story is allegory, and exaggeration inscribes the meaning. In this case, it is a parable of ideal familial attachment: the father as self-sacrificing, the son as devotee.

Neither Izaak nor Mendel could live up to the virtuous ideal, humans that they were. My father insisted that he and his siblings were thoroughly dedicated to their parents. "We were very devoted," he told me. "Like nobody else." Those who left Jedwabne and left their parents never turned back, he said. "They never wrote a letter to their parents, they forgot about their parents. They didn't want to know anything about their parents." For all his talk of a child's duty to devotion, my father's living parent (Priwa) during my lifetime was strikingly absent from our lives. She lived to her nineties, but I have no record of her death or where she is buried. I have no personal memory of her, and while there were

occasional visits, I know her only from a very few photographs, my father's stories, and only two letters in my family archive. One of the two letters is a mother's
grievance about a neglectful son. Though clear in statement about devotion, my
father was vague on its substance. He left me wondering, how is devotion exhib-
ited? How is it revealed?

It seems Izaak could also fall from grace, his righteousness tinged by human
passion. Straying from his fixed depiction one day—and he told me this story
only once—Mendel revealed to me another side of Izaak Wasersztejn:

> My father liked to go to bed with people, not Jewish women but the Polacks.
> This was in Jedwabne. Wednesday was market day. Everybody busy. My
> father would go in the stable. I saw him. He was coming out of the stable
> and he was with a woman. My mother didn't care. She didn't want to have
> sex with him. She didn't like him.
>
> Everyone knew because it's a small town, and we would know. He went to
> Christian women, a lot of times. He was a very sexy guy.
>
> How do I tell you what happened? My father didn't come to sleep one
> night. Chaim was the oldest, and he went to look for him, and he found
> him with a girlfriend. She had a husband and he slept with both of them,
> in the same bed.

At this point in our conversation, I asked if Izaak had sexual relations with
both the woman and her husband. Mendel was appalled at the thought! "No!"
he responded, startled by the question. Izaak "was friendly with the husband and
had sex with the wife!"

Delicate memory. There are fragments and there is full-fledged recall. Individual memory can be fragile and fixed, sometimes at once. It is always distorted,
yet somehow honest. Memories are works of the imagination that are rooted in
real life and layered with meaning.

My father had not told me the story of Izaak and his sexual encounters with his
neighbors before my first trip to Poland. He revealed that story four years later.
Both times—the summer of 2001 and the summer of 2005—he did address the
matter of Polish Christians and Jews.

We know from my father and from the historical record that in market towns
like Jedwabne in the 1920s, Polish Christians and Jews most often came together
on market day and in the market square, a confluence of farmers and crafts-
men (producers), traders and brokers (distributors) and people buying, selling, exchanging, eating, and socializing, sometimes even intimately. At these
moments they were together, even as they were apart—a social dynamic poi-
gnantly described by my father's stories of separation and alienation, Jew from
Christian in Jedwabne.

Mendel consistently referred to non-Jewish Poles as "Polacks," a term considered derogatory in the English-language context. Knowing his disdain for Poles, it is possible he used the offensive word purposefully, and the insult became habit. On the other hand, my father was at one time a fluent Polish-language speaker, having learned it at his integrated public school. It is possible, therefore, that for him, "Polack" was "*Polak*," the Polish masculine word for Pole, though he did not use the feminine form "*Polka*" when referring to women. Izaak "liked to go to bed with the Polacks," Mendel said of the women in Jedwabne who were not Jewish. This suggests he had every intention of invoking the insult whenever he used the term "Polack."

"The Polish were very antisemitic," was my father's refrain. I believe his boyhood stories of fraught, hostile tensions between the Polish Christians and Jews of his time. His own experience may be true, but his conclusion is mistaken. In it he is guilty of demonization, the flip side of idealization. His conclusion does not illuminate history but erases it, naturalizing what are historically specific and contingent tensions between the social groups. Antisemitism is neither timeless nor is it an explanation. I did not know that as I prepared my first trip to Poland, my father's exhortation echoing in my mind. It would take time and this project for that truth to reveal itself to me.

3

The Voyage Out

A wall of family photographs extends the length of the center hallway of my home. It shows parents, grandparents, children, and grandchildren across three generations and ten households. There are old, faded, black and whites, and newer, color photos. The handcrafted Italian frames complement both types, giving an intensity that's sometimes missing from contemporary snapshots, and emphasizing the rich historical and cultural qualities of the aging photographs.

I took one off the wall to show my father. It's the only photograph we have from the time his family lived in Jedwabne. I could identify most of the people, but I wanted to know more. Who was the guy sitting all the way on the left side? Did Jedwabne have a photograph studio? Why did the family have the photograph taken, and why does everyone look so somber?

"Oh, by God!" my father cried out, cradling the precious artifact. "It's another long story, this picture. You have to understand, it goes back to Motl. Let me explain," he said, a new excitement in his voice.

1924. There would be no more immigration to the United States because, Mendel said, "evidently they got scared of Polish refugees running to America." He was disappointed his dreams of heaven were not likely to come true.

Priwa had more immediate concerns, worried that her strapping young sons would be called into more war. Isn't that how she lost her own parents, maybe not directly, but anyhow? And the big world war was fought on the very steps of her house, on the paths where her children passed the round of their daily lives.

Hadn't those soldiers lain dead like rats on the street? Even after the Great War, hadn't the new Polish nation gone to war with the Russians once again?

Mendel explained about how the United States made a new law making it almost impossible for Jews from Poland to go to America. Mendel shrugged, "Who knows why?" But people talk and from the gossip Priwa heard about a place called Cuba. It's not far from America, they said. First you go to Cuba and then you get to America. Priwa made arrangements for Motl. There was no need for Chaim to leave because the army wouldn't want a boy with a limp. Besides Chaim would never leave his father's side after all that the old man had done for him, saving his leg and carrying him from place to place, from specialist to specialist.

It was different for Motl. He was eighteen and vulnerable, ripe for the pickings of the Polish military. The arrangements were made, and Motl was set to travel with another boy from Jedwabne, also heading to Cuba. This way the two boys wouldn't have to go alone across the land, across the ocean to a place one can only imagine what it is. They left, getting themselves to Warsaw first, then to a port city in France where they were to hop the ship.

The voyage was long and rough. Word floated back to Jedwabne, back to Priwa, that one of the two travel mates had perished. They had been in Vigo, another port city on the far eastern Spanish shore when it happened. But who was it? Which one? Her child? Another one of her babies she would have to bury? It took some time before the families knew which boy died and which boy lived.

It was not Motl. He was the survivor, and arrived safely in Cuba. It took almost a month before the ship pulled into Havana harbor. Motl disembarked with three dollars in his pocket! That was it! He knew nobody, nothing. "He was a greenhorn," Mendel explained. "His only education was how to pray! That's all he knew."

The Havana air was moist, *very* moist, and lay thick in Motl's throat. The scent was tropical, with fragrances from red blossoms and the sweetness of fruit. The buildings were graceful and elegant as if they were copied from an important city in Europe. He walked the streets of Havana with their strange names: *Muralla, Neptuno, Luz, Sol*. Not at all like the ones back home: *Przestrzelska, Cmentarna, Łomżyńska, Sadowa*.

Motl found his way to a place called HIAS, which was there to help Jewish refugees from Europe. HIAS was an American organization and for immigrants like Motl it meant "Hebrew Shelter." HIAS (Hebrew Immigrant Aid Society) had been in Cuba for several years. They gave Motl a meal. They gave him a bed. And they looked for a job for him. And he worked and he saved. He saved as many pennies as he could.

It was good that HIAS helped Motl get started. But naturally, he was lonely for his family. He didn't know if he would ever see them again. So he wrote and asked them to send a photograph. At least he would have that. Maybe it would help with the loneliness.

Back in Jedwabne, the family prepared for the photograph. They would have to take the horse and wagon to Łomża where there was a studio, a nice one called The Rembrandt. This was a special occasion and so to take the photograph, the family wore the best clothes they owned, saved generally just for Rosh Hashanah and Yom Kippur. This was like the high holidays, a special time.

The package with the precious photograph arrived. Motl could see his father Izaak, sitting in the front row all the way to the right. As always, his beard was trimmed neatly. Oh yes, because Izaak was always an orderly person and very fussy about cleanliness. Motl might have remembered the times Izaak wouldn't let the children buy breads from the neighbor's bakery because he thought they were sloppy. Maybe he remembered how when the family passed a well-kept house, Izaak would say, "This man is a *baalabus!*"[1]

The Wasersztejns (ca. 1926)

He sees there Priwa, his *mame*, sitting to the left of her husband at the center of the photograph 🔎, at the center of the family.[2] She was a beauty. High cheek bones, blue eyes, creamy skin. It's hard to tell in the photograph because she is wearing a *sheitl*, just as they all did, the Jewish wives. It wasn't that his *mame* was a religious woman. She wore a wig because if you were a good Jewish wife, that is what you wear.

There's Chaim, the big brother, the devoted son, who stood behind Izaak and Mendel whose arm leans on his father's shoulder, a light touch. It is possible the photographer posed them, but it is no accident that Chaim stood protectively over the eldest and the youngest. Sarah, closest in age to Mendel, stood behind her mother, their bodies close to one another. They were used to being close after all those nights nestled together on the straw sack.

Then there's Yankl seated, with Josef behind him, and sister Fagel, by then married to Label Wenguer, who sits at the far end slightly apart from the rest of the family. Fagel stands behind him, holding their child, another blond!

And Mendel is there too, the baby of the family. He was thirteen, bar mitzvah age. Funny he's holding that booklet from *Biblioteka Narodowa*. What is it? Looks like Niemcewicz's famous old play *Powrót Posla*, the one about Polish politics, and war and revolution.

It was time for Motl to go to work. He worked construction on a site that would eventually become famous. Motl was one of thousands of laborers to build the Cuban National Capitol, the one designed to look just like America's, in Washington. It would be a big building, and for Motl that meant something steady, a good start.

He was on the job but had some problems. It was not the work. He didn't mind working hard. It was not the long hours. He didn't have anything else to do anyway. His problem was the language. He didn't always get it right reading gestures or guessing what to do. One time, the foreman called out to him, "*Traeme aquellos, esos clavos alli*." The boss motioned, offering a quick wave of the hand and a few encouraging nods of the head. Motl thought he understood. He headed over to the right spot. In front of him was a huge sack of cement. He bent down, pulled the bag over his strong shoulder, hauled it over and plopped it down. A puff of white dust rose after the low thud of the drop, dusting his eyes. "*No, no, no, chico*," the foreman said, chuckling. "*Traeme los clavos, los clavos*," he repeated. Oh. Nails. That's what he wanted. Bring him that box of flatheads, sitting on the ground near where the heavy sack once lay.

Later Motl became a street peddler, selling anything, selling *tchotchkes*.[3] "Maybe it was shoes or candy," Mendel suggested, "whatever it was, whatever he could sell." Motl passed a movie theater. He had never been to a movie, and thought he'd go in. He opened the doors to the movie house. Just then, right in front of him, a mob of horses came running towards him! He quickly closed the door and left. What is this movie business? Those horses were about to mow him down, Motl thought.

He gave up on the entertainment. Instead, he would save all his earnings. And he saved little by little, *poco a poco*, penny by penny.

Finally Motl saved enough to send for Yankl. Yankl had been training as a tailor in Poland. By the time he arrived in Cuba, he was highly skilled. They both worked and saved more money. Then they sent for Josef. When there were the three of them, they managed to have a few dollars between them.

Soon it was time to send for Mendel. The girls, their parents, and Chaim would have to wait for later.

Mendel's turn came in 1930 when he was seventeen years old. By then, Mendel, who had been working diligently on his studies, had gotten honors in school. He was accepted into the Druskin Gymnasium in Białystok where the better class of Jews used to go. It was just as he had hoped, his going to study there. No more than six months later, his brothers sent for him with assurances that in Cuba, Mendel could continue his studies. In Cuba, they explained, education was free and he would surely make his way.

Mendel kissed his weeping mother good-bye, and Izaak took him to Warsaw. "Don't forget us," Izaak warned his youngest son before seeing him to the train and stepping away. Before he left, Izaak asked around the older people to keep an eye on his boy, worried someone might steal the few dollars his son hid in his pocket. Mendel traveled southwest across Europe to Le Havre, the port in France where the ship was waiting.

The voyage out was horrendous. Of course, Mendel was a steerage passenger, one among hundreds and hundreds of strangers who traveled together in filthy, cramped quarters. He was assigned a bunk, and tried sleeping in it. He felt trapped, barely able to breathe. Like his father, he suffered from asthma, and these conditions did not help with that. The place was not fit for the dead, he thought. Lying there, Mendel felt one among the dead, and the bunk seemed like a closed coffin. The sweat of the bodies near him, the rough swaying of the big ship and the fear of being trapped overwhelmed him. He sneaked out of steerage to the upper levels, on deck where lounge chairs were set out for wealthier passengers now tucked into dreamy quarters. Night after night Mendel made his way on deck where he swayed and slept and waited.

It was late summer, early fall of 1930 that Mendel left Poland for Cuba. That was just the time the Dominican hurricane hit the Caribbean with legendary fierceness. Mendel's voyage took longer than expected because the hurricane had slowed them down. Worse than that, the thunderous waves and incessant rocking of the ship left Mendel in a near-permanent state of nausea.

From a distance in the middle of the night, Mendel saw the lights of Havana. The little lights shining in the ocean were heavenly. It was then Mendel knew he was entering a different world.

The ship docked in Havana harbor. Mendel walked out, weary but ready for his new life and anxious to be with his brothers. That would have to wait just a bit longer until he got through the immigration process. Meantime, Mendel caught sight of Motl from the distance. Motl saw him too, and they waved across the fence that separated them.

It took four days to get processed through immigration. Motl came every day to see if he could retrieve his brother. As Mendel waited, he allowed his thoughts to drift to school, his education. He so wanted to study, to *progress*. So far, he did what he was supposed to do. Study in Polish schools. Graduate. Get honors in school. "If you study, you're a somebody," he thought. He wanted to be a somebody. "A lawyer, or maybe a writer. A lawyer who defended people," he thought. That would be good. He wanted to defend anybody who is honest and decent and should not be punished—those who were underneath. Now that would be righteousness!

He awoke from the daydream to make his way to the gates of Havana, there with his valise. Then he glimpsed Motl on the other side of the fence. "Motl! Motl! It's me Mendeleh!" he shouted. The brothers were finally together after six long years, embracing and kissing one another.

"We're going to a place called Manguito," Motl explained. "It's a ways away from Havana."

"Manguito has a university?" Mendel asked.

Motl didn't answer. He just laughed.

Mendel kept quiet.

Motl was right. Manguito was quite a distance from Havana in an altogether different province of Cuba 🌐, the island much larger than the boy had imagined.[4] First they traveled to Colón, a city in the province of Matanzas about eighty miles away. Then they would travel from Colón to Manguito, a distance of only twenty-five miles. The last leg seemed an eternity since the unpaved roads challenged even the best of spirits.

It took forever to go the short distance from Colón to Manguito because the road was so bad. The old jalopy did the best it could, bumping and banging on the stones along the path. The trees were magnificent. They were Cuban Laurels, grand with thick roots curving from the base out towards the road, making travel even more difficult. The Laurels lined both sides of the road, facing each other. Their grey trunks, massive and thickly ridged, supported a canopy of weeping branches that met above the riders.

Mendel took notice of the clusters of deep green and pale ruby leaves, and he thought: "This is out of this world. It must be heaven. When I get out the other side, I will be in heaven. Heaven must be a paradise! *¡El cielo debe ser una paraiso!*"

Routes

Motl went to Cuba. His story is not "Motl went to the United States." This is not to say that the consequences for Motl, as an individual case, were better or worse than they might have been had the 1924 US immigration law not been put in place. Listening to my father's rendition of Motl's voyage and of his own voyage out, I couldn't help but think about how legislation and the policies that result shape the course of human lives.

It's what I try to convey to my students in courses I teach at the college where I'm an anthropology professor. Many of my students are immigrants themselves, some with legal documents in place, some without. They know it first-hand, just like my father and Motl did. They have the experience of leaving a familiar place, of saying goodbye to loved ones, of traveling great distances, sometimes alone, and of starting over in a new, strange place. They know this part, but don't always know what's behind what makes one place unlivable or at least undesirable, and another livable or at least imagined as a golden land of opportunity. They don't know why certain laws are in place, sometimes to draw them in, sometimes to keep them out, and sometimes to push them underground.

My father was not aware of why he was kept out; he only knew that he was. Unlike my father or many of my students, I will never know the immigrant experience. But I do know there are structural forces that fashion the contours of a field of action, making some things possible, or impossible, or nearly impossible for individuals. It is on that constructed field of action, structured by abstract and often invisible forces, that individuals *make* their lives. Here I turn to a discussion of law as one among that set of powerful forces.

The law is neither neutral nor moral, but reflects interests, and builds on precedent. Slavery provides a vivid example. Rooted in English common law of property, US laws provided the institutional infrastructure to support the economic phenomenon that was slavery; without it, the practice of slavery could not have succeeded.[5]

Although precedent and interests rather than humanist principles are often the driving forces of law, that empirical truth gets lost, sometimes on purpose (deliberate cover-up; conscious mystification), sometimes inadvertently (use of dense, bureaucratic language), and sometimes by wishful thinking as ordinary people keep hold of preconceived ideas that law equals justice.

In a fascinating article that traces assumptions underlying federal Indian law, legal scholar Steve Newcomb provides a detailed examination of federal and state decisions over several centuries. His data and analysis are illuminating, revealing the uses of precedent to protect interests. In one case, Newcomb quotes from a decision by the Tennessee Supreme Court in 1835:

> We maintain that the principle declared in the fifteenth century as the law of Christendom, that discovery gave title to assume sovereignty over, and to govern the unconverted natives of Africa, Asia, and North and South America, has been recognized as a part of the national law, for nearly four centuries, and that it is now so recognized by every Christian power, in its political department, and its judicial . . . Our claim is based on the right to coerce obedience. The claim may be denounced by the moralist. We answer, it is the law of the land.[6]

In the decision, the Court explicitly acknowledges what holds sway: *precedent* (the "law" set out by Christendom in the period of European "discovery"); and powerful *interests* (the sovereign control of the land by conquerors and subsequently their inheritors, not the interests of the colonized, indigenous peoples). The Court also makes explicit its role in upholding the privileges of its European and Christian predecessors by means of the law.

Legalese may read objectively, coolly, and seem distant and impartial. The law itself is not, as slave, Indian, and immigration laws illustrate. The Immigration Act of 1924 offers a case in point. In the sixty-eighth Congress of the United States, Session I, Chapter 190 and in 32 sections, the Immigration Act of 1924 was written into law.

SIXTY-EIGHTH CONGRESS. Sess. I. Chs. 185, 190. 1924.

CHAP. 190.—An Act To limit the immigration of aliens into the United States, and for other purposes.

May 26, 1924
[H. R. 7995.]
[Public, No. 139.]

Be it enacted by the Senate and House of Representatives of the United States of America in Congress assembled, That this Act may be cited as the "Immigration Act of 1924."

Immigration Act of 1924.

NUMERICAL LIMITATIONS.

Numerical limitations.

Sec. 11. (a) The annual quota of any nationality shall be 2 per centum of the number of foreign-born individuals of such nationality resident in continental United States as determined by the United States census of 1890, but the minimum quota of any nationality shall be 100.

Annual quota, 2 per cent of resident nationality in 1890.

Excerpt, US Immigration Act of 1924

The excerpt 🖉 above gives the title, the opening summary statement of purpose of the Act and, in Section 11, a key provision.[7]

The provision created a permanent quota system for immigrant entry into the United States, basing the number on the 1890 census. Several questions come to mind: What prompted the legislation? Why institute a quota system? Why base the number on a much earlier census (1890) rather than one closer in time to the 1924 law (i.e., 1920)? As Congress debated enactment of new US immigration policy, whose interests got heard, and how?

The Office of the Historian, US Department of the State, offers a succinct statement on the main objective of the law: "In all of its parts, the most basic purpose of the 1924 Immigration Act was to preserve *the ideal of American homogeneity*" (emphasis mine).[8] This was a period in American history when labor unions had gained momentum, the economy had contracted and entered crisis mode (recessions and depressions), and socialism and communism posed threats to the established social relations of capitalist production. The lawmakers, subject to the perceived political, economic, and ideological pressures of their time, had something specific in mind, imagining that "homogeneous American ideal."

Senator David Reed, co-author of the 1924 Immigration Law, published an article in the *New York Times* on April 27, just a month before the legislation would be enacted. The article is designed to share with the American public "the wisdom of [this] policy of exclusion," a "good" judgment Reed based on distorted facts, racialized understanding of foreign "others," and the desire for a "more homogeneous nation":[9]

> There has come about a general realization of the fact that the races of men who have been coming to us in recent years are wholly dissimilar to the native-born Americans, that they are untrained in self government—a faculty that it has taken the Northwestern Europeans many centuries to acquire. Thoughtful Americans have been despondent for the future of our country when the suffrage should be exercised by men whose inexperience in popular forms of government would lead them to demand too much of their Government, and to rely too heavily upon it, and too little upon their own initiative.
>
> America was beginning also to smart under the irritation of her "foreign colonies"—those groups of aliens, either in city slums or in country districts, who speak a foreign language and live a foreign life, and who want neither to learn our common speech nor to share our common life. From all this has grown the conviction that it was best for America that our incoming immigrants should hereafter be of the same races as those of us who are already here, so that each year's immigration should so far as possible be a miniature America, resembling in national origins the persons who are already settled in our country.

In one fell swoop, Reed racializes and naturalizes the legitimacy of the established leadership (Northwest Europeans), casts worker rights as parasitic (they demand too much), and locates causes of poverty and sources of social discord in the foreigners rather than in the systems and structures that engender destitution and conflict. It is brilliant rhetoric, classic scapegoating, and, most importantly, it worked.

In the article, Reed explains that the quota system will use the 1890 census: "The reason that that date was fixed is that the 1890 census of foreign born bears a closer resemblance to the national origins of our whole population today than does any other census." The later census would reflect the influx of immigrants that occurred at the turn of the new century. It was those "kind" of immigrants Reed sought to limit from entering the US, the undesirables who would pollute the pure, homogeneous American race and nation. Those turn-of-the-century undesirables were Southern and Eastern Europeans: the Italians and the Jews. The 28-year-old male Kromberg from "Jedwobno" who entered Ellis Island on February 25, 1902 got in, but twenty-two years later, his nephew Motl would be cast as an alien, a foreign parasite, racially inferior, and intellectually and constitutionally unfit for the American way of life.

In case there is doubt the legislation was cast in such terms, it is worthwhile to read the explicitly racist argument put forth by one staunch supporter, Senator Ellison DuRant Smith of South Carolina, excerpted below.

> Who is an American? Is he an immigrant from Italy? Is he an immigrant from Germany? If you were to go abroad and some one were to meet you and say, "I met a typical American," what would flash into your mind as a typical American, the typical representative of that new Nation? Would it be the son of an Italian immigrant, the son of a German immigrant, the son of any of the breeds from the Orient, the son of the denizens of Africa? . . . I would like for the Members of the Senate to read that book just recently published by Madison Grant, *The Passing of a Great Race*. Thank God we have in America perhaps the largest percentage of any country in the world of the pure, unadulterated Anglo-Saxon stock; certainly the greatest of any nation in the Nordic breed. It is for the preservation of that splendid stock that has characterized us that I would make this not an asylum for the oppressed of all countries, but a country to assimilate and perfect that splendid type of manhood that has made America the foremost Nation in her progress and in her power, and yet the youngest of all the nations.
>
> I think we now have sufficient population in our country for us to shut the door and to breed up a pure, unadulterated American citizenship. I recognize that there is a dangerous lack of distinction between people of a certain nationality and the breed of the dog.[10]

Senator Smith invoked the dangerous rhetoric and pseudoscience of the eugenics movement that had gained favor in the early twentieth century. While some in the Congress refuted Smith's views on grounds of principle, the legislation passed. While some in the larger society refuted the pseudoscience behind these views, those critics went unheard. Franz Boas, considered by some to be the father of American anthropology, is a case in point.

Boas was a member of the Dillingham Commission (1907–1911), a federal commission formed to examine the impact of immigration on US society.[11] The anthropologist designed a comprehensive study of head size and shape among "the Hebrews" and "the Italians"—the Eastern and Southern European members of the darker races who had been deemed inferior and unassimilable. In an enormous, nearly 600-page report, Boas concluded that human biology is adaptable

and changeable, not static and frozen into random categories on which race labels
could be tacked. His findings and voice were drowned out; while Boas contested
the rationale used to justify the proposed new laws, the Commission and parts
of the various reports it produced were used in precisely that way—to support
restrictive immigration policy.

In terms of his views, Franz Boas—not Senator Smith—was the outlier. Henry
Fairfield Osborn, President of the Museum of Natural History, wrote a letter to
the *New York Times* in April, 1924 he titled "Lo, the Poor Nordic!" stating his position on "the immigrant question."[12] Osborn, unabashed in his eugenicist beliefs
and affiliations, effortlessly conflated political power with racial superiority. "In
my opening address as President of the Second International Society of Eugenics," Osborn writes, "I laid down certain principles to which I now desire to call
attention." Among these principles is the "right of the State" to preserve and
protect the *racial* integrity of the nation, particularly those descended from the
Northern races (e.g., Nordics), clearly of superior stock. Like Senator Smith,
Osborn makes claims about the natural superiority of the Nordic "race," their
contributions to democracy and the need to protect the nation from those "unfit
to share the duties and responsibilities of our well-founded Government." Once
again, Boas stood up to the distorted arguments and spurious evidence in a letter
posted by the *New York Times* five days later on April 13, 1924.[13] While the anthropologist's position has stood the test of time, Osborn's logic predominated in
the politics—and immigration policies—of their time.

Both Boas and Smith referred to Madison Grant in the communications cited
here. Smith urged his Senate colleagues to read Grant's book *The Passing of a Great
Race* for the power of its argument to support the immigration legislation then
pending. Boas, on the other hand, is dismissive of Grant. In the *New York Times*
letter, Boas writes, Osborn's "whole claim, which is entirely in line with the vaga-
ries of Madison Grant . . . that every cultural achievement of the Mediterranean
people is due to Nordic influence, is historically untenable."

In the years to follow, eugenics and scientific racism of the sort propounded by
American scientists and politicians would have disturbing effects on law and social
policy in the US, including but not limited to forced sterilization of "problem"
populations.[14] In the years to follow, eugenics and scientific racism would also be
implicated in the mass murders perpetrated by the Nazis during the Holocaust. In
the introduction to his biography of Madison Grant, Jonathan Spiro offers this
chilling account:

> At the conclusion of World War II, the American Military Tribunal at
> Nuremberg indicted Major General Karl Brandt of the Waffen-SS for
> conspiracy to commit war crimes and crimes against humanity. Brandt had
> been Adolf Hitler's personal physician and the most important medical

authority in the Third Reich . . . In his defense, Brandt introduced into evidence a book published in Munich in 1935 that had vigorously advo- cated and justified the elimination of inferior peoples . . . upon reading the book, the Führer himself had announced, 'This book is my Bible' . . . Brandt's defense exhibit was actually the German translation of a work originally published in the United States in 1916: *The Passing of the Great Race* [by] Madison Grant.[15]

In the US, Grant served as vice-president of the Immigration Restriction League (IRL), an advocacy organization that forcefully lobbied for restrictive immigration.[16] The IRL was a national organization with chapters in major US cities where its influential leaders launched anti-immigration campaigns in the first decades of the twentieth century. Their platform was consistent with the pol- icies that would be put in place with the Immigration Law of 1924: keep out the Eastern Europeans and Italians. Harvard University's archive of the Immigrant Restriction League's communications reveals the organization's high-powered and politically connected leadership, its racist logic, and its policy demands they specifically tie to the interests of powerful economic elites.

Motl lugged sacks of cement to build *El Capitolio* that in its size, architecture, and function recalled its counterpart in Washington, DC. The timing was right. Since the end of the War of 1898, Cuba was now firmly located in the US sphere of influence. Meantime, in the hallowed halls of the United States Capitol, sena- tors and congressmen discussed and decided upon ways to shut out rubbish like Motl and his brothers, including my father Mendel.

4

The Shopkeepers

I flipped over the slip of paper with the green markings, the one that named Jedwabne my father's hometown. The flip side read, "Manguito Prov. Matanzas" .[1] My father named the other place that had played a formative role in his life, and about which I had no first-hand knowledge. Manguito, so many thousands of miles from Jedwabne, one in the old world, so to speak, the other in the new world, so to speak. Yiddish and Polish in one place, the Spanish language in the other place. He was so young to have crossed the ocean by himself. I'd been

thinking about my own children, could not imagine letting them go like that, letting them go *alone*, a *teenager*, in *steerage*, with little money, and no way to call me!

I hadn't really realized how important his dream of studying had been until I sat down with him to talk about his voyage. I also wondered why he had never brought us to visit Manguito, those years we had traveled to Cuba. Yes, Cuba is a large island, but it's not that large he couldn't have brought us there, to see where he had begun a new life. For now, I could close my eyes and, while listening to my father's stories, imagine Manguito.

The old jalopy, *"una guagita,"* Mendel called it, made it to their destination. Mendel and Motl came out of the Cuban Laurels and right away entered "the shtetl Manguito" as Mendel described the little town in the plantation region. They were greeted by a little park just to the right of the road. It was lush there, green, hot and wet. They drove a little ways further and stopped just before the plaza.

Mendeleh slid out of the little bus. He was a scrawny immigrant whose spindly legs began to shiver. His thin, shaking body could barely move but his eyes were bright with energy and excitement. "It's Manguito!" Mendel said, recalling the first moment of his arrival. "Manguito's right here. Yankl's right there, wait-ing for me to arrive. Everything is shocking! Everything is new!" Mendel never dreamed he would see his brothers again. Yet there they were, and his new life too.

In Cuba, Motl had become Manolo. Then there was Yankl, Yosef, and Chaim who became Jacobo, José, and Jaime. Fagel became Fela. And Sarah? "Well Sarah is always Sarah," Mendel said. In Manguito, Mendeleh became Miguelito. Before long, Miguelito caught onto the language of this new land.

It seemed the Wasersztejn brothers had already started to extend their reach into several regions on the western side of Cuba. After Jacobo arrived, he and Manolo opened a store in Bejucal, a city just south of Havana. It would be the first of many ventures in shopkeeping for the Jewish brothers from Poland who loved each other deeply and clashed with even greater intensity.

Once José arrived, the brothers began to feel crowded in that little shop in Bejucal, famous as the final stop on the old railway line from Havana. Jacobo moved beyond the family partnership to open a nice men's suit factory with an acquaintance, "a Jewish man named Leff," Miguel noted. Then the brothers heard about Manguito, a small town in the important sugar-producing province of Matanzas with an *ingenio de azúcar*, a sugar refinery near hectares and hectares of plantations. Dark-skinned laborers worked the cane fields in an industry that found new life on the island after the Great War, though it slumped again dur-ing the trying times of the late 1920s. Still, where they make sugar, people buy things, the brothers had heard, and Jacobo was willing to give it a try.

The store was called El Cañón Alemán—the German Cannon. They gave it that name because in the beginning, people in Cuba thought the Wasersztejns were Germans because of their German-sounding name. Besides at that time, the Jews favored the Germans since "the Germans were good to the Jews in those days," Miguel remarked.

Miguelito was shown his cramped, bare quarters in the back of El Cañón Alemán and right away he got to work.

Maybe it wasn't heaven after all.

But he felt safe in Manguito, a place rich with *limón, naranja* and *plátano* (lemon, orange, and banana). "As long as there were no Polacks," Miguel noted, none of them throwing stones at him. There were a few Jewish families, not enough to have a synagogue but "nobody was looking for that anyway," he pointed out.

Before long, folks began asking where he was from. Miguelito told them: Poland. So they gave him a name: "*Polaco*," or more often than not, "*Polaquito*." Miguelito kept it quiet that he was Jewish, worried they would start hating him, the way it was in Jedwabne. He didn't want them to hate him so he didn't offer up that part.

Miguelito tended the store and the Cuban people always came in with a smile. "*¡Hey Miguelito! ¡El Polaquito!*" And all the girls! They would come in looking for Miguelito crying, "*¿Donde está? ¡Mira, alli está!. Que guapo!*" (Where is he? Look, there he is! How handsome!) Flush with the flattery, but still too timid to respond, the *Polaquito* would retreat to the back of the store.

Manguito was a small town, with a population of 2,000, maybe 3,000 if you count the townsfolk and surrounding cane workers altogether. In those years— 1930, 1931, 1932—the laborers made barely 80 cents a day to cut cane.

"Do you know what it is like to bend over all day cutting cane?" Miguel asked, drawing attention to the brutality. "And the people were poor, *muy pobre*. When the people came to buy in the store, they were desperate. They only had enough to spend a few pennies."

Miguelito learned the business, working twelve hours a day. He arranged the merchandise for display—cheap shirts, cheap shoes, cheap pants. Cheap *lienzo* fabric, the cheapest, coarsest fabric in the world. They sold this coarse muslin for five cents a yard. The better quality was six cents a yard. Eight cents a yard was very good quality. Ten cents a yard was the finest. The farmers were so poor they would buy a lot of yardage and make everything out of muslin: clothes, tablecloths, bedspreads.

Miguelito had a knack for making displays to attract customers. He dressed up the mannequin, and placed it outside the door where it would greet passers-by: *Un pantalon. Una camisa. Un sombrero. Un par de zapatos. Un par de guantes. Y un tabaco en la boca por la venta nueve centavos* (pants, shirt, hat, pair of shoes, pair of gloves, and a cigar in his mouth for nine cents).

Business was good only some of the time and dead most of the rest. That's because there was only one season when people could buy: *zafra. Zafra* was the time of the harvest when there was work for the laborers and a little bit of pay for them too. *Zafra* lasted maybe three months when El Cañón Alemán sold shirts for twenty-five cents, pants for fifty cents and shoes for fifty cents too.

The store was in a good location not far from the plaza. It was on the first floor of a two-story building, right next door to a bakery. The second floor had a balcony that gave shade over the sidewalk beneath. Several buildings in a row, one after the other, were connected, and so were the balconies. The balconies, held up by pillars, created a long gallery down the sidewalk. The pillars looked like Greek columns, smooth, slender, and topped by two carved volutes, which gave the poor place an important feel.

Inside the store, Miguelito took the ladder and climbed the tall display cabinets. With an old rag, he wiped away the dust from the old wooden shelves. There was always a lot of dust and it aggravated Miguelito's asthma. Sometimes he was so short of breath he thought he would be left with none at all. At night his breathing became even more belabored. Lying there, his body would make a pathetic one–two dance: a weak gasp for air, then a sucked in chest; a shallow gasp, then a sunken chest.

Miguelito started out skinny in Manguito and only got skinnier. Between the asthma attacks and the problem with the food, it was hard to fatten up. Jacobo arranged that Miguelito get his meals from the little place nearby, the only restaurant in town. For fifteen dollars a month Miguelito would get breakfast, lunch, and dinner. The food was greasy and stewy and had things in it that couldn't be identified. One time the cook came by the store. His eyes brightened when he saw Miguelito's cat saunter out the back of the shop. "Oooh! Aaah!" the cook said admiringly. "What a beautiful cat to make *arroz con gato!*" (rice with cat). Miguelito got even skinnier.

As a matter of fact, Miguelito got so thin and so weak, his body nearly collapsed completely. Jacobo realized something was terribly wrong and sent his brother to a farm in San Miguel de los Baños where he drank spring water, ate fresh food, and breathed clean air. In two months, Miguelito gained twenty pounds!

Then he was back in Manguito with its slow pace and small adventures, like his scary encounter with a ferocious dog. The baker next door had a German Shepherd that always seemed ready to eat someone up. They let him loose at night to keep watch, but he was chained up by day. Miguelito's room was in the back near the baker's kitchen, by the backyard where he'd go to wash up early each morning before getting to work by 6. At dawn one morning, he was in the back by the outdoor sink, busy with his morning ritual, hidden from the neighbors by a shuttered window. He heard some steps. They were getting closer, ominously closer. Miguelito flung open the old wooden shutter. It was the dog! He looked straight at Miguelito, ready to pounce. Miguelito was breathless. "Oh by God," he recalled thinking, "He's going to eat me up!"

Miguelito made believe he was dead, thinking if he moved, the dog would grab him and eat him right then and there! He closed his eyes and relaxed his face, letting it droop as if in eternal sleep. Is the dog still there? He opened one eye. He didn't see the dog but that didn't mean he wasn't close by, ready to tear into Miguelito's hide. Miguelito began to move, slowly. One shuffle step. Another shuffle step. A peek. No dog. He tip-toed slowly, slowly towards the door to his room. Miguelito was almost there but he knew the dog must be somewhere near. A pause and a deep breath. He ran for it, got in his room, locked the door and was safe. It took about an hour to go a few steps! This was a funny story he'd have to remember to tell his children and maybe even grandchildren someday, if he'd be so lucky.

Little by little Miguelito and Jacobo brought in some money. The whole year they hadn't sold anything but in just three months during *zafra* they made $2000, a sum that would have to support the four brothers for the year. That was it for the whole season. By then Manolo was traveling to and from Havana, Bejucal and Manguito, buying merchandise from the big city to sell in the two shops.

Manolo was in charge of the receipts. He took the cash from the season to deposit in Havana where the money would be safe and secure in the bank. He placed the cluster of bills in his back pocket and took off in a shared car back on the rough country road. As always, the vehicle bumped and banged, shaking and rattling its passengers. As always, the long journey made Manolo tired and very thirsty. The first stop was Colón, from there Manolo was to hop the bus to Havana. In Colón he stopped at a little place for a quick *bebida*, slipping onto a stool at the bar. He patted the pocket where his money was tucked. It felt awfully flat. He patted again, not wanting to acknowledge what he already knew. The money was gone! The season was finished. He was desperate. He ran out the shop and down the street looking for the taxi. There it was. It was still in town. And there was the packet of money, sitting just there on the running board! He practically fainted, that Manolo, imagining *what if*.

It had been a rough year between Jacobo and Miguelito only because the younger one had not given up his plan to study. Miguelito pestered and he begged his brother, only five years his senior. "Can I go to Havana?", "Can I go to school?", "When can I get out of here and start my studies?"

The answer was always the same. Jacobo was stern, "I cannot afford you. We cannot afford you to study."

One time there was a get-together with Jacobo, a doctor and a lawyer who all commiserated about Miguelito's ambition. "You don't want to become a doctor," the doctor said. "I'm a doctor and I cannot afford to support my family." The lawyer told him, "Come on! Forget about it! I'm a judge and I barely make $100 a month."

That was the mid-1920s era of Machado, Miguel said, "the worst president when nobody was making much of anything except the big shots. At least the doctors and judges got something. The teachers, they didn't get paid at all! After Machado came, people were practically dying from hunger."

Still, Miguelito felt pretty miserable with this conspiracy to shoot down his dreams although he slowly came to accept it. He learned to keep quiet. What else could he do?

In between working and sleeping there were some comical moments. One time two *campesinos* rode into town on their horses. They tied them up to the pillar in front of the store. Meantime, a new law was passed by the *municipio* that you cannot sell after twelve o'clock on Sundays. Before that El Cañón Alemán would be open every single day from six in the morning until twelve midnight! "Now all of a sudden, on Sundays you have to close 12 o'clock," Miguel recalled.

It was in the *tiempo de zafra* when people had money to buy. Two men came with their horses just around noontime, and they wanted to shop. Jacobo and Miguelito would not miss a sale because of some law. They sneaked the customers into the store through the baker's shop next door.

"Miguelito, I'm going to the post office," Jacobo said, heading to the train station to pick up the mail with the Jewish newspaper from Poland. "Lock the door, Miguelito, in case the Kaufmans report you to the police. Watch out for the police knocking on the door. Prepare yourself," he warned.

Miguelito took care of the first *guajiro* (peasant), and then the customer left. The young shopkeeper started with the second man when what does he hear? Knocking at the door! That must mean only one thing—it's the police! Miguelito had to be quick on his feet. He shuttled the customer to the back where they kept the inventory. There was a stack of cheap mattresses piled high. Miguelito pulled off a bunch, ordered the guy to lie on the *colchónes* that remained, and then covered him up again with six top mattresses. This way, in case the police came in, they wouldn't find a customer after 12 o'clock. A good plan. But the man could not breathe. He started to go insane, choking and squirming. He tried escaping from under the heavy mattresses but Miguelito pushed him back underneath, screaming "Don't take your head out! Get covered—the police are coming! They will take you prisoner—both of us will go to jail!"

They kept knocking at the door. Miguelito heard it knock-knocking. It did not stop. Knock. Pause. Knock-knock. Pause. Miguelito made believe he was sleeping in his little room out back in case the police barged in. Time passed. Nobody entered. The knocking continued.

Suddenly, there was yelling at the door. *"¡Miguelito! ¡Miguel! ¿Qué te pasó?"* Jacobo shouted, sounding desperate. He was thinking that after all they had gone through, it all ends now, this way—the *jíbaros* killing his little brother.[2]

"Whahhhh, waah," Miguelito muttered as if asleep.

"¿Miguel, donde estás? Where are you?" Jacobo shouted again, becoming hysterical. Was Miguelito moaning, half dead?

"I'm here," Miguelito responded so his brother would hear but not so loud to think he was fully awake.

"Did you see the police banging at the door?" Miguelito asked his brother once the two were reunited inside the store. The police banging at the door? Why it was Jacobo all along, sitting on the rocker, reading the paper, swinging the chair back and forth, the legs knock-knocking the door. Knock. Pause. Knock-knock. Pause.

Then he remembered the guy, the customer. Miguelito ran to the back and pulled off the mattresses. Jacobo looked over his shoulder to see the man stuffed between. The guy was terrified when he saw Jacobo. Dripping in sweat, the poor man ran out and off.

Jacobo told the neighbors the story and everyone had a good laugh. They all thought Miguelito was so smart with his clever plan, slapping his back and congratulating him.

The story of the mattresses kept folks entertained in Manguito for quite some time. There wasn't much else to do in the quiet town. Once a year maybe there was a movie. Every once in a while they would bring in a famous *orquesta* so everybody could dance. Miguelito wanted to be prepared so he arranged for someone to show him how to dance, especially how to do the Cuban *son* with its soulful, festive rhythm that was all the rage. He fumbled with his lessons but he got a bit of the hang of it. The night came for the *orquesta* but Miguelito chickened out. He got as close as the entrance to the dancehall, then backed away and headed back home to his little room.

"I was afraid," Miguel recalled, "After all, I was just a *jíbaro*."

Before long, Miguelito would come of age and Jacobo would help him along. After Miguel had been in Manguito a year or so, Jacobo left his younger brother to tend the store on his own. The older brother was off to start a new venture in the city of Matanzas where he was to take a bride, the magnificent Eva, not yet fifteen years old.

Before he headed to Matanzas, Jacobo showed Miguel the way with women. The nice Cuban girls would have a chaperone, and unless you knew what you were doing, it was best to leave them alone. Their brothers were looking to get Jacobo or José or Miguel to marry their sisters.

"We were white and had a business," Miguel explained, "and the girls went crazy for the young men from Europe. If you talk to a girl, right away she was crazy."

But there were others you could go to, the prostitutes from the next town over. Jacobo showed Miguel where to go, taking him there, showing him. That first time, Miguelito was too timid to do it himself. He just looked around. Later, he would know where to go and what to do.

That was the way to learn sex, by going to prostitutes. Everybody went to prostitutes, and sometimes, a bunch of boys would go to the same one. When they went in a group, Miguel liked to be the first because he "didn't want to get shmeared up with a venereal disease." And he wouldn't go to the prostitutes in Manguito because he was embarrassed the neighbors might see him. After all, it was such a small town. He preferred to go to the ones in the next town over.

Miguel thought he was pretty subtle about his visits to the next town, imagining people didn't catch on to what he was doing. Remembering those times many years later, Miguel realized how obvious he likely was, and it embarrassed him to no end, even as an old man in his nineties. One time, after his sister Fela had come from Poland, he suggested they go visit that nice Jewish family in the next town, *pretending* he wanted to see *them*, and figuring Fela would be a good decoy. They go, and, after what seemed a polite lapse of time, Miguel slipped out for a half hour. When he returned, everyone gave him a look, but nobody said a thing. But they knew. And what a fool *he* was thinking he fooled *them*!

But it was the maid in Manguito who really showed him the way. She was just a bit older than Miguel, and he believed she adored him. Somehow she'd find her way to his room after his shower, when he went to lie down. She'd come over, "*¿Qué pasa Miguelito?*," and she would dry him and she would play with him. And then she got pregnant, but Miguel took her to his sister Fela who handled the situation. The girl had an abortion, Miguel was quite certain about that.

Soon after Jacobo left town, Miguel brought a fellow named Ramon Simo Coto to work with him in the store. Ramon, who went by the nickname "Fito," was struggling because his father had been a Machado loyalist and now things weren't going so well for the dictator and his affiliates. Fito was nice, a good friend and honest.

Together the two of them thought they were hot shots. Miguel and Fito made great plans to venture into Havana and get a true taste of the nightlife. Then people started to talk: Watch out for the toilets! Watch out for diseases! Don't even take a shower! Fito and Miguel got to Havana and checked into a cheap hotel. They looked around the seedy room, down the dark halls, and into the communal bath. They were afraid to take a shower! Afraid to use the toilet! Afraid to get a venereal disease! After three days tiptoeing around Havana, the brave guys returned to Manguito, back to the girls the next town over.

Meantime, things were happening. The Wasersztejns began to *progress*. They were no longer Wasersztejn but Waserstein. Soon after Fela arrived, Sarah took the journey to Cuba. At one point Sarah flirted with the Zionist movement, and even joined a group that had a nice-sized branch in Jedwabne. But her brothers found her calling in the new world: marriage. After she arrived in Cuba, they arranged it with a nice young Jewish man named Herman. They helped Herman open his own store in Matanzas. He was a good husband to Sarah, and they had a beautiful marriage, a beautiful life.

"Lovers when they marry should only have a marriage like theirs," Miguel observed.

Miguelito was feeling his oats. He made a couple of important decisions. He'd go to Havana and start a new business there. He had some connections now— his brothers, Fito, other young Jewish men looking to make a business or to grow a business. The girls in Manguito liked him so much, it was likely the ones in Havana would too. He would learn to dance—*really* dance. He would venture out. He would be ambitious. He could be on top of the world. He would never turn back.

Miguelito left Manguito for good in 1936. Next time he saw Manguito it would be sixty-four years later.

Return

My father was eighty-seven years old when I returned with him to the settings of his Cuban life. We traveled with a contingent of anthropologists, our permits from the US Department of the Treasury in order. I had submitted the applications for the two of us, the father and daughter, co-researchers on an anthropological study. The descriptions (our bios and purpose of the trip) were true, though presented in scholarly terms; there was little trace of the intimacy at the heart of the project. Miguel loved his new, short bio, and he tacked it on a wall in his home. He thought it made him sound important.

We flew from New York to Havana late at night, July 21, 2000, eighteen months after President Clinton expanded exchange opportunities between Americans and Cubans. I worried how my father would fare after all the years and his experiences. It felt peculiar to be up in the sky heading to Cuba. The pilot announced the final approach, and it seemed unbelievable. I squeezed my father's hand tightly, overcome for a moment with intense sadness. He seemed calm and relaxed, almost reserved.

It *was* real. We arrived and before long were on our way to the hotel, driving through sleepy, darkened towns in the middle of the night. We met up with my brother David who was also able to make the trip. A cinematographer, David would use my home video camera to capture our stay on film.

The three of us headed to Manguito 🖉 after making arrangements with a driver named Ricardo.[3] We passed the Valle de Yumury with its great vista and new bridge through the city of Matanzas and then stopped in Colón for a beverage, just as Manolo had done so many decades past. We were all ready for this rite of return, and the mood in the car was upbeat and sociable. "How many girlfriends did you have in Manguito?" Ricardo wanted to know. Miguel began to reminisce. "I had only one *novia* in Manguito," he answered, the conversation in Spanish. "Aida Fundora. She was very beautiful and played piano. She played piano for *me*," he said with emphasis. "The poor thing died of cancer," he told us.

The Cuban Laurels no longer created a canopy on the two-lane highway to Manguito, though both sides of the road were lush with palm trees and laurels and stretches of cultivated farmland.

We pulled into Manguito 🖉.[4] Miguel got quiet, looking side to side out the car windows. Ricardo slowed down to a crawl so we could take it all in: the train station, the park, the main street called Calle Real, and the plaza at the center of town.

On the road to Manguito (July 2000)

We were looking for an older person and what he or she might remember. Not five minutes in Manguito, we found him. In just those first few minutes, word about us— the visitors—had already spread. Saul approached Miguel. "You lived in Manguito?" he asked firmly. Yes, my father explained 🔗 about the store he used to have, the one called El Cañón Alemán, and his *novia* who lived just here by the plaza.[5]

"Ah! El Cañón Alemán," Saul replied. "They were *Polacos*." Then Saul named the girlfriend before my father could utter another word. "Aida," Saul said. Aida Fundora. She died of cancer."

"*¡Mire, como sabe este hombre!*" my father exclaimed in disbelief. Look what this man knows!

Saul walked us to a private home, a simple, single-story house surrounded by fruit trees and tropical flowers. Hilda was sitting in her living-room rocker when the crowd entered her home. Saul began to make introductions, reminding Hilda of the *Polacos* who had once lived in Manguito. "¿José?" Hilda asked, looking up at my father, seeming to recognize him. Nobody had yet mentioned José. Saul answered for her. "No. This one's Miguelito," he said, "*el Polaco bonito*."

"I didn't dance with you, Miguel," Hilda 🔗 said flirtatiously. "I danced with José!"[6] Then all the old timers were talking at once, Hilda and her husband Orestes, Saul and his wife Migdalia, Miguel and a troupe of adult children crowding around. They recalled this girlfriend and that shop, this in-law and that jealous lover, and even the corner restaurant, Las Cardenas—the one with the cook who had eyed Miguel's pet cat. They had a big laugh. "*Miguelito era mas flaquito!*" Saul said, remembering the days gone by when my father was so skinny.

"I'm going to cry," Miguel sighed, "I'm going to cry out of *alegria*," he said. Happiness 🔗.[7]

The group of us walked towards the plaza, and beyond it to find Miguel's old store on Calle Real, and where he used to live. We had driven right past, coming into town. There it was, an empty shell but the pillars 🔗 outside still stood tall, almost elegant in their decay.[8]

We peered inside the empty building 🔗—the father, daughter and son, but none of us spoke.[9] I thought back on the old stories: the scary dog, the horses tied up outside, the mattresses, and the cheap *lienzo* fabric.

Miguel walked away and, as he crossed the street, briefly looked back where the store once stood. An old man in a brown hat emerged from a building heading toward us, looking a bit confused. Saul reached out to explain. "This was the *Polaco!*" he said. The old man's 🔗 eyes cast downward for just a moment, then up again, brightening with a memory. "*¿Miguel?*" he called out in a soft but sure voice.[10]

It was amazing the old man remembered my father. The last time he might have seen Miguel was sixty-four years earlier when my father was twenty-three years old. Who was this old man with his wrinkled, dark skin and sharp memory? Maybe he had shopped in El Cañón Alemán. There was no opportunity to ask amid the clamor of this short reunion. I only managed to get the old man's name: Luciano Blanco 🔗.[11]

Most likely, sugar was the hub around which these old acquaintances had once come together. In his recollections of Manguito from six decades before, my father expressed a certain awareness of sugar's role in their lives and his: the seasonal round of production, the *zafra*, the poverty, hard labor, and rural workers he variously referred to as "farmers," "*campesinos*," and "*guajiros*." As with all his stories, my father's account of Manguito suggests a broader and brutal history, this one with sugar at its center. Like Miguel and Luciano, sugar has a social life that can be traced. I would turn to other sources to flesh that out.

Fernando Ortiz is well known in anthropological circles for *Cuban Counterpoint*, a book published in 1940 that became a classic study of the two most important products in Cuban history: sugar and tobacco.[12] Sugar, he explained, is a vegetable turned commodity. Its history reveals key aspects of Cuba's history and its place in the emerging global economy of the last several centuries. Like any other commodity, sugar requires land, labor, machinery, and money. The Cuban story lies in the specific combination of these elements, and the key questions center around *whose* land, *whose* labor, *whose* machinery, and *whose* money.

Sugar has its own unique features, Ortiz pointed out. In the way it is cultivated, it is like no other product. In the way it is processed, it is unique. In what it demands of the human factor, sugar has particular requirements. His study of Cuban sugar led Ortiz to identify the commodity's specific attributes: Sugar looks out for itself. It demands seasonal, not steady work. It requires extensive cultivation, which means many hands are needed, but only intermittently. It requires unskilled labor and strong arms, which made it particularly suited for the slave trade and slave labor. It calls for machines and brute force. And it needs large swaths of land to support such extensive cultivation.[13]

Unlike other agricultural products, there is no set time for the sugar-cane harvest. It is a bit flexible that way since "the season is not so exact nor the hour so important. At times it waits for months, and at times over a year, and it is always done by the light of the sun of working hours."[14] But when the harvest time arrived, it came with a frenzy, the slashing of stalks, machetes gleaming, across the great acreages of the sugar plantations.

With the last stalk falls to the ground, the work of the "sugar-raiser" is done. After that, time is of the essence. The next step requires *speed*: the product needs to get *quickly* off the ground and transported to the mill for processing. Ortiz explained why:

> The cane must be ground as soon as it is cut or else the yield of juice shrinks, ferments, and spoils. Not a moment is to be lost . . . cut cane begins to rot in a few days. The operations of cutting, hauling, grinding, clarification, filtration, evaporation, and crystallization must be carried out one after the other, but without interruption; nearly all of them are going on at the same time in the mill.[15]

Sugar requires a lot—a lot of land and a lot of people to work quickly in a short amount of time, and for a short while each season. In the early decades of the nineteenth century, Cuba yearned to be a player in the sugar industry. It had much to offer sugar. It could satisfy many of its demands: it had the land (the largest of the Caribbean islands), the climate (proportion of sun and rain; temperature), and the money (imperial, planter and merchant capital, tools and technology). But Cuba was missing one important ingredient: labor.

Cuba also had some competition. The sugar industry was already well established in rival colonies, the British and French key among these. But they were having problems of their own. Those sugar-producing colonies were not getting the support they had enjoyed before the Napoleonic wars, there was a worrisome debt crisis among the British planter class, and there was a revolution in Haiti, among other troubles.[16] "The scene was set for the Cuban sugar boom," notes anthropologist Verena Martinez-Alier.[17] If only they could resolve the labor problem.

They did. They solved it by means of another global exchange—the transatlantic slave trade. After that, Cuba became the top Caribbean sugar producer for the world market.[18]

When the sugar plantation got to Cuba, it came with the violence of occupation and of slavery. The plantation, large in size, production and processing, was invasive because it supplanted prior forms of agriculture, and it used enormous

numbers of slave laborers transported from West and East Africa. "Two-thirds of
the slaves shipped to the Caribbean worked on sugar plantations," anthropologist Eric Wolf states, "almost two million [were] transported from Africa between
1810 and 1870, many of them destined for Cuba." When the British abolished the
slave trade in 1807, "more than 600,000 slaves still went to the Spanish domin-
ions in the New World—550,000 of them destined for Cuba."[19] The triangular
trade meant the forced departure of slave labor from one port (Africa), the sugar
product departed a second port (Cuba), and consumption and capital accumula-
tion occurred in the third port (Europe). In this way, "tropical produce became
everyday staples" for Europeans and even North Americans.[20]

Cuba would not abolish slavery until 1886, among the last countries in the
Americas to do so. There were various and contradictory forces at work that led
to the abolition of slavery there. Some among the planter class came to regard
"free" labor as preferable to slave labor. Considering the slave trade had succeeded in transporting an enormous number of workers to the Caribbean, under
"free" labor conditions, the burden of feeding, clothing, and housing workers
would no longer fall to the slave-owners. Workers would be on their own in that
regard, sustaining themselves in a low-wage economy. Worried about debt, the
planter class was also looking to become "emancipated" from the burdensome
ties they had with slave dealers. There was also grass-roots resistance to slavery.
Slave revolts were frequent—strikes, uprisings, and full-fledged rebellions. Also,
a powerful independence movement developed during this same period. White
Cubans were looking for autonomy from Spain; many among them believed "the
emancipation of the slaves [was] a precondition for their own emancipation."[21]

There were still other factors involved in the transition from slave to wage
labor in Cuba. In the second half of the nineteenth century, the United States
had its eye on the island. Struck with manifest destiny fever, the US fully engaged
in expansionist political and economic enterprise whether through purchase, by
commercial domination or by war (e.g., US–Mexican War of 1846–48). President Polk looked to purchase Cuba from Spain but was turned down, and in
1882, "a North American, Atkins [became] the first Yankee planter of Cuba."[22]
Fifteen years later, war would again bring swift change, reconfiguring power
in the Spanish Caribbean. The Spanish–American War (1898) would see the
defeat of Spain, the near-destruction of Cuban independence, and the growing domination of US economic and political interests in the region. The US
intervention in the Cuban struggle for independence from Spain had specific
consequences, including that it "created the conditions for the replacement of
planters' capital with corporate capital brought in from the United States."[23]
Those US corporate entities included the United Fruit Company, the American
Sugar Refining Corporation, Cuban American Sugar Company and the Hershey
Corporation, among many others.[24]

Manguito is situated in the province of Matanzas, perhaps the most important sugar-producing region in Cuba during the nineteenth century. When the
American corporations entered the market, they moved the industry east to
Camagüey and Oriente where large tracts of land were especially cheap as was
the migrant labor from islands nearby. The east became sugar king central while
the mills in the west struggled to keep up with the competition.[25]

By the time my father arrived in Cuba, Matanzas had long passed its sugar-
industry peak, though it did see a short-lived upswing in the aftermath of World
War I. That's what Manolo and Jacobo had heard about, and why they opened
shop in that district. My father walked into this history and these changes in the
depression years, selling cheap goods to low-wage, temporary workers, themselves barely scraping by.

"*¿No te mueres sin conocer Manguito, si*?" Saul asked my father. Don't die without
knowing Manguito, he said as the two old men walked arm in arm across the
little plaza.

5

Young Man in Havana

My father  never answered my question about
why he had returned to visit Manguito only in
his memories and the anecdotes he shared.[1] In
the years his children could have seen his Cuban
hometown for themselves, why hadn't he brought
us there? He gave me no words in response, but a
small shrug of the shoulder, a sign I should move
on and ask a different question. Maybe there was
no time for return visits to Manguito. Maybe he was
just too busy getting through everyday life to give
much attention to what went before.

Decades later, he could focus on what went before, and this project meant
we could venture there together. I would preserve the tales he told and try to dig
deeper, go beyond them. He seemed to like the dynamic: he told me what he
wanted me to hear, and I marked it down, like a dutiful secretary.

My father's description of his adolescent sexual adventures in Manguito is
a case in point. His account did not surprise me, and we both seemed to be
comfortable talking about it, a gendered dance with him doing the telling, and
me doing the listening. I wasn't surprised because I had heard about his exploits
before, from both my parents. My father believed men should be proud of their
conquests, and didn't shy away from sharing such information, even with his
own daughter. My mother believed that the young maid, the woman whose name

he would not say and who gave him such pleasure, did not actually have an abortion but gave birth to his child. There's no evidence to verify my mother's belief, and my father dismissed the suggestion with a brusque wave of his hand.

It was more difficult for me to imagine my father as the timid one, too afraid to enter the dancehall, too shy to venture out on the dance floor. I couldn't imagine there was ever a time he didn't know how to dance—wasn't he born with that skill? "Dad," I asked, "so how did you get to be such a good dancer?" "In Havana," he snapped back as if I should have known that fact already. I wasn't taken aback by his impatience, but it never failed to hurt. Most likely he did not notice the momentary cloud that passed across my face. He was in his own world. Now he prepared to tell me more. He looked at me, the blue of his eyes suddenly lighter, "It was when I got to Havana . . ."

Jacobo had put his foot down on Miguel's formal education. Anyway that dream was fast fading. The youngest brother had more immediate ambitions. Before leaving Manguito for good, and with Fito helping out in the store, Miguel visited Havana more and more frequently. He passed by the shopping district, strolling the famous streets—Muralla, Neptuno, San Rafael. There was El Encanto 🖊, the elegant department store, always with an exclusive clientele.[2] To see those gorgeous dresses, those gorgeous windows! And there's La Moda Americana on the esquina San Rafael and Amistad. American fashion. How modern! What progress!

He began to shed his fears, and gained purpose. He threw away doubt and caught adventure. He came out of himself. On the streets of Havana, Miguel walked and talked with new confidence.

The Waserstein brothers were so devoted to one another, but each was moving up and out and beyond. Jacobo would marry Eva, and once that happened, "he was only for himself," Miguel noted. Miguel could no longer expect much from him except criticism. Same thing with José. No matter what ideas or suggestions or ambitions Miguel had, the two older, more important brothers would criticize him. "That's a bad idea." "It's no good." "You did that? Garbage!" Everything that had to be done had to be because Jacobo declared it. If Miguel said it, it didn't mean a thing! José a little less so, but still he was quick with the insults.

They still had business together but things shifted. Jacobo spent more time in Matanzas before moving to Havana. Manolo and a partner began manufacturing men's shirts. They closed the shop in Bejucal and José moved to Manguito where he decided he should be boss. For Miguel, the itch was getting worse. It was time for him. Time to make a move.

He spoke to his friend, someone he met in San Miguel de los Baños where Miguelito had gone to fatten up. His friend was a businessman from Havana, a wealthy Jewish guy with a partner who manufactured shoes for wholesale that Miguel sold in the store.

The friend separated from his partner, and decided to go into ready-to-wear. The fellow would open a factory and he would manufacture dresses. At that time—Cuba in the 1930s—there was nothing in ready-to-wear. Everybody made their dresses by hand, doing the sewing themselves because there was no work and no money to buy much of anything. Ready-to-wear 🖉 was something special, Miguel thought, and it was new.[3]

Yes, ready-to-wear would be Miguel's future, he imagined. He would open a store in Havana and the manufacturer would supply him with dresses. Miguel had been saving his pennies, little by little, *poco a poco*. He had two thousand dollars saved! Two thousand dollars! He had sacrificed to save that much. In Manguito he didn't even spend five cents to buy a Coca-Cola. Except that one time when Jacobo went to Havana and Miguelito took a coin from the cash register to buy himself the soda. It was a nice change, that Coca-Cola. The rest of the time Miguelito squeezed lemon onto ice when he needed a tasty drink.

That was the only time for Coca-Cola. It was too much of a luxury spending *centavos* on such things. It was worth the sacrifice. Now he would start his own venture in the big city. It was sometime in 1936.

Miguel opened a store on Neptuno, *Numero* 455, right in the central shopping district near all the important stores in Havana. He poured his heart and his life-savings into the small shop with its specialties, just like they had at the big department store nearby: Ladies Dresses. Ladies Coats. Ladies Underwear. Pocketbooks. Perfume. He started with four pieces of underwear in Ladies Underwear. He started with six pocketbooks in the pocketbook department—all different colors—red, green, black. A lady came in. She bought the black pocketbook. Later, another customer came in. She also wanted a black pocketbook—not the red one, not the green one. She wanted the black one because black goes with everything! That's how Miguel 🖉 learned.[4] He told her, "Come back next week. Next week I'll have black."

Miguel had in his mind *La Moda Americana*. *Americana*. American. He hadn't given up on that part of his dream. He would give the store an American name. Maybe he would give himself an American name! From Waserstein to Waterston, an *Americano*. *Tiendas Waterston*. That would be how to name the store. He would add the tagline, "*Templo de la Elegancia femenina*," Temple of Feminine Elegance, signaling this would be a sacred, special place where a woman could become the classiest, most stylish, most graceful of all. A woman could be *transformed* entering the hallowed shop doors of *La Moda Americana*.

The owner of Tiendas Waterston paid attention to the styles, *all* the styles, all the *changing* styles. He looked carefully at the dresses in the windows of El Encanto, and the way the American men walking into that store would dress. Miguel would see an American tourist and think, "*He* must be close to God!" Miguel tried to dress the way they did—white slacks, a sports jacket and wingtip *dancing* shoes 🖉.[5]

Tiendas Waterston 🖉 *"Temple of Feminine Elegance" (ca. 1938)*[6]

Miguel became even more popular with the girls in Havana than he had been with those in Manguito. In Havana he went to a dance school, and by his own assertion, became an expert after only a few months of instruction. He learned *son, rumba, cha-cha-chá, merengue*—which is really Dominican—and the *bolero* where he could hold a girl close to him, moving her with his fluid, confident motions. Miguel was lucky he had found a special teacher who also taught him the *paso doble*, a spirited Spanish dance that would become Miguel's specialty—he the matador, she his cape.

In the beginning, Miguel danced with all the girls—pretty, homely, those who asked him to dance, those who he asked, Jewish or Catholic. "As long as they were white," he noted.

"I want to dance with *you*, Miguel," the girls would say 🖉.[7] Sometimes he would head over to Centro de Israelita de Cuba, the Jewish Center, but only when they had evenings of music and dance. If he had a bit of cash in his pocket, he would make his way to Casino Deportivo 🖉, Hornedo's country club 🖉, aplenty with girls and dancing and romance.[8]

Many girls chased after Miguel. "After a while, they were a bother," he said, "always with their crying, 'I want to dance with you! I want to dance with you!'" But there was one that was special. Anita. She was also a very good dancer and she was a beauty besides. For many, many years, Miguel kept her photograph with those simple words of heartfelt affection: *"A Miguel con el sincero afecto de Anita"*—for Miguel with sincere affection from Anita 🖉.[9]

In the meantime, Miguel's friend supplied him with dresses, and they sold, little by little. It wasn't perfect, and they both made mistakes. But they learned.

And Miguel thought he might buy better dresses. He thought maybe one day he could go to New York where, he said, "they sell you wholesale," and ship the goods to Havana. Just like at El Encanto where they had merchandise from all over the world—from New York and Paris, and from all the best designers.

Before long, José closed up the shop in Manguito for good and moved to Havana where he joined Miguel in another venture, a little shop named El Tropico. They became partners though they rarely saw eye-to-eye on things. While Miguel wanted to sell fine things, José wanted to stick to *shmatas*.[10]

Miguel had an idea. Maybe his uncle in New York, "the Golden One," could help him get nicer merchandise like he saw in the windows of El Encanto. "Oh by God," Miguel thought, "if I could get dresses like that, I would sell them right away." He sent a letter to *onkel* Yitzhak and *tante* Golde at their home: 1552 Carroll Street in Brooklyn. That address would forever be imprinted in Miguel's memory. He wrote asking his uncle if he knew somebody who could ship nice merchandise to Havana.

It turns out Yitzhak Kromberg wasn't so golden after all. "He worked all his life in a factory sewing garments," Miguel explained, not admiringly but with contempt. "And he wasn't so smart either," he added. Uncle Yitzhak turned the case over to Harry, his son-in-law, "a chintzy guy who was a crook and a bastard," Miguel noted. Uncle Yitzhak wrote to Miguel: "Harry will take care of you. He's in the business too." Miguel was excited.

The merchandise arrived in Havana. It was garbage. Harry took the garbage they used to throw away, and sent it to Miguel. And he overcharged him for it too. He figured Miguel's a greenhorn, he wouldn't know any better. He figured he could take advantage of him and send damaged goods. Miguel wrote to Harry: "The dresses came torn." Harry didn't write back. Harry didn't tell his wife Adele about it either. She might have stood up for her cousin, the young man in Havana.

Miguel figured it was time he went to New York. He could meet his relatives in person and confront Harry, the crook. Jacobo was planning a trip too, so the two brothers could go together. In those days it was a sea voyage from Cuba to Miami, then a long train ride to New York. Miguel made preparations—tickets, luggage, and the addresses in New York. He took his Cuban citizenship document from its safe spot, the leather-bound permit carefully put away with other important papers. It had been waiting a few years to be used, Miguel's passport *out* 🖉.[11]

August 21, 1936 🖉.[12] That's when he got it. Nearly three years later, Miguel would see it stamped by an American immigrant inspector. "Admitted," it was marked, "at Miami, Florida on 6/26, 1939, under Paragraph 7 Section 3, Immigration Act of 1924 for 2 weeks."

Miguel and Jacobo made their way to Carroll Street not too far from Eastern Parkway. It was a short visit, just those two weeks permitted by Immigration, but a good enough sample. Despite the shabby apartment in the drab neighborhood, Miguel liked the taste of New York.

His confrontation with Harry didn't get anywhere, but Miguel was finished with him anyway. He learned soon enough the bastard had sent him closeouts. Over the next few years and the next few trips, Miguel was introduced to others of his cousins, some who became close allies and good friends over the years—like Frances, for example. And Samuel Smoller.

Samuel worked as a buyer for Ohrbach's on 14th Street, and was married to Miguel's beautiful cousin Alma. Sam acted like a big shot especially in front of Miguel who, when he got to New York, "was a nothing, a nobody," as Miguel put it. At dinner, Sam would show Miguel the fork and the spoon as if Miguel didn't know what those were or what they were used for.

"What did he think?" Miguel asked rhetorically. "In Havana they don't use forks?" In front of everybody, he would show Miguel how a refined person should use the fork and the spoon, as if Miguel's the jerk and Sam's the big shot. But Miguel took the lessons to heart anyway, and would remember to pass down the finer points of etiquette to his children and maybe even his grandchildren someday, if he'd be so lucky.

Sam also taught Miguel the ropes around the garment district. They'd go together to Seventh Avenue, more or less around 38th Street and walk fast over to Broadway, more or less around 40th Street. 1400 Broadway. That was an important building for ladies ready-to-wear, for dresses Miguel hoped to sell in Tiendas Waterston.

Sam showed him and taught him and guided him, and Miguel was quick to catch on. Miguel had a good eye and became a skilled buyer, venturing out on his own without Sam. He knew what the customers would want before they themselves knew, and he had an eye for style, for color, for fabric.

His visits to New York were becoming more frequent—"every five months, every six months, every four months," Miguel explained, though he couldn't stay beyond the visa permit, generally a few weeks at a time. But he wanted to stay. When he came for visits, he stayed with *tante* Golde, especially in the beginning, and began paying her when the stays extended from weeks to months. In her home, he spoke Yiddish but forced himself to learn English and to speak it. He took night classes when he could, and back in Havana, studied with an Englishman. Each time Miguel returned to New York, he "grabbed" the language faster and faster.

There was the matter of the partnership with José. They had an arrangement that helped ease the fighting: Miguel would be the buyer in New York, and José would stay back in Havana with the store. The two brothers still argued, and José still criticized, "Why did you buy this?" Why did you buy that?"

It was always the same problem. Miguel had big ideas. He had visions for the display windows in the store. Then he would go on a buying trip to look for the nicest merchandise—things that would sell better than the same old *shmatas*. And they *were* selling better. The goods were selling nicely. Miguel would buy dresses wholesale for a dollar each, or $1.25, or $1.80 if it were a much nicer dress. One time Miguel entered a showroom, a very famous name. They wanted $4.00 for each dress! That was a shock. Who heard of that? Miguel felt adventurous and contacted his partner. "José, let's buy these dresses." He was bursting.

"Are you crazy? Four dollars?" his brother shouted back.

"José," Miguel explained, "I'll put it in the window. You'll see. It's going to attract all the customers!"

"No," José answered firmly.

"Yes," Miguel insisted.

"No!" José refused to give in.

Miguel bought the $4.00 dress anyway. "Son-of-a-bitch," José called back at him.

And that's how it got to be with the two brothers until they stopped talking to each other altogether. In business, none of the brothers got along so well. Starting with Jacobo, Miguel said, "they all thought they were big shots." In the end, they went their separate ways—Jacobo had El Figurin, José would run El Tropico, and Miguel would have his own dream shops.

In the meantime, other things were happening to rally the family. Izaak, Priwa, and Chaim—thereafter to be called Jaime—were the last of the immediate family to arrive in Cuba from Poland, settling into Havana. They had come in the nick of time. Soon even Cuba would close its doors to European refugees like the old man, his wife, and the son with the lame leg.

And then the war broke out.

The Power of Privilege

My father was ambitious, energetic, intuitive, and sometimes strategic. From my insider vantage point, I could observe these traits. He repeatedly spoke the language of aspiration, of wanting "the best," to be on top, successful, and powerful. His body moved with energy. He did not walk like most people. He ran, rushing toward his destination no matter what it was. I see examples in flashes of my own childhood memories: a little girl on the busy streets of Havana struggling to keep up with her father who was weaving several paces ahead (I was terrified of getting lost); a young woman and her father zigzagging New York City's garment district, an exhausting ritual. He did not study the trends, but *felt* them: what's admired, what's passé; where's the benefit, where's the drawback; who's an ally, who is not. He trusted his gut, and his judgments were quick and fierce.

He had neither the time nor the inclination to examine his place in the social order of the worlds within which he found himself. His energies were devoted to negotiating within those worlds, not to analyzing them. But I could. Stepping back from one man's life history, his personal struggles and resilience, the challenges he faced and his temperament as an individual, I would try to place him and his ambitions in broader context. I'd start with his *social* attributes, moving out from there to study a longer and deeper history. I followed the research.

As an eastern European Jew in the first decades of the twentieth century, my father embodied an "alien other" in the land of his birth. In the Poland of his early childhood, my father's "kind" was perceived as threatening to the newly born national body. In his time and in that social, political, and economic environment, it was difficult for him to find spaces of privilege.

In Cuba, my father enjoyed a different social location. His new life on the island began in a rural area with a mono-crop specialty produced first by slave labor and later by low-wage rural proletariat. He and his brothers walked into an agricultural sector where they found an occupational niche and an improved social position. They were merchants, not plantation workers. They descended from Europe, not Africa. They were white, not black. In the Cuba of my father's time, these attributes mattered. Taken together, my father's advantages accumulated, like the small savings he had managed to collect.

The race issue in Cuba was not altogether black or white. In the anti-slavery, anti-colonial, pro-independence period, racialized alliances crossed institutionalized prejudice. "Black" in nineteenth-century Cuba signaled occupational location, which at that time was intimately tied to slavery. Anthropologist Martinez-Alier explains, "The negroid phenotype . . . formed the basis for discrimination . . . racism [can be explained] as a pretext for economic exploitation."[13] In contrast, "white" referred to *criollos* (creoles; Cuban-born of European descent); the elites among them flourished with the sugar industry and the slave laborers they possessed. For blacks in nineteenth-century Cuba, ending slavery was their primary freedom struggle. For creoles, the freedom struggle was a nationalist movement to escape the economic and political fetters of the waning Spanish empire. There were moments when the interests of both groups came together. At those times, they fought side-by-side against a common enemy. The Cuban national hero and *independentista* José Martí worked towards that ideal, forging "an effective united front for Cuban independence, forming the Partido Revolucionario Cubano out of a coalition of racial and social forces."[14] The Afro-Cuban movement, under the leadership of Gen. Antonio Maceo and mobilized by the Directorio Central de las Sociedades de la Raza de Color, also participated in the struggle against Spain alongside its own "struggle for equality."[15]

Over the years, scholars and social observers have taken a fine-toothed comb to untangle the complicated strands of race in Cuba. Despite nationalist ideology of inclusion, systematic exclusion by race continued apace, even as there were some spaces for mobility among the darker races there (e.g., Antonio Maceo, a "colored" leader of the rebel army). More often than not, white solidarity was strategic, not principled, and the white creole elite dreaded *their* new nation becoming like Haiti—a *black* republic. Historian Alejandro de la Fuente describes the extent of late nineteenth-century racial "fraternity" in Cuba:

> Whites, including many members of the Liberation Army, subscribed to the myth of racial equality and a raceless nation, but they also identified Cuba's future progress and prosperity with the whitening of the country. As anywhere else in the North Atlantic world, an appropriate racial composition was perceived as a precondition for progress and modernity. In this way, the act of hiding and silencing individuals of African descent within a racially inclusive notion of nationhood was not only a purely ideological exercise. At a more concrete level, blacks and blackness were attacked through a program of state-encouraged immigration that sought to dilute them in a torrent of white blood.[16]

The twentieth century brought more confusion and contradiction to the nationalist and racial questions in Cuba once the United States became firmly implanted in Cuban space. Indeed, the US was fast becoming a major international player across the globe by means of its growing commercial interests, expansionist "land grab" policies and mounting political power. In this regard, US interests in Cuba were clear-cut although how to ensure hegemony was not so obvious. From Washington's perspective, Cuba could no longer extend beyond the US sphere of influence; debates among the powerful centered on how best to guarantee it.

In the lead-up to US intervention, Spain had been taking its last gasps of control in Cuba. In the wake of a slow Spanish retreat, the rebellion made headway despite the setbacks of losing its major leaders (Martí was killed in 1895; Maceo in 1896). Then, in February of 1898 the USS *Maine* exploded in Havana Harbor, triggering the US decision to go to war against Spain the following month. Over one hundred years later, the verdict is still out on who or what caused the explosion, and it remains unclear why a battleship was sent to Havana in the first place. "The Spaniards were entirely unprepared for the visit of the Maine," the *New York Times* reported in 1911. "Once in the harbor she had the city and its defenses at her mercy, for all the modern guns in the surrounding fortifications faced the sea and none of them could be brought to bear on her."[17]

This was a short war and a long victory for the United States, which in three months managed to capture Puerto Rico, the Hawaiian Islands, Wake Island, Guam, and the Philippines, compensating Spain with $20 million.[18] The US installed a four-year military occupation in Cuba during which time it established

hegemony, and upon its departure, "granted" Cuba conditional autonomy, subject to the terms of the Platt Amendment of 1903. The "agreement," which Cuba
signed under duress, allowed for US political and military intervention in Cuba at
its own discretion. "This Nation asks nothing of Cuba, save that it shall continue to
develop as it has developed during these past seven years," wrote President Theodore Roosevelt in 1906. "Our intervention in Cuban affairs will only come if Cuba
herself shows that she has fallen into the *insurrectionary* habit"[19] (emphasis mine). As
Roosevelt's communication indicates, under this treaty Cuban independence was
a legal fiction.[20]

In this period, another layer was added to Cuba's complicated relationship
with race: the US racial imaginary. Recall that in the first decades of the twentieth century, the United States instituted immigration restrictions, purportedly
preoccupied with maintaining "racial purity." While the US began fencing in
its borders, protecting itself from racialized others, it engaged in political and
economic imperialism, penetrating other countries.

Ideologies of race helped resolve that contradiction. Without assistance from
a superior authority, the "colored" nation of Cuba would be unable to manage
itself, to install and maintain democratic principles of government, to develop
an advanced economy, or to become civilized. Cuba represented a classic case of
social Darwinism, becoming the "white man's burden." It *needed* the US Government of Occupation.

Yet Cuba's formal independence gave it a certain degree of autonomy. The first
five decades of twentieth-century Cuba were marked by internal political struggles
and growing economic disparity. All the while, the Cuban leadership "rose and fell
based on the blessings of Washington."[21] The criterion for Washington was not the
presence or absence of democracy, corruption, sustainability, or inequality, but
"friendliness" to US interests. As historian David F. Schmitz notes, the United
States has historically supported right-wing dictators such as Cuba's President
Machado (and later, Batista) in exchange for "being on our side."[22]

Cuba would discover that it was difficult to serve multiple masters. A major
aspect of US "interests" was economic, especially the corporations that controlled
a large proportion of the sugar industry as well as a significant percentage of the
national territory. When these powerful companies needed immigrant labor, the
Cuban government assented, despite internal opposition, resulting in "the massive introduction of West Indian laborers in the 1910s and 1920s."[23] The internal
resistance to migration had a racial cast. White Cuban elites feared the new immigrants from Haiti and Jamaica who constituted, in their racial imaginary, "a black
'invasion' of the country and a deadly blow to the whitening ideal."[24]

My father arrived in Cuba in 1930 when the country was in the midst of
reconfiguring its racial and national identity in the context of neocolonialism
and its peripheral status in the global capitalist economy.[25] Miguel knew what

he saw on the surface. Machado was a strongman and he was corrupt. Machado was "the worst president" who let his people starve while living high on the hog.

What my father observed was true but his vision was limited. Cuban wealth did not just line the pockets of the Cuban political elite, but was extracted from the island nation by powerful outsiders. United Fruit and the rest made great profits while "Machado" didn't pay the teachers, the latter a fact my father noted with horror. Machado is like a fetish, imagined as the cause of the country's woes while structures of economic and race inequality remained intact, generating and regenerating social suffering. Some may dismiss the notion of "structures" as too abstract; locating the source of inequality in a person (a president and "his" policies) seems more real. And thus the fetish lives on.

By definition, a privilege is something restricted and special, enjoyed by some, but not all. Built into the various structures of inequality are privileges for some at the expense of others. There are different domains of privilege— class privilege, race privilege, gender privilege, for example. The same indi- vidual may have privilege in one domain and not the others or another. The fact that "privilege" emerges systemically out of structures of inequality is made invisible by rhetorical and ideological device (the cult of individualism, presup- posed "deservedness," demonization of the disadvantaged). As a result, those with (class, race, ethnic, gender) privilege can take these for granted. In this way, privilege becomes something natural, a given.

Those without privilege (in all or some of the domains) may very well be aware of its absence and the constructed nature of "advantage." Those without privilege in one domain may have it in another, and take the latter for granted. Being con- scious of one's disadvantage does not guarantee awareness of some other advan- tage. Those without privilege may contest the system of advantages that unfairly accrues benefits to some over others. More often than not, in such a system, those without advantage yearn to acquire it, and will defend the little privilege they may have over the next person. This is not a natural state of affairs but a relatively predictable pattern of behavior under conditions of scarcity where privileges are prized and may even be essential for survival.

My father yearned to acquire the privileges he did not have and seemed oblivi- ous to the gender and race advantages he possessed in the Cuban context. He assumed his male prerogatives and would never imagine dancing with a black girl. He took a look around, saw what "counted" and what did not. He would be on the side of the victors, and move forward as they had been able to do. The winners were god-like, he thought. He tried on their identity in name and in appearance. In search of privilege, Miguel allied himself with the most powerful entity in his midst: the United States of America.

An American Soldier

If I didn't have the old photographs to prove it, I would never have believed my father donned the best fashions of his times. By the time I knew him, he was pragmatic about such things, and made sure his children valued the frugality he modeled for us. "See these shoes? I've had them for thirty years. Thirty years! And look what perfect condition they are in. Perfect! They don't look a day old!" he'd tell his children. We'd grit our teeth, mutter, "Yes, daddy," and exchange knowing glances with each other. To us, the shoes *did* look thirty years old. Although they were well cared for and in perfect condition, there was no getting away from their age. They were dated. Couldn't he tell?

Now I held his old, pale-blue guayabera shirt in my hands. The label read "Radiadic Fashion," size "M," and the hem was terribly frayed. I decided to keep it, a relic and a memento.

Sometimes, the intimate nature of this project wore on me. Jane Lazarre, another daughter of an immigrant East European Jew, warns that the dangers of this kind of project are always underestimated and that its intimate nature would make it "far more exhausting than safer, more distant studies."[1] I entered familiar turf, but it was so strange. I entered unfamiliar territory, but I recognized it. I loved my father deeply, but couldn't stand him. I was drawn to the story, but not satisfied to leave it at that. I couldn't help but see history in him, but couldn't reduce him to that either. Like my father's ever-shifting identity, this project refused one label.

I found amongst my father's papers, "A TRUE COPY" letter dated June 23, 1944 from W.E. Nelson, WOJG, USA, Personnel Officer, to the Adjuntant

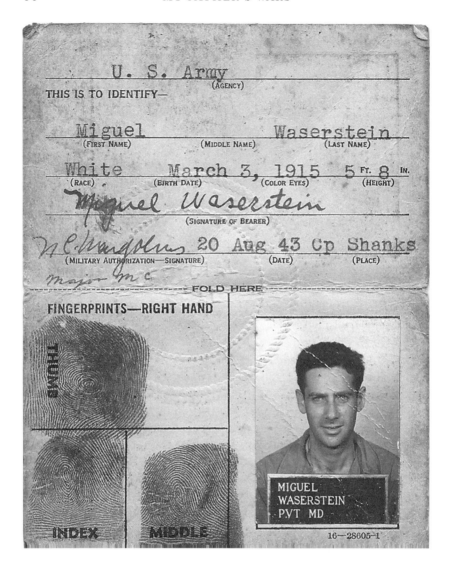

General in Washington, D.C. It is the official declaration of my father's new name. I had been putting the pieces together, and needed my father's help. "Tell me about the war ✎ years," I asked.[2]

His voice quieted, and the wet of his eyes began to shimmer. He turned his face towards mine. "Do you know my parents barely made it out in time? Do you know how much they suffered?"

Izaak saw the doctor in Warsaw. "What do you think? Cuba is around the corner?" the physician pressed the frail man, weakened by the asthma that had plagued him for so long. Izaak wanted the doctor's blessing to travel but that would not happen. "You cannot go," the doctor said, "You are too delicate. You will not make it from here to there."

He went anyway. Izaak and Priwa and Chaim. And they made it across the ocean, all three of them. As the ship docked in Havana, the passengers caught a glimpse of their new lives just as had their brothers and sisters, their sons and daughters over the previous fourteen years. It was 1938. At long last, the Wasersteins were all together.

And the doctor? He died years before Izaak would. The doctor died because of the war.

Priwa and Izaak settled into their new home in the Santos Suárez district of Havana, a pleasant place with a nice balcony and an extra bedroom. Miguel moved in and slept in the spare room, at least for a bit. The young man had been a bit of an itinerant in those years. He sometimes stayed at Jacobo's, sometimes in a cheap rooming house, sometimes at *tante* Golde's in New York, sometimes in a residential hotel on Manhattan's west side. With his parents new in town, Miguel settled in with them, at least before his next trip to New York.

Izaak suffered terribly with his asthma. And the rest of the family didn't know how to help him. There were many times Izaak couldn't breathe. In the middle of the night sometimes, he'd call out for Miguel to come help him. Miguel would sit him up, and put pillows behind him so he could sit up better, maybe catch his breath. They were nice, fluffy, feather pillows.

"Feather pillows! Can you imagine how that made it worse?" Miguel exclaimed. "Feather pillows are a poison for a person with asthma! In later years, anyone with asthma would tell you that. But back then, nobody knew. They didn't know any better."

Moisés Waserstein had also come from Jedwabne, just before Izaak, Priwa, and Jaime. Moisés was the oldest of dear aunt Chajcia's children, and would establish himself in Matanzas. The younger one, Shmulke, was still in Poland with his mother, waiting to get clearance to come too.

The new arrivals came with little news from back home. It seemed things were not so good, but not completely unbearable. Still most everyone was looking to move. The five sisters from Łomża, the mean Kromberg daughters who walked away from the Wasersteins dying of typhus in a barn—now *they* wanted help. "Can you get us to Cuba?" they begged. This time the Wasersteins did nothing. It was their turn to look away.

Not long after Miguel's parents arrived, Cuba closed its borders to the refugees. Chajcia and Shmulke would not be able to leave Jedwabne after all.

Miguel was down by the docks the day in 1939 the *St. Louis* was in Havana harbor. He went to see the ship. He remembered seeing the people who were desperate to get off it.

"But it was that goddamn president of Cuba," Miguel said. "It was Laredo Brú—he was the worst president."

Rumor had it Laredo Brú accepted money so the Jews could not get off the ship, could not get into Cuba. Miguel watched as the ship backed out of the harbor to return to Europe with all those desperate people, almost a thousand of them. Some jumped over the sides into the ocean, they were that desperate.

Even in Cuba the propaganda of the times was seeping in. Those were the years "Hitler made propaganda against the Jews," Miguel said, and in Cuba the German Ambassador spread it. Miguel didn't advertise that he was Jewish. "As a matter of fact," he said, "sometimes I hid it."

Right around that time Miguel met a nice Cuban girl. They met at the doctor's office and he talked to her because she was very attractive. She invited Miguel to her home for a little get-together with her friends. Miguel went. Her friends were all Cuban, and some of the guys started saying bad things about the Jews, about how the Jews took things that belonged to the Cubans. Miguel protested what they were saying but tried not to reveal he was Jewish. He just told them, "You're wrong. That's not true." Finally, Miguel had heard enough.

"I want to tell you," Miguel said, his eyes straight on the one with the loudest voice and lowest opinion of the Jews. "I am Jewish too."

The guy was shocked, and then he apologized. That didn't stop Miguel from hiding his Jewishness. He thought, "Why should I advertise it? Why should I get into arguments?"

Instead of getting into arguments, Miguel traveled back to New York, eventually becoming the buyer for all the Waserstein brothers who were expanding their enterprises. As business improved, so did Miguel's circumstances. Sometimes he still stayed with *tante* Golde in Brooklyn, sometimes he'd stay in a cheap hotel, and later he got a better hotel, right in front of the Hudson River on Riverside Drive in Manhattan. The place had beautiful views. It was like heaven.

Miguel had his fair share of girls in Havana and his fair share of girls in Manhattan, and he didn't want to lose steam with any of them. When in New York, he'd send notes to the ones in Havana ; when in Havana he'd send reminders to the ones in New York, even photos of himself so handsome and dapper .[3]

What with the war and all, Miguel noticed the girls really went for the men in uniform. It started to be that if a man didn't have a uniform, nobody looked at him. People even distrusted the men who weren't in uniform.

But everyone trusted Jimmy Stewart, the movie star, and *he* wore a uniform. Miguel explained, "Jimmy Stewart gave up being a movie star to join the military and look what happened to him! Wherever he went, all the girls ran after him. They admired him so! They praised him and they gave him respect."

On account of Jimmy Stewart , Miguel decided he would join the Army too.[4]

He was in New York when he made the decision, and the war frenzy was in full swing. There were signs and advertisements and promises every place he looked. Miguel sent a letter to Priwa and Izaak, breaking the news to his parents. It was terrible. Priwa was beside herself upset. After getting her sons to safety, away from war, one of them decided to step right into it. Izaak begged him not to go. Miguel wouldn't budge. "I wanted to be an American," he explained, "I wanted to speak English. I wanted everything the best." Izaak sent messages with Jews traveling to New York from Havana: "Your father asked me to come see you and tell you 'Come back to Cuba.'"

"No, I won't go back." Miguel didn't waver. "I made up my mind," he told the messengers. He signed up at the Local Board of the Selective Service on Nostrand Avenue in Brooklyn, and soon received a postcard in the mail, addressed to "Miguel Wasserstein, Class 1A-available for unrestricted service."

Miguel had some time before he would be sent overseas. Fito came from Havana, and the two friends explored the city, strolling through the parks and the piers, taking photographs of one another posing in front of the ships docked on the Hudson. A policeman approached them, these two foreigners with accents and no uniform, taking photographs of the river way. "Why are you taking pictures?" the officer demanded. "Don't you know there's a war going on? What are you—spies?" he asked them, as he detained the pair. Hours later they were released, after Miguel explained over and over again, "But I just enlisted! I'm going to the war!" They rushed back to the residential hotel—Miguel's place on Riverside Drive, the place with the views on 80th Street. The police hadn't even confiscated the film but now the pair thought their innocent photographs were too dangerous to keep. They ripped the film from the camera, cut it to shreds and flushed it down the toilet. A close call.

One day Miguel went for a drive upstate with his cousin Herman. Herman had a serious girlfriend and was dreaming of buying something for himself when he heard about a dude ranch for sale. Miguel donned his new sports jacket and shoes, and hopped into Herman's car for the day trip. "When are you going to get married?" Herman asked Miguel. Not so soon, Miguel told him. There's no rush. He's the baby of the family and all the others needed to be married first.

They pulled into the dude ranch and walked to the little restaurant on the property. Herman wanted to talk with the proprietor, a woman who seemed to be the boss even though her husband was right there too. Miguel wanted to talk to their daughter, the young waitress sitting on a bench just like a little angel. She was a beauty, and so sweet, and calm, peaceful, quiet and respectful. "A girl like that could only be nice," Miguel thought. While Herman chatted up the wife, Miguel approached the husband. "May I take your daughter on a date?" he asked the older man.

And then the military called him for service. It was February 11, 1943. Finally Miguel would see the world!

He was sent to Camp Shanks where he was processed and given a Medical Department identification card to keep with him at all times. Then he was shipped to England. Miguel recalled the first days of his stint in the English countryside

as bitterly cold, sleeping in a tent out-of-doors. They asked the recruits questions about what they did in civilian life, about their skills and expertise. Miguel
told them about Tiendas Waterston and his visions for a shop he would call El
Imperio. Soon enough, Miguel was put in charge of the tailor shop. When soldiers needed clothing they came to Miguel. He made sure all the clothing was
in good shape, washed and pressed. Miguel even slept with the clothing and not
with the soldiers in the barracks. And then it was in the line of clothes duty that
Miguel was injured in the war.

The camp was in central England. Miguel would often hitch a ride in the
military ambulance to take clothes to London for special washing and dry clean-
ing. Night-time driving in England meant you took your life in your hands. The
fog was treacherous, and there was always fog. An English road in the night fog
during wartime was as pitch-black as could be.

The evening of the accident, Miguel had finished his business with the clothes
in London, and hitched a ride back to camp in the ambulance, as usual. He
tossed the clothing in the back and got comfortable next to the driver. Then
he dozed off, lulled by the movement of the vehicle along the country road.
The next thing he would remember was the hospital bed, opening his eyes to
a surgeon peering down on him. "I did a good job. You won't see a thing," the
surgeon smiled proudly. The accident was pretty serious and Miguel's wounds
severe—his head split open when the ambulance turned over in a ditch. The surgeon was right. He sewed him up just fine, and Miguel was soon back at camp.

Miguel was popular with the British girls just as he had been with the Cubans
and the Americans. Only now he had a uniform. One gal approached him, asking him sweetly where he was from with that unusual, Yiddishy Spanish accent.
"I'm from Texas," Miguel told the British beauty, "this is how we talk in Texas."

Her name was Pat and she was a nurse at the
hospital across from the camp, a married gal
whose husband was off to war. They met one
late afternoon when the day was just waning.
Miguel was riding a bicycle—he avoided cars ever
since the accident. Dressed in his military best,
Miguel headed by bike to the local pub, looking for a companion, looking to enjoy himself.
That's when he saw Pat, standing outside the
hospital. It was a nice afternoon, and Miguel
wore sunglasses. He wore sunglasses because
his blue eyes were always light sensitive and the
glasses helped with the glare, especially at sunset.
Pat called out to him, "Oh, how much sun we
have in England!" she teased.

Michael Waterston 🖉 *(ca. 1945)[5]*

Miguel stopped the bike and approached her. "Do I have to advertise it, announce that I have only one eye?" he asked her, looking to get her sympathy and her attention.

"Oh, I am so sorry," she responded, a bit flustered, "I'm very sorry."

"Do you recognize which one it is?" Miguel flirted back at her.

"This one!" she exclaimed.

"You're right!" Miguel winked. And they went off for a drink. And they went off for more than a drink, more than one time. And then she got pregnant. But she was a nurse, and she knew how to handle the situation. The nurse had an abortion, Miguel was quite certain about that.

Pat had a married sister, and Miguel had a friend named Cris. He was a handsome, simple guy from a small town in Pennsylvania. "He was a *jíbaro*, you know, he didn't know anything about girls," Miguel said. Miguel introduced Cris to Pat's sister. He showed him the way, how to do it, how to go slowly, how to be with a woman. Miguel was no longer the greenhorn, but the expert, a Latin lover .[6]

Miguel was in the Army for three years. Just before he and the other soldiers in his unit left England, an officer asked them: Do you want to be a United States citizen?" Yes, of course they answered.

The officer said, "If you want to change your name, the way you say it now is how it's going to be."

"My name is Michael. Michael Waterston," Miguel said.

Michael Waterston. "It sounded so much better than the names some people have," Michael said. "Like Kreplach. It sounds ridiculous—like from Poland! What kind of a name is Kreplach anyway—kreplach is a meat, you cook it. Yes, in Havana, Kreplach changed his name to Kress! Of course it's much nicer, Kress than Kreplach."

"Of course it's much nicer Waterston than Waserstein."

Michael had a lot to think about. Unlike his brothers, he was the sophisticate, a cosmopolitan man who had been to places, who had seen the world. If the Waserstein brothers had gotten along in business, Michael believed, they could have conquered the world! They could have been bigger than El Encanto. They could have been better than the finest stores in Manhattan. But the brothers could not work together. Michael had different ideas than his brothers, and they did not show him respect. He would go his own way, and build El Imperio—The Empire.

Textil Blumin, S.A. would become the name of his own venture with two stores he would build in Havana. They would be centrally located, one, a corner store on Calle Muralla, *Numero* 424 on the *esquina* Villegas, and the other nearby at Muralla, *Numero* 360. They would have windows and he would make displays to attract customers. He would have fabrics but better merchandise too, more ready-to-wear, more departments. The stores would follow the

"American system"—have a table with merchandise and a sign, "special price for the day." One shop would be called Blumin, but the store on the corner would be named El Imperio.

Michael repeated the name, "El Imperio, the Empire. The accent is on the second word. You barely mention 'El' you say 'l'imperio,' so people hear *imperio*, empire, just like in any other language."

Michael was also thinking a lot about that girl he had met, the one from the dude ranch, the sweet one. He had taken her to a nightclub and she enchanted him. She wasn't a good dancer, but it wasn't important the way she would get him out of step.

She was a fine girl. Michael remembered how he had asked her back to his apartment and she wouldn't go, and that impressed him. She must be a very fine girl, he thought, not going to a man's apartment. The second time he took her out, he asked her again to see his apartment—just to see the glorious view from Riverside Drive. She wouldn't go, and seemed insulted that he asked. It annoyed him that she didn't trust him. What did she think, that he would force himself on her?

Now he couldn't get her off his mind and told his buddies about this girl in Manhattan with a *tante* in East New York, Brooklyn, but it was driving him crazy that he no longer had her address, couldn't locate her, or remember the name of the street to send a letter. "Why East New York's my neighborhood!" said Phil Forman, Michael's army buddy. Phil had his sister scour the neighborhood for the girl's aunt, a Betty Gross, married to a rabbi with five children, none of them her own. No luck. Phil's sister couldn't locate her. Next he tried his sister-in-law, she might know better.

Next thing he knows, Michael received a letter. It was from Louise, the nice girl, the one so peaceful and refined, the one who didn't go—who wouldn't go—to a man's apartment. It was Victory in Europe Day that Michael received her note.

The Lost Ones

A question kept forming in my mind across the conversations I had been having with my father: "Who am I in relation to the Other and to my past self?"

I kept thinking about how my father's life intersected with the violences of the twentieth century, an epoch of brutal upheaval.

I wondered if violent contact produces a crisis of identity—and whether this was as true for cultural groups as for individuals.

I thought about the fact that my father lived, and that hundreds of millions of others did not.

I realized that it was simply because my father was among those who lived that he had a lifetime of stories to tell. My father's life included the dead (those killed by war, conflict, genocide) as a "present absence" even if the dead barely appeared in his narrative.

It struck me that the life-stories of the war dead are always cut short, creating a void around which the living "remember" them, and craft their own lives. It seems the stories of those killed are so often "disremembered"—told by others in the service of something disconnected from the dead themselves. Memorials may be erected in their name but these are not necessarily true to the lives of the dead or to their experiences. Some among the dead are lost entirely, unaccounted for and forgotten.

These thoughts led me to other questions. What was it about the twentieth century that made it so deadly? What is it that makes people believe that war is a reasonable, *normal* course of action? How do people wipe from their consciousnesses the bare fact of the destructive force of war? I did not pose these questions to my father. Instead I looked to history, poetry, and the social sciences to help me understand.

I learned from this literature that the twentieth century saw the consequences of centuries of violent contact between empires, and between emerging nation-states and new empires vying for land, labor, wealth, and power in the modern period. No statement can capture the ferociousness, the terror, or the horror of the century. No narrative can capture the full effects of the violence on human lives or the subsequent effects on social groups in places where there was war.

The numbers of dead offer a declaration of the extent of the violence: "231 million people died in wars and conflict during the twentieth century," war scholar and research scientist Milton Leitenberg estimates.[7] The numbers are beyond comprehension. I find it hard to imagine so many human lives lost to war, or to comprehend the destructive forces that go along with it: starvation, disease, genocide, trauma.

In her "different kind of war story," anthropologist Carolyn Nordstrom makes the sharp observation that "most writing about violence in western theory never deals with actual violence . . . in most of these cases people are writing from the safety of a nonviolent situation."[8] Nordstrom is herself an exception, having spent decades as an anthropologist in war zones. She theorizes the violence of war while keeping hold of the "'wild cr[ies]' of terror, passion, mystery, rage . . . despair" that real people in real wars experience.[9] Her contemporary ethnographic projects bring readers to the places where bullets are fired, where flesh is torn, where blood, brutality, and death are intertwined. We need to go to that place and sit with it, learn from it. It is raw and tangible, the content that must be absorbed before we can go to the abstract.

On war, Virginia Woolf wrote, "Dead bodies and ruined houses are not an argument [but] a crude statement of fact."[10] Dead bodies and ruined houses are war for ordinary people, the civilian and combat soldier. We need to understand the ways in which war is the clash of classes, armies, and empires played out on structurally uneven killing fields. We must also see that war is complete torment, a truth made cliché by fatigue, indifference, misrepresentation, and abstraction.

Knowing the sheer numbers of dead is essential but inadequate. A number is still an abstraction; 231 million can lull because it does not hold the wild cries of terror and despair that surround the death and destruction. Sometimes poetry and fiction can shake us from the lull. "But all limped on, blood-shod. All went lame; all blind," wrote Wilfred Owen, the prolific poet–soldier killed in World War I at age 25, one among hundreds of thousands of young men who died in that war.[11] From Siegfried Sassoon, a surviving soldier who was also Owen's friend and fellow poet, came "The Hero":

> Blown to small bits. And no one seemed to care
> Except that lonely woman with white hair[12]

He who was blown to small bits was one of an estimated 13–15 million people killed in the course of that war.

The notion of "progress" as humankind's inevitable trajectory was firmly entrenched in twentieth-century western thought, political rhetoric, and economic practice. Social theorist Jeffrey C. Alexander considers the idea of progress as the "underlying motif" of the twentieth century:

> We must clarify what initially marked the west off from other civilizations, the modern west from earlier periods in its history, and the twentieth century from earlier western modern societies. This distinguishing notion is 'progress' and the possibility of perfection it implies.[13]

It is a powerful idea to which people have become habituated, justifying and naturalizing exploitation, conquest, and the spectacular violence of war. The significance of this belief is that it tolerates blindness to the horrors that fall in the wake of the march towards "advancement." Historian Howard Zinn posits a series of questions to challenge "the excuse of progress" that reached great heights in the "beastly century":[14]

> Was all this bloodshed and deceit . . . a necessity for the human race to progress from savagery to civilization? Perhaps a persuasive argument can be made—as it was made by Stalin when he killed peasants for industrial progress in the Soviet Union, as it was made by Churchill explaining the bombings of Dresden and Hamburg, and Truman explaining Hiroshima. But how can the judgment be made if the benefits and losses cannot be balanced because the losses are either unmentioned or mentioned quickly?[15]

For so long, modernity was imagined as a key expression of progress. Reason and rationality—not superstition or magical thinking—would hold sway, and new tools and efficient technology would bring humankind to the highest levels of civilization. In the natural order of things, the advanced ones were the rightful leaders of the civilized world. They would usher the backward ones (those without advanced technology; those guided by primitive beliefs) into modernity.

In some quarters, the enormity of the violence of the twentieth century unsettled these assumptions and called into question the legitimacy of the new world order. For example, anthropologist Alexander Hinton refers to the multiple genocides of the century as "the dark side of modernity."[16] And Zygmunt Bauman's widely known and important thesis in *Modernity and the Holocaust* suggests the violence was not an aberration but part and parcel of "advanced" social relations of production and the governance mechanisms in place to protect it. In the case of the Holocaust, Baumann argues, "the social norms and institutions of modernity . . . made [it] feasible. Without modern civilization and its most central essential achievements, there would be no Holocaust."[17] The critics' voices have been stilled by weak counter-arguments (humankind has always been violent, though the archeological record contests this assertion; it is human nature to be violent; the Holocaust was a deviation; etc.), temporary salves that shield harsh truths and reinforce trust in contemporaneous authority.

My father was not unaffected by the forces that left so many dead, and which his life history reveals. He stood in uncomfortable relation to the forces of history, to the obstacles he faced, to the opportunities available to him, and to the dead. He did not create the social formations in which he was situated, but maneuvered within them for advantage (survival, mobility), at times silencing aspects of his self (as Jew, for example), emphasizing others (whiteness, for example), and inventing still others (Americanness, for example). In a social formation characterized by hierarchy, advantage/disadvantage lie along it where one's gain is likely to be at another's loss. No one escapes untouched.

My father became an American soldier, and by means of it metamorphized from Miguel to Michael. Crafting his life, Michael looked to thrive within the parameters of what was in front of him. And what was in front of him, at that time, in that historical moment was the possibility of an American life. Europe was in decline; the United States was emerging more fully as the central global power. Michael wanted that—the power, and the good American life. Before, he did not qualify to become an American (in the midst of the 1920s Depression years, neither his labor nor his military participation were needed). Later, the world went to war. The military became his entrée, and war gave him the opening to become Michael Waterston.

War cannot happen without the participation of those who enact it and the compliance of the masses that stand on one side or the other of the battle line. Participants need to be pressed into service, and consent and complicity need to be roused. There is a mobilization process where lines are drawn, potent language is utilized, groups are demonized and dehumanized, justification is put on spectacular display, duty is summoned, virtue invoked, trophies bestowed, and the satisfaction of real or perceived needs is tied to outcomes. There is a repertoire of rhetoric upon which to draw—war in the name of God, evil, country, democracy, freedom, or security. It is calculating, but, as war scholar R. Brian Ferguson notes, "the values are true to local culture," values that are inculcated, harnessed, and exploited.[18]

Some people go to war because it is the law of the land (a legal draft). Some join because they consider a "just" war is possible, and believe in a specific war's purported purpose. Still others participate out of blind duty (patriotism, jingoism), basing their decision on "trust" (leaders know what is best). Some are lured by images of glory—victory, heroism, and manliness. The uniform itself signals these attributes; positive response to the sign can be very reinforcing, especially for those with few or no other roads to social respect. Some participate because they are promised something specific in exchange (an education, citizenship) or have been specifically targeted by marketing campaigns. Of course, these are not mutually exclusive motivations and an individual may be moved by a multiple of incentives.

My father's decision to go to war did not have to do with principle, patriotism or jingoism. Michael joined the military to be accepted and acceptable. When under suspicion by a New York City policeman for taking photographs by the piers, Michael invoked his military contribution to prove loyalty and belonging (he was not an outsider; he was not a spy). By means of the military, he could demonstrate his manly virility, and his eligibility as an American; the uniform would at once entice the girls and display his allegiance. He longed to be a part of a war effort that would create his "path to citizenship"; in this way, the law structured Michael's choice.

My father's war stories are light-hearted, almost carefree. They aren't morose, and are devoid of the horrors of war probably because he did not witness them first-hand. They center on flirtations, friendships, and small adventures, a surprising choice considering the time and the place for them. Michael, focused on his individualistic life, does not mention the dead though they number between 65 and 75 million during World War II.[19]

What are we to make of this, and of him? My interest is not to criticize or condemn but to glean insight from the individual case. My father was not a world leader, a poet, or an important figure in history. He was an ordinary man, a refugee who knew what it felt like to be the object of scorn, who experienced war at his childhood doorstep, and who suffered hunger, loneliness, and disappointment. He was an exile in the sense that Edward Said has described: a state of being, in a jealous state, with resentment, always out of place, he felt his difference.[20] Sometimes these kinds of feelings and experiences can bring one to awareness or empathy, though not always, perhaps not even usually. Sometimes these kinds of feelings and experiences make people believe it gives them a right to the good life, no matter if war is the only path to it. Before, they were the ones to suffer; now it's their turn to be on top, regardless of the casualties.

"Even in the darkest times," Hannah Arendt wrote, "we have the right to expect some illumination."[21] She found illumination in the lives and works of certain women and men, including Bertolt Brecht who "was more struck by the misfortunes of the time than his own unhappiness."[22] In "Beyond Personal Frustration," Arendt offers up an excerpt of the poet's "To Posterity," a poem that helps us *see* too.[23]

Indeed I live in the dark ages!
A guileless word is an absurdity. A smooth forehead betokens
A hard heart. He who laughs
Has not yet heard
The terrible tidings.
. . .
You, who shall emerge from the flood
In which we are sinking,
Think –
When you speak of our weaknesses,
Also of the dark time
That brought them forth.
. . .
Do not judge us
Too harshly.

It is easier to judge from the vantage point of a future time than to see human failings in the present. Looking back at the dark times, how many have asked: Where were *they* amidst the dying? What were they *doing*? Why didn't they speak up, act or resist? How could they just stand by and let it happen? How could they be so *disinterested*? How could they participate, contribute, *collaborate*?

"In a world of conflict," Howard Zinn wrote, "it is the job of thinking people, as Albert Camus suggested, not to be on the side of the executioners."[24] The challenge is to identify who they are since in that world of conflict multiple executioners operate at once. The presence of war offers evidence that executioners are involved.

Zinn took up this challenge. He served in World War II as a bombardier. He was twenty-one years old when he enlisted, thinking, "This war was different. It was a war against the unspeakable brutality of fascism."[25] Later, he came to realize "there is no such thing as a just war," and recognized that World War II is "the supreme test" of that conviction.[26] Howard Zinn came to this realization because he studied history, and would become an important historian. Zinn describes the process of his illumination:

> I began consciously to question the motives, the conduct, and the consequences of that crusade against fascism . . . I was reading history. Had the United States fought in World War II for the rights of nations to independence and self-determination? What of its own history of expansion through war and conquest? The United States had observed Fascist expansion without any strong reactions [Ethiopia, Spain, Austria, Czechoslovakia, Poland, Nanking] . . . Did the United States enter the war because of its indignation at Hitler's treatment of the Jews? . . . the English and Americans had not shown by their actions that they were terribly concerned about the Jews . . . Behind the halo of righteousness that surrounded the war against fascism, the usual motives of governments, repeatedly shown in history were operating: the aggrandizement of the nation, more profit for its wealthy elite, and more power to its political leaders . . . Perhaps the worst consequence of World War II is that it kept alive the idea that war could be just.[27]

In the dark times, my father's social world was imbued and framed by an expanding culture of militarism. He did not question it. He was too busy surviving and adapting to study history. The war was background and he paid it little mind. For him, what stood out were beauty, romance and success, and the figure of his own imagined future.

In Love and War

I picked up the red Saks Fifth Avenue 9 x 12 gift box, about two inches thick and overflowing with letters wrapped with rubber bands in bunches. One grouping is from the fall of 1945, the sheets of stationery pretty sturdy considering their age. There are envelopes too. Some had 3-cent stamps with a white eagle on a lavender background, its wings forming the shape of a "V," a victory insignia across its front with the words, "win the war," and the bird surrounded by thirteen stars. These letters were a correspondence between Louise and Michael .[1]

I had just come from a frustrating interaction with my father. There may once have been a time when I could have gotten my father to talk about Louise without the conversation becoming too difficult to continue. But that would have been long before I got this project underway. Now I had to rely on other sources to learn about what happened that spring day in 1945 when Michael received the fateful letter from Louise.

"Tell me more about Louise," I asked him that day. "What happened after she wrote you?"

"*Luisa* tramped around with a lot of people," he answered, his voice low and tight. Suddenly, his lips were taut, his jaw shifting to one side as he unleashed the venom that never fully left. "I want you to listen. The neighbors talked about her. I didn't realize. I trusted her. I believed her. She was beautiful. I thought she was intelligent. But she comes from a family where sex—she comes from a different, different, different background. Her father is a half gypsy. Oversexed [image]."[2]

"Enough about that," I blurted, stopping him from elaborating the depiction I found offensive and did not want to hear. "We'll come back to it another time," I said trying to regain my composure.

Eventually, I was able to gather the story, pulling details from the letters, from Louise and from my father himself.

Louise Maude Steinberg, the nice girl, the one so peaceful and refined, the one who didn't go, who wouldn't go to a man's apartment, had heard from Miguel's cousin Frances. "He's lonesome," Frances told her by phone one early April day in 1945, "He'd love to hear from you." Louise didn't mind. After all, she had been sending letters to soldiers she didn't even know to help them through the loneliness of war, and she made extra cash posing with servicemen who were on leave in Manhattan. The soldiers would stop by a photo booth in Times Square with a fake background made to look like the Blitzkreig Bar. Louise would stand there and smile seductively, cigarette and bottle in hand, with the soldier by her side. Flash! The boy got his New York souvenir [image].[3]

She remembered meeting Miguel. It was 1942, and he was from Cuba. She thought he had gorgeous blue eyes. They met at Rushbrook Lodge up the line in Tuxedo, New York. Louise was there waiting tables, helping out her father's new wife Sarah. The Lodge was Sarah's place, and Louise could make extra cash.

She thought Miguel was very polite. He even asked her father for permission to invite her out in New York. When he came to visit Louise the first time, *tante* Betty was very suspicious of him. Even though he said he was Jewish and spoke Yiddish, she thought he had a very strange accent. "What is this Cuba place?" her *tante* asked. "I never heard of such a place. Maybe he's a *spy*."

The couple had an evening date, and went to the Havana–Madrid nightclub for dinner. Louise was eighteen and Miguel was twenty-nine. He ordered cocktails and bought her a pack of Luckies from the cigarette girl. The live show of Latin music, and his smooth, controlled dancing seemed so sophisticated. Louise felt like a movie star.

But then he kissed her. He did it with such passion, with such intensity that it scared her. He was very forceful, frightening even. After a few dates, Louise decided not to see him. He called and she didn't answer the phone. He called and she had her sister Sylvia say she wasn't home even when it was very late at night and it was obvious she was there. He wrote, and she ignored his postcards.

It was different now. It was wartime, and Louise thought she would give him a chance. Actually, she tried giving him a chance a year or two after their first, fateful dates. She couldn't quite get him off her mind.

That was during the war years when Louise and Sylvia had their own Manhattan studio apartment. As children of divorce, the sisters had been on their own for a long time—Louise in advertising, Sylvia an artist. It was a tough time for a young, Jewish girl to make headway, but Louise was managing.

Louise adored her father, Maxwell, and the two would often have lunch in the city. "I've been thinking about that young Cuban," Louise told her father. He suggested she give the fellow a call. Louise did—at that residence hotel the Cuban kept pushing her to visit. A woman answered. "He left for the war," the woman said. Louise figured he had gotten married, and the woman on the line was his American wife.

It was a busy spring for the 21-year-old, the season Roosevelt died. Louise's baby brother Maurice was put on active duty, Miguel's cousin Frances had called, and her darling father was suddenly, unexpectedly, and shockingly diagnosed with a malignant brain tumor.

By his bedside, Louise would sit with her father, and sometimes read to him. His health had deteriorated at rapid speed, and he seemed blank, this man who had filled his mind with poetry and history and philosophy. One day, he seemed a bit more responsive and Louise read to him the letter she had received from the young Cuban.

May 10, 1945
Dear Louise,

It was V.E. Day. I got up in the morning but found no difference in the atmosphere from any other day. It rained heavy (usual English weather) . . . Phil came in with a smile on his face. I understood that he must have good news for me. Then he handed me your letter.

. . . I can only say, Louise, that I was in heaven and I thank you very much. Everything seemed to turn to the gay side. It stopped raining and the sun started to shine through. . .

You know, sometimes I was thinking you've already married after hearing about the many quick wartime marriages back there. Three years have gone by but I am sure you're still the same sweet little gal as before. I still remember your beautiful face, with your dark eyes, long hair and that sweet smile. I wish I could have a picture of you, so I could look at you with my open eyes.

. . . with all my best wishes to you, I say,

Cheerio—
Sincerely,
Michael

P.S. Please notice how my name is spelled. I changed it when I got my citizenship papers.

Maxwell perked up for a moment. "A prince of a fellow," her father said.

Louise—the one with the beautiful face and the dark eyes and the long hair and that sweet smile. Michael thought she was the *perfect* woman .[4]

Michael would not be alone changing his name. Louise, an American girl from Brooklyn, had done so as well. She made the change during that same busy spring of her twenty-first year. In those days, in that part of the world, many people weren't so good to the Jews. It was especially true if you were trying to make it in certain industries or in the top advertising agencies. Between her sex and her Jewishness, Louise knew

Louise Maude Stone (Steinberg) (ca. 1945)

she was likely stuck as a clerk, phone operator, or secretary. At her first job, the kindly boss suggested she make the change since a Jewish name like Steinberg would not bode well for employment, much less advancement. At another job— the famous Wendell P. Colton agency—she learned why.

That day Louise filled in for the receptionist and greeted a young Jewish girl from Brooklyn applying for a bookkeeping position. The applicant was interviewed by W.P. Jr. himself. Afterward, the boss reprimanded Louise. "Don't send *that* kind to me anymore," he told her. Louise knew what he meant. She nodded, and felt deep shame. W.P. didn't know Louise was a Jew since she used an alias and lied about her religion.

And then she officially changed her name. It was an easy process. She petitioned the court in March, and by April 25, 1945 she became "validated": Louise Maude *Stone*.

The spring turned into a summer of significant events. Maxwell Steinberg died on June 14, just before his 57th birthday. Louise was devastated. It was all too much, unbearable even, and she was lost in grief. Though by then her parents had been divorced for nine years and though Maxwell had been violently abusive to his former wife, Louise's mother came to the funeral. Louise approached Marjorie. "I need to be here," she told her daughter. "No matter what," Marjorie said, "I loved your father with all my heart. He was the father of my children."

And then Louise and Michael intensified their courtship, a love affair by mail. Michael returned to New York for a brief moment in September, traveling across the Atlantic on the *Queen Elizabeth* with the thousands of other returning troops. By this time Louise had met Frances and some other of Michael's cousins—Edith, Milton, Shirley. The group of them took Louise to see Michael at Fort Dix in New Jersey. The couple kissed, deeply and long, while the cousins looked on. This time Louise welcomed Miguel's passion. They were to marry—that they had decided in letters they wrote over the previous four months.

Michael was given a permit to visit his family in Cuba before heading to a military camp for the discharge process. He wanted Louise to come with him to Havana, a vacation they both needed before the wedding. Louise refused. "She's very fine," Michael thought. "A very fine girl."

The Waserstein family was thrilled. Thrilled that their Miguel came back from war in one piece. Thrilled that Miguelito, the youngest, would be married, the last among the brothers and sisters to do so. It was okay the bride was from New York—as long as she was Jewish, that's what mattered. After all, it was an age-old imperative that Jews should marry Jews, even for the not so observant among them.

The weeks away turned into the fall months when Michael was sent first to Camp Crowder in Missouri and then, just before his release, to Walter Reed Hospital in Washington, D.C. The packet of letters got thick; their notes were loving and tender.

> Louise my dear darling,
>
> It was so good to hear your sweet voice today. I only wish I could have you close to me holding you tight and look at your beautiful eyes. After that pleasant talk we had I walked back to the barrack and still could hear you saying "I love you." So do I, honey dear and you know it.
>
> . . . Cheerio sweetheart.
>
> All my love and kisses.
>
> > Your
> > Michael ✎[5]

> Michael dear
>
> . . . The radio is on now—and it so happens they're playing an old song that's very sweet—"I'll see you in my dreams." I guess that I'll have to confess—that I see you. Ye Gods, I miss you a lot. Last night we turned out the light at 12:30—at 2:30 a.m. I was still awake—thinking of you. You really shouldn't interfere with my sleep that way!! Won't you please hurry back????
>
> I hate to have to end a letter to you—because when I write I feel that you're nearer—but I have to close some time.
>
> Cheerio-dear—and goodnight with Love and kisses—
>
> > Louise ✎[6]

It was a movie-picture romance, and the soldier and the young beauty met again in Washington. Louise finally agreed to visit him so long as Michael arranged accommodation for her in a private home. It was Christmastime and there were celebrations all around. Louise played piano for Michael and he listened with great satisfaction. Together they attended the holiday gala sponsored by the Walter Reed Hospital, dining on roast young turkey and oyster dressing, candied yams, and custard pie.

At last, Michael was honorably discharged from military service. It was January 9, 1946 out of Fort Dix. The next day, the couple was married at City Hall, a modest affair celebrated at the St. George Hotel 🏊 in Brooklyn Heights. Before the wedding, Michael had taken Louise there for a swim in the pool.[7]

"I wanted to see her in a bathing suit before I married her," Michael said as if the reason should be obvious.

Honeymoon 🏊 *(1946) Varadero Beach, Cuba*[8]

Louise wondered if he thought it a kind of *mikveh*, the bathing ritual to ensure his new bride's purity.

The gloss on their great love would get tarnished the very first night they were together as husband and wife. Louise was not a virgin, and Michael was appalled. She begged his forgiveness, and he gave it. She promised to be the kind of wife he expected her to be, and he seemed satisfied.

The honeymoon was glorious, the lovers captured in photographs from their two months in Cuba—at the famous Varadero Beach, with the Waserstein family, at the Tropicana nightclub.

Before the honeymoon was over, before they were back in New York, Louise would be pregnant.

Before the honeymoon was over, Michael would be back at work, planning a new buying trip and dealing with his brothers once again. Jacobo was the rooster of the family, and his mother Priwa fawned over him. "Oh how smart you are!" she would say to Jacobo, infuriating the rest of her children. More than that, Jacobo always tried to put himself on top. One time, just after the war, Jacobo stopped by Miguel's store. Miguel was excited. He had set up his store American style and the merchandise was flying off the tables. "The trouble with you, Miguel," his brother told him, "You think you're a big shot now. Remember, I'm the one sent those generals in England *los cigarros* so they'd treat you right!"

One day, Shmulke Waserstein walked into the store. It was not long after the war had ended, and his brother Moisés, now settled in Matanzas, had managed to get him out of Europe. Shmulke was Chajcia's son, and Chajcia was the favorite aunt who had tried to find help for the Waserstein family stuck with typhus in a barn in Łomża so many moons ago.

Shmulke told Miguel what happened in Jedwabne, an unimaginable story.[9]

"They never dreamed such a thing could happen. We never dreamed this could happen," Miguel repeated over and over as if in a trance. "Through all the mish mash in Europe, they didn't have any idea what went on. The real truth," he said, "was when Shmulke came to Cuba."

Shmulke told Miguel, and from then on, Michael would tell his children and his grandchildren about the horror of July 10, 1941.

The Germans had been moving east in Poland, violating their deal with the Russians, marching into town after town. The Germans entered Jedwabne. There were only a few Germans in Jedwabne because, after all, it was just a small village.

"When the Germans came," Michael recounted almost breathlessly, "it gave the Polacks the freedom to do anything they wanted with the Jews! So they killed them! They killed them all!"

Shmulke was saved. He went to a Catholic farm girl and she helped him. Shmulke described everything—how he was hidden in the bushes and how they killed the Jews, maybe 1500 or 2000 of them.

Michael said, "Shmulke saw how a woman walked into the pond. She drowned her baby and then she drowned herself."

"He saw when they killed the Jews," Michael went on. It was a very hot day. "They had them in the marketplace—the whole day standing in the heat. Shmulke told how a woman stood all day, her dead baby in her arms hour after hour. All of them were standing in the heat, while the Polacks were preparing the stable to burn. And then, at the end, when the stable was ready, they pushed them into the barn and burned them."

There was a little girl. She was the little sister of Michael's friend from so long ago, from when he was Mendel. A Polish guy wanted to pull the girl away from her family. The guy wanted to save her. She was a beautiful little girl. And the girl said no, and she burned with her family. She burned with the rest of them.

There was another girl Michael once knew, a beauty named Sarah. "Sarita Zefko," he remembered. She had gone to Russia and danced ballet. "She married a Jewish guy who was an intellectual—you know, the intellectuals were Communists. The Polacks got him too. They put him on the ground, they cut out his tongue, and took out his eyes," Michael recounted.

And Chajcia. They burned her in the stable too.

And Abram Hirsh Kromberg, Priwa's brother who was a World War I hero, the one with the selfish wife and daughters. He and his wife and his daughters were murdered in Jedwabne too.

Michael continued.

> Then when the stable wasn't big enough for all the Jews to be burned there, they took out the younger people—you know, 13, 14, 15, 18 years old, and they took them to the Jewish cemetery. They made them dig a ditch. The boys had to dig a ditch, and they put them in a row and they put them with hammers: "Next!" and "Next!" and each one of them . . . each and every one of them . . . screamed out, *Shema Yisroel Adonai Elohenu, Adonai Echad!*"

"The Polish were very antisemitic," Michael said, "They had to relieve themselves to get rid of the Jews."

Postwar

"What?! You slept with the enemy?" my Jewish doctor exclaimed hearing I'd stayed with a Polish Christian family in my father's old *shtetl*. It was the summer of 2008. Just a few years earlier, the same thought might have entered my own mind had I entertained such an idea. For me, as for my physician, Poland had been "fixed in my Jewish imagination as the land of unreconstructed anti-Semitism" to use Eva Hoffman's words.[10] To think differently about Poland and Polish Christians would signify disloyalty of the worst kind: betrayal of the sacred memory of the persecution and suffering of the Jews, a suffering, we have been taught, that extends into thousands of years of the Jewish plight. My first visit to Poland was colored by these images and feelings.

That first trip in the summer of 2001 coincided with a series of critical events in Poland around the release of Jan Gross's book *Neighbors: The Destruction of the Jewish Community in Jedwabne, Poland*. One month before my arrival in Jedwabne, a commemorative ceremony was held on what became a sacred and contested site: the spot on which the Jewish townsfolk were set afire in a barn exactly sixty years earlier.

By the time I arrived in August, the ceremonies were over, and a new, controversial tomb-like monument was in place. But my trip was not triggered by Gross's book or the intense debate and discussion in Poland that resulted. I was there as part of the project behind this book, a daughter–anthropologist's story of her father's life and the social history that surrounded it. Though the English-language edition of Gross's book was published in 2001, the story of the Jedwabne massacre was not new to *me*. I grew up on it, hearing from an early age what happened that sweltering day in July 1941. Shmulke's testimony had become family legend, passed from one generation to the next.[11]

Shmulke's postwar testimony, archived in the Jewish Historical Institute in Poland, also provided the basis for *Neighbors*.[12] Gross's slim volume packed a huge charge. In Jedwabne, it was not the Germans who annihilated the Jews but the Polish Christians who had slaughtered their Jewish neighbors. There were draggings, knifings, and pummelings and then the major event: Jews burnt alive in the barn. "In July 1941," Gross concludes, "half of the population of a small East European town murdered the other half—some 1,600 men, women and children"[13]

As my project evolved, the time came for me to confront my conflicting emotions of loyalty to and betrayal of my father and to my sense of collective identity. I began to see my father's reflexive attachment to the experience of Jewish suffering even as he reinvented himself in new circumstances. Over and over I listened to my father's rendition of the massacre:

> When the stable wasn't big enough for all the Jews to be burned there, they took out the younger people—you know, 13, 14, 15, 18 years old, and they took them to the Jewish cemetery. They made them dig a ditch. The boys had to dig a ditch, and they put them in a row and they put them with hammers: "Next!" and "Next!" and each one of them . . . each and every one of them . . . screamed out, "*Shema Yisroel Adonai Elohenu, Adonai Echad!*"

I hear in his narrative only a partial account of events—the "happenings;" the tension between myth and fact is evident in his recitation. In my father's telling, the story becomes a legend, even as it "speaks truth" to the violence and horror. In this storyteller's hands, Jedwabne is a parable of heroism and suffering, with each young boy-hero shouting the main statement of his Jewish belief (the *Shema*) at the moment of their deaths. The narrator invokes the sacred, not as protection from the violence of the world but to move the now-dead boys to another, more exalted place, immune from, detached from the wounds of the flesh. This maneuver shifts the secular dynamic to sacred ground, thereby leaving the whole history behind the event untouched by critique, analysis, or insight. And yet, throughout his life my father remained burdened by the defining events of the century, including the massacre in Jedwabne, and his earliest experiences of war on Polish soil. He had recurring nightmares of being chased, and so often described himself and his family in the process of running, suffering, barely surviving. "Run Miguel Run" he dubbed as his own nickname. Relentlessly pursued by annihilationists, always on the edge of ruin, my father embodied the *diasporic* Jew whose *habitus* drove his desire to repeatedly tell the stories that kept him faithful to the emotional suffering he really did endure.

I would also attempt to confront my conflicting emotions and sense of collective identity by expanding the focus of my inquiry beyond my father's life history: I would sleep with the enemy.

Serendipity played a part in the next stage of my project. On a cool autumn day in 2005, I began sharing "my father's story in history and anthropology" with a group of undergraduate students in my 59th Street City University of New York classroom. In the middle of the lecture, one student shot up his arm. "What?" I asked, slightly annoyed at the interruption at a key moment in my narrative. "I'm from Jedwabne," Stasio Danielski said. I was shocked. Though I had already been to Poland, been to Jedwabne, it still struck me as a mythic place. How could there be a real-life, flesh-and-blood, Polish-Christian *person* from Jedwabne—my student, someone in my care, in my trust?

Thus began my effort to gather voices of Polish Christians, and my return to Jedwabne with Stasio (his name and the names of his relatives are pseudonyms).[14]

Stasio and I stayed with his uncle Nelek and aunt Elka in Łomża. Nelek and Elka were generous hosts, insisting I use their bedroom while they moved into the living room, sharing that space with their nephew. Things moved *very* slowly in the Danielski household. The food, vodka, and conversation flowed but it seemed forever before they would take me to Jedwabne. The delays were a form of resistance and an expression of fear, I think. In the aftermath of *Neighbors*, how could they be sure the nice (Jewish) professor would not bring them danger?

Finally the day did arrive. We pulled into Jedwabne. Nelek drove to the monument, though I hadn't asked him to do so. Elka dug into a grocery bag, pulling out a glass memorial candle and placing it gently at the foot of the stone.

A short distance away is the old Jewish cemetery. Seeing it for the first time seven years earlier was for me a stark emblem of Jewish extermination on Polish soil: the graves untended; broken stones the only remnants. This time even those relics were unseen. I could not find them buried beneath the overgrown grasses that I slogged through while Stasio filmed me from the sidelines.

We walked to the well-tended Christian cemetery to visit the graves of Stasio's family and those of aunt Elka's relatives: Stasio's grandma and grandpa, Nelek's sister, Elka's parents. Elka wiped the headstones, swept dirt off each grave, and laid her candles on them. The grocery bag was now empty. Together, we lit each candle.

Afterward, we wandered through the cemetery and came upon a startling find. There, in a condition much more ragged than the Polish-Christian graves yet in much less a state of decay than in the Jewish cemetery, were the graves of German soldiers killed in Jedwabne during World War I. Rustic wooden crosses, bouquets of plastic flowers strewn about, and the remains of memorial candles marked this cemetery .[15]

Though the Jewish cemetery looked different from the time of my first visit, the Jedwabne massacre monument looked the same as it had seven years earlier. Joanna Michlic has written about the sequence of events from the time Gross's book was published in Poland in May 2000 to the commemoration ceremony on July 10, 2001. She notes that Gross's volume ignited an intense, difficult, disturbing, and ongoing debate in post-communist Poland about Polish Christian and Jewish relations and the Holocaust, particularly the role of ethnic Poles in colluding with or resisting the annihilationist project. Participants in this "battle over the memory of Polish–Jewish relations and the Polish collective self-image" include representatives from secular and religious segments of Polish society— priests, presidents, scholars, and intellectuals, politicians and journalists.[16] It has also involved interested observers outside of Poland, including rabbis and politicians as well as scholars and members of the post-generation like myself.[17]

Michlic posits two approaches to the "rewriting" of the history of Polish– Jewish relations: a self-critical stance in which Polish Christians face their "dark past" in relation to Jews and they come to terms with the distortions in their "collective self-portrait . . . solely as victims [of the Nazis] and [as] heroes"; and a self-defensive stance that effectively silences any questions about the past, collective memory and Polish national identity. Among those in the self-defensive camp, Michlic explains, are right-wing nationalists many of whom are virulent antisemites, and who have a large presence in the right-wing media in Poland.

In the midst of this politically and emotionally charged discussion came a decision from the Polish state authorities: "*an appropriate commemoration* of the Jewish victims of the Jedwabne massacre" would be installed, and marked with the words, "To the memory of Jews from Jedwabne and the surrounding area, men, women and children, inhabitants of this land, who were murdered and burned alive on this spot on July 10, 1941" (emphasis mine).[18] More than that, the new monument would replace an old plaque in place since 1963. That plaque, its message now refuted by Jan Gross's revelations, had been inscribed with these words: "The place of destruction of the Jewish population. Here Gestapo and Nazi gendarmes burnt alive 1600 people on 10 July 1941."

In his eloquent essay "Grave Discussions," biographer John Matteson describes how public memory is shaped and enshrined by monuments that look like graves, and how commemorative ceremonies sanctify a particular reading of the past. Examining how and why monuments to the American Revolution were developed in nineteenth-century New England, Matteson writes, "commemoration [is] a word that means 'to be mindful together' . . . 'together' is key, for commemorative objects . . . establish common cultural ground . . . the monument tries to place . . . limits so that we truly may be mindful together."[19]

But that was in *New* England, the British enemy by then far away, and the "we" referred to the making of an American citizenry in context of the making of a particularly "American" national narrative. In Jedwabne, the Jews came back to haunt; the monument was the product of a dynamic interaction between memory and politics, narrative and history, and the sacred and the secular. The result was that sacred memory in Poland was forced to shift, implemented by secular authority.

For Jews, the sacred—that which must be protected from criticism—is upheld in the "appropriate" commemoration in Jedwabne: memories of the Holocaust, its victims and perpetrators, and is consistent with a larger Jewish motif: the root of the problem—the root of the massacre—lies in antisemitism. At the same time, Poles were called upon to confront "their dark past" now inscribed with a new narrative. For some among them, the sacred memories of Polish identity and faith were defiled, and the monument a sacrilege.

It is difficult to get beyond the impasse.

We may never know the full extent of what "happened" in Jedwabne in July 1941; discussion seems to have stalled around a relatively narrow set of issues and partial bits of evidence. The number of dead, for example, returns as a significant point of contention. Did the dead number 200, 400, 1,600? In the wake of Gross's book, Poland's Institute of National Remembrance (IPN) launched an exhumation at the site of the mass burning in May 2001.[20] One month later, the IPN called it off in response to objections by some Jewish religious leaders who considered the exhumation a "desecration of the dead."[21] At that point, 200 remains had been found; for some, proof that the number of dead is significantly fewer than 1,600.

There was also the matter of bullets of German make pulled from the site, evidence, some argued, that the Nazis had committed the deed, not the Polish neighbors, although later the bullets were revealed to be of a type used by Germans in World War I.

Were these bullets parts of the weaponry, I can't help but wonder, that played in the deaths of soldiers buried in Jedwabne's cemetery of the German war dead from World War I—the dead soldiers my grandmother Priwa saw strewn on the street in front of her home?

Can there ever be a "being mindful together" in Jedwabne? It strikes me, listening to the words as well as the silences of my new friends in Jedwabne, that the monument and how it evolved ruptures as much as it might heal, creates new silences as much as it opens up dialogue. For those who live in Jedwabne, the monument stands as an unbearable accusation even if for the rest of Poland it opened up a space to dialogue about "Poland's dark past." Jedwabne and its current residents—one, two, even three generations after the event—seem to be bearing the brunt of that dark past. "Jedwabne is cursed," Poland's Chief Rabbi Michael Schudrich told me in an interview (2008) as if to quarantine the problem and locate it in the township. The public dialogue offers folks from Jedwabne little consolation; only the right-wing nationalists seem to lift the burden of guilt off their shoulders, entrapping them further into hostile relations (imagined or concrete) with Jews.[22]

Despite the strengths of Gross's book and despite the fact that it opened the possibility for critical self-reflection in Poland, it also helped re-inscribe Polish antisemitism as ubiquitous, a monolith, and as an explanation. Blinded by "the burden of [my own] instilled memory," I also accepted that image and that argument by uncritically accepting Gross's assertion that half the town literally murdered the other half.[23] But sleeping with the enemy has made me see things differently, revealing that easy explanations and blanket accusations seep in easily but are off the mark. That does not mean I pretend antisemitism doesn't exist. It does not mean I ignore the reality of the massacre in Jedwabne— a slaughter that took members of my own family.

The Polish Christians and Jews were torn apart, and the Polish Christians and Jews tore each other apart. Some might consider the destruction an inevitable instance of ethnic conflict, causal in its own right, a reflection of timeless, tribal hatred and enmity that seethes.[24] This is the primordialist view, an explanation that carries great weight in our times though sophistry, not evidence supports it.

But ethnicity does not by itself structure hostile (or peaceful) social relations nor does it by itself produce the violent polarization that left the Jews of Jedwabne dead. For that we need to go back to that longer and larger Polish history recounted in the first chapter of this book. We need to more deeply understand the social relations of land and labor in Poland; Poland's relations with its neighbors over centuries of European war; the partitions of Poland as the spoils of war and the effects of these historical processes on the polity, the Polish national identity, collective anxiety, and the making of "Poland's threatening Other"—the Jew.[25] We also need to examine the workings of Jewish collective memory steeped in a Jewish people "consciousness" and for some, "a set of sacred and inviolable truths"—collective memory that was (and is) itself situated in nationalism and violent nation-building projects.[26] This is a deeper, more nuanced understanding of violent history that may help reveal what made Jedwabne possible even as it requires confronting the sacred.

8

American Dreams/Dreaming in Cuban

My father and I had a few minutes to ourselves at my kitchen table before the rest of the family would arrive and interrupt us. It was April, and we had just celebrated Passover a few days earlier. My father often expressed disdain for those Jews who made a show of it (by their dress, by their insularity, by praying all day), and at the same time, expressed pride in being a member of the tribe. In one breath, my father could exalt Jewishness and in the next, disparage it.

I asked him what being Jewish meant to him. He paused, thinking for a moment before he began to speak. "Maybe it's a good thing that you ask me," he started.

"Do you know I don't believe in religion?" he asked, not waiting for my reply. "It's good to be Bar Mitzvahed," he said, switching gears. "It's a good tradition, because the boy respects the parents and the parents respect him," he added.

"Religion should not exist," he continued, shifting positions again. "None. All religions they should eliminate, because of the fighting," he declared.

"I'm a Jewish person," he stated. "I grew up, I was told the Jews were *best* in the world," he went on, agitated, unleashing what seemed a long-held resentment. "The Jews in Poland banged into my head that we are the only religion direct to God. But there's no such thing as God and no such thing as heaven—it's all baloney! It doesn't exist. The world exists for billions of years. And how long is the Jewish religion—five thousand years, ten thousand years? They made it up!"

"Sweetheart," he added, "I know because I know the truth! The spirit is when you're breathing."

Yitzhak Izaak escaped the war, missed the massacre in Jedwabne, and survived the transport from Poland to Cuba, but he would not be long for the world. He smiled for the camera standing on the wide boulevard in Miramar, but he suffered terribly with asthma. He would try anything to get relief from the suffocation. It's hard to imagine drowning, enveloped in the oxygen you cannot breathe. The air surrounds you and it's a life force but you cannot grab it or swallow it or push it through the pathway that will keep you alive.

So Izaak did whatever he could, whatever anyone advised that might offer a chance to stop the smothering, to be free of the panic, and to breathe. A visitor came from New York and suggested a special medicine. Izaak swallowed it though it was terribly bitter. Nobody knew what was in it, only that it came highly recommended. Everyday Izaak took the bitter medicine that was too strong and most likely poisonous.

Izaak began losing weight. He got skinnier and skinnier until he was just a skeleton. He had become delicate.

It used to be Izaak and Priwa visited their sons in the stores that lined the best shopping district in Havana. Then it got to be too much for Izaak and he sat home most of the time.[1] One day, he wanted to get out of the apartment. Instead of going to the door, he walked off the balcony. And that was it! He was dead.

Some say he killed himself but it was the asthma made him crazy and the medicine made it worse. He was seventy-three years old.

After the war, the old were dying and the old ways were sloughing off. Michael mourned what was lost, and then moved on. He had the future to accomplish—a business to build, a wife to love, children to bear, and a home to buy. He stood at the cusp of the American Dream, straddling the past and the future. Louise called it the peacetime things they were looking for.

This new life would require some navigating, negotiating, and administrating what with the business in Havana and the home in New York. Things were moving at a fast pace. Marsha Linda was the firstborn, a tiny baby in their tiny studio apartment on 89th Street.[2] She was named for her grandfather Maxwell, but the family called her "Linda" like the Spanish word for pretty. Linda was a toddler and Louise was just pregnant with Jessica when Izaak died in February of 1948.

Michael was knee-deep in his Havana–New York commute, and had established a buying office in Manhattan where he'd buy merchandise for El Imperio and Jacobo's Havana store, El Figurin.[3] By the end of the decade, the couple had two small children, and soon another would be on the way. They were growing, moving up in the world. Upwardly mobile, that's what they were.

It wouldn't be easy, but the times were pretty good for ambitious, visionary, hard-working young couples like Michael and Louise Waterston. On the outskirts of New York City, new homes were being built—lovely, sturdy, even affordable houses in luxurious bedroom communities. And the Veterans' Administration was on their side, guaranteeing a big chunk of their loan, making it very likely they'd qualify for the mortgage.

The 1950s had arrived.

The young couple gathered their small girls and toured the suburbs in the green Dodge they had managed to buy despite the shortages those first years after the war. There were many possibilities: the five towns of the south shore, and more expensive homes on the north shore of Long Island, in the village of Great Neck or the hamlet of Manhasset. There was Westchester, with its small cities and charming villages. Louise was partial to a red-brick colonial, but those seemed out of their price range. She imagined twelve thousand dollars must be their maximum.

In Havana, Louise found it very disturbing the way people gambled away their nest eggs on craps and roulette, so easily seduced by the glamour and the gaudiness of the place. How many wives did she see crying in the bathroom because their husbands lost a fortune? One gal was beside herself, sobbing. Ten thousand dollars, gone. The dream house gone, just like that.

Mike gambled too, but penny ante stuff. Well, he'd be a big shot and play twenty bucks. Louise found it annoying. It wasn't so long ago that twenty dollars was her whole week's wages.

Before long the young wife and mother would forget about the twenty dollars. Her Mike, her Miguel, brought her to the best nightclubs like Sans Souci or the Tropicana where stars crooned Cuban love songs and half-naked beauties entranced the audience. They'd dance to boleros like Cómo Fue .[4]

Cómo Fue—How did it happen—
one–step–two–step–three step-rest
no sé decirte cómo fue—I can't say how—
one–two–three–rest
no sé explicarme que pasó—I can't explain what happened—
one–two–three–rest
pero de ti me enamoré—but I fell in love with you—
one–two–three–long rest.

And they'd dance to Besame Mucho. Louise said it was their special song.

Back in the States, there was little time for nightclubs and dancing. Michael was on a spending spree, lavishing his new family with "everything the best"—a movie camera to document the happy girls and growing brood, a diamond wristwatch for the lovely wife, and the dream house, a love nest, his family homestead.

Michael's budget was twenty-five thousand dollars. "What do you think you can get for that?" remarked one snippy realtor. He was holding out for what he wanted, for his dream. Another agent told him about a new place, just finished that he might like, a red-brick colonial built by the owner. He wanted forty thousand for it. Michael was interested.

The early fall day was dreary and wet, and the girls were asleep in the car when the couple pulled up the quiet little street. It took two years of searching, but when Michael walked into the house on Meredith Place, he knew it was his.

The house was spacious and bright despite the dark day. The front had bay windows flanking the pretty door and entranceway. The living room had a huge picture window offering a view to the back with a large yard, tall trees and a brook running through. There was a formal dining room, French doors, an eat-in kitchen, four bedrooms, a bathroom here, a bathroom there, and even a first-floor bedroom suite the builder called "the maid's room." The girls woke up, running up and down the stairs and out the back.

Michael made an offer, then and there, writing out a deposit check for the realtor to pass on to the owner. They heard the owner turned it down. A few days later, the family went yet again for a drive in the County. Louise remembers coming upon the same house but never knew how they managed to find it. There was a man tending the yard outside. The owner! They discussed terms. There had been another offer, and the owner promised to hold out five more days for that buyer to make arrangements. Next Thursday would be do-or-die day. Michael didn't sleep all week. If he got that house, he pledged, he would never sell it. It would remain in the family *forever*.

Thursday came, the wait was torturous, and finally the call came in: the house was theirs for thirty-seven thousand dollars. On the last day of October 1950, six months before baby number three would arrive, William Kaufman sold Michael his dream house .[5]

Michael's long trips to Havana were not a disruption but a normal pattern in the family's round of activity: three weeks away, two months home. In between, there were diapers to change, auctions to attend, neighbors to greet, and holidays to celebrate, some of them in Havana with the growing family. At Maslow Freen's Fine Furniture, the couple bought grand pieces (an enormous mahogany oblong table with two leaves, Empire chairs, a three tier cabinet with inlay), and at auction they picked up antique accessories and superior tableware (bone china, crystal vases, claret glasses, porcelain figurines, sterling flatware in an oak chest).

The gold wall-to-wall carpeting practically shimmered. It clashed with but gave opulence to the downstairs rooms with their textured damask wallpaper, an elaborate covering with curlicue *fleur-de-lis* in off-white on a steel-blue background.

Louise seduced her husband in this house. Everywhere. On the soft gold carpeting in the dining room, on the grass outside in the backyard, in the bedroom where their bodies were reflected in the Venetian mirror. He had told her about the maid in Manguito and how the Cuban girl had served and satisfied him. Louise found the story offensive, and it aroused her. She would do for him then what the maid had done before.

The third baby arrived in the spring of 1951. Another girl. Louise worried Michael would be disappointed she hadn't produced a boy. But he was thrilled with Alisse, a name Louise devised from "Alice" so the child would be called "A-lease" and not Alicia during their trips to Cuba. As with all his babies, he cradled the third daughter in *Oyf'n Pripetshok* , adding his own words to the old Polish-Jewish lullaby:[6]

You are my *shanalee*, my *shana maydalee*, ay lu lu lu lu.
I love my little *shana babaleee*, ay lu lu lu lu .[7]

Michael's house in the Empire State was located in the town of Eastchester, though Meredith Place had a Bronxville mailing address. This gave the home extra cachet since Bronxville was such an exclusive area, reserved for the finest of the fine (in those days, in that part of the world, Bronxville didn't much like Jews *or* blacks). People would be impressed with the address, though the children would attend the Tuckahoe—not the Bronxville—school in Eastchester's District 2.

One season followed another and the children were blossoming. New joy came to the household when David was born in 1954. Finally, a boy 🖉!⁸ The father came and went across the ocean, and the mother tended children, smoked cigarettes, drank coffee, socialized with the other mothers in the neighborhood, and cleaned house with Inez, the maid from Mt. Vernon.

They became a fully assimilated, American family, Jews by identity and not particularly observant. They were members of the Free Synagogue of Westchester, a reform temple in Mt. Vernon whose rabbi was Leon Jick, famed for his civil rights work and studies of Reform Judaism. They celebrated Passover, Hanukah, and Christmas. Each fall, the parents attended High Holiday services, and the children had a photo shoot with Santa.

For Michael, there were always aggravations with the business. El Imperio was booming despite the pressure to pay off "the goddamn president of Cuba" with every shipment of merchandise he had coming from the states. That was the time of Batista, "a military man," Michael pointed out. "He was the worst president."

Each package of merchandise obliged two payments. A shipment would come in, and Batista's gangsters would say, "This is our package." They'd put it off to the side, promising to bring it to Miguel later. But first Miguel had to pay. There was the official duty that needed to be paid, and then there was the other payment, the extra fee, the unofficial duty. In those days it was the only way to stock the store.

Back home was paradise. The children were beautiful and Michael was so proud of his accomplishments. He regularly captured the family on his 16 mm home movie camera. First he'd have Louise get dressed and dress the children. Then they'd all go to the set: in Cuba it might be Varadero Beach 🖉, poolside at the Rosita de Hornedo hotel or next door at Casino Deportivo; in New York it might be a backyard bar-b-que, the elegant living room or, if it were wintertime, on the frozen pond down the street.⁹ Michael was the director, and Louise was generally driven to tears. He wanted the girls to pose in just such a way, or maybe dance for the camera. The irritation does not show in the final, picture perfect shots.

The decade was coming to a close. Louise was smoking intensely and more constantly. Most often a cigarette dangled from her rosebud lips. She'd light one to answer the telephone, while another smoldered in an ashtray by the stove. She faced a mini-crisis during a hurricane in 1958, considering the empty pack of smokes on one hand and the house full of children on the other. Should she drive through the storm or stay with the kids? Though the branches were falling

Posing  *(mid-1950s)[10]*

and the rain was pounding down hard, Louise managed the trek to Cozy Corner, the five and dime in nearby Chester Heights.

There were things on Louise's mind. One of Michael's favorite cousins and her husband were among the couple's closest friends. In Louise's basement laundry room one day, the husband grabbed her and forced his mouth on hers. Louise was disgusted. She shoved him and called him crazy. And then he did it to her daughter who was only twelve years old. "Keep away from my children," Louise warned him, though the two couples stayed friends. In fact, the cousin and her husband would still be the children's guardians should the Waterston children become orphaned.

Each spring Louise and Inez would scrub the twenty-eight windows in the red-brick house. Louise found herself restless, though she claimed these were the happiest years of her life. It was annoying to hear that the wife of the famous TV comedy writer up the street was attending law school while Louise and the neighborhood gals had their coffee klatches, gabbing about their children, their homes and their husbands over Maxwell House and Lucky Strikes. Then, someone would say something, and Louise would wince: "Make sure no Negro children come to the birthday party, Louise," her neighbor cautioned; or "Mommy, my friend [from Bronxville] told me she never saw a Jewish person before," her child reported.

Linda got very grown up, a fifties teenager who learned to slow dance to the likes of Richie Valens's *Donna* and *Tears on My Pillow* by Little Anthony and the Imperials. With her dark, large eyes and short black hair teased into a puffy bouffant, Linda looked like a cross between Elizabeth Taylor and Natalie Wood. She followed the styles of the times, favoring a short, close-fitting black skirt topped by a skin-tight, black pullover sweater.

Michael was appalled. You look like a tramp, he told her.

Habitus

I think I remember Linda dressed in that tight, black outfit, standing in the downstairs powder room teasing her hair, right before dad started yelling and calling her names. It was early morning and a school day so we were all scrambling. I scooted down the narrow hallway toward the bathroom but stopped to straddle the wall. Place one foot perpendicular to the floor on one side of the wall and the other foot on the other side. If you get a good flat foot grip, you can go up the wall one side step at a time until you reach the ceiling. Oh! What my mother let us kids do. I can't imagine having let my own children climb the walls (one of my mistakes?). She even let me write on my bedroom wall—in pen, pencil, marker, and even lipstick for goodness sake! I wrote mostly in pencil (easy to rub out) and sometimes in pen (but then I'd have to cross out or peel off the wallpaper in the spot I wanted to erase). I so often changed my mind about those I wrote about, or if it was a rant about a friend, had to hide the comments before she came to the house to play. Lipstick was reserved for writing about my mother. Had I dared go and take it from her make-up bag? I guess so. I know it was a rich red color, and that I used it to write:

I ~~Love~~ Mommy
~~Hate~~
~~Love~~
~~Hate~~
Love

In my mind's eye it is easy for me to tour the red-brick house so seared is that place in the deep layers of my memory. It's not just that I lived there my early years, but later it was where I raised my own child the first decade of his life. I can close my eyes and go back to the center hall light reflected as a bold stripe on the long, blank wall, a view from a child's bedroom. I can trace the contours of each bathroom, nicknamed for the primary color of the tile: the yellow bathroom had pale lemon-colored ones with a white mosaic floor surrounding a center black tile; the pink bathroom had baby aspirin colored tiles with maroon accents. I can almost smell the roast beef in the oven, the damp grass, and mother's Arpege.

Of course I have these memories. My mother was there, a steady presence. On the rare occasions she went out, I'd lie in her bed, my face in the pillow so I could smell her sweet perfume. I missed her. She taught me with her patience and assurances to trust myself and have confidence in my dreams and capabilities.

My father had a different style. I remember how he molded me—shaping, carving, instructing, expecting. He began teaching me the art of thorough housekeeping when I was six years old. In the bathroom that meant start high up and work your way down until you're on your hands and knees scrubbing the floor with elbow grease (it may take me awhile, but to this day when I'm done with a bathroom, you've never seen it cleaner). He wanted to be sure I'd be a good *balabusta* or maybe an ambassador's wife.

He was very specific, my father, having special skills he wanted the daughters to develop—dance ballet, play the piano, and how to set a lovely table. After all, one of us would be crowned Miss America some day, and to get there, he had us practice. Practice how to walk, how to sit, how to smile, and of course, how to play piano—the most refined of the talents, and besides, the pianist always wins! Books were for balancing *atop* our heads while we climbed up the stairs and down again, keeping proper posture.

My parents tended to their children each in their own way. My father offered cures from Poland, Cuba, and sometimes his own syncretic inventions. A child with a fever would be immediately put to bed, socks on the feet (keep them from getting cold because the feet go first when a person dies) and covered in blankets to sweat it out. The head should be cooled by placing chilled, sliced potatoes across the forehead, held down with a man's handkerchief wrapped around the child's head. Potatoes draw out the fever, and children who complain about the dank smell of the warming vegetable should be ignored. The child should also gargle with warm salt water and lemon at least three times a day, a remedy not just for the young or the ill, but for all who want to avoid getting sick in the first place. That's because gargling takes out all the poison from the body. For the child with fever, the final step is to drink a glass of *guggle muggle* that in my house was pronounced "googamoogl," a potion made from warm milk, a raw egg, a dollop of butter, and gobs of honey. "Honey is the most important ingredient in googamoogl," my father would say.

On a regular basis, my father would haul out a huge metal sunlamp, with a wide brown base and a narrow pole topped by a strange case holding bulbs that gave off a peculiar, subdued light and equally peculiar odor, something like iodine. He insisted the machine killed germs and brought us good health. The operation took place in one of the children's bedrooms. First he directed the light onto the bed, stripped of blankets but with the bottom sheet covering the mattress. The lamp zapped all germs from the sheet. Then each child would enter the room, one at a time. The youngest children would be naked (the older ones wore underpants) except for the plastic goggles with greenish-rose-colored lenses, making the experience altogether strange. The child scrambled on the bed, lay on her back, arms down by her sides while the light encased her body for several minutes until it was time to turn over and have her back done.

Somehow along the way, each child learned her or his place in the family. The beautiful one. The daydreamer. The smart one. The rebel. The nervous wreck. The practical one. The drama queen, the troublemaker, and the stubborn one. One could not be of a type when it was proclaimed on another though one could have multiple traits. At times, the lines around these roles were quite rigid, like the piano pieces we were given, then claimed as our very own (Linda had Malagueña so no one else could play it, just as Für Elise belonged to Jessica, and Chopin's Waltz Op. 69. No. 2 to Alisse). [11]

Yes, I do remember Linda dressed in that tight, black outfit, standing in the downstairs powder room teasing her hair, right before dad started yelling and calling her a tramp. Maybe there were many mornings like that, I'm not quite sure. I am sure it was around that time things began falling out of their place.

That morning, Linda was getting ready to go to Tuckahoe High, the local public school comprising working-class Italians (though some were up-and-coming), up-and-coming Jews (though some were working class), and working-class, working poor African Americans. One time, Linda attended a dance in the gymnasium. My mother went to the school to pick up her daughter at the end of the evening. A uniformed guard at the door stopped her. "Your child has been dancing with colored boys all night long," he said in more or less those words.

Not long afterward, a black teenager came to our house. He had been sent by the school principal to apologize to my parents for dancing with Linda. My mother was taken aback but had enough presence of mind to try and assure him, "You have no need to apologize, no reason to apologize."

Later, there would be hell to pay. Hearing the news, my father grew increasingly suspicious of Linda, now tainted in his eyes, and worried what the neighbors were saying. He had such high hopes for her! What was she doing? What was she trying to do? *Destroy his dreams?*

Oh, how difficult it is to grasp the meanings of what was going on in these scenarios involving actors, bodies, selves, histories, and collectivities. Much is

happening at once, even in the small domestic scenes portrayed, making it hard
to understand and very tricky to "explain" without oversimplifying or coming off
as reductionist. The famous anthropologist Bronislaw Malinowski wrote about
"the imponderabilia of actual life and of typical behavior" nearly one hundred
years ago, suggesting it may be impossible to account for what the ethnographer
observes on the ground, in real life.[12] Since Malinowski's time, scholarship has
come a long way. We've now got better conceptual tools, more documentation,
improved access to information, and a greater number of voices so that it is possible to approach a deeper understanding of what we experience and observe.

The scene of my 1950s childhood includes who gets center stage, and who is forgotten or barely considered. There is what is said and what isn't. There are the signs
of discontent and anxiety, the undercurrents of dissatisfaction beginning to stir.
There are the intimacies, including the quality of the interpersonal relationships.
There is the central social unit, its function, and how it is comprised, imagined,
and played out. There are other social groupings, how these are categorized, and
how belonging and "otherness" are determined. There is the dynamic tension
between the individual and the larger social. There is social process. There are the
inequalities of race, gender, and class, inequities that are structured systematically
and form the violence of everyday life, in peacetime. There is silence and *habitus*.

The scenarios I described were implanted in a specific moment in time and
place: in the postwar, Cold War, New York variation of the American suburb, and in
postwar, Cold War Havana, both sites on the verge of social, political, and economic
eruption. It is a commonplace that life in the suburbs circa 1950s was not the idyllic scene we often think it pretended to be. I'm not so sure those living through it
believed it was as idyllic as all that, especially those whose voices had long been shut
out, muted. Like Linda's classmate, for example, the black teenager whose forced
subordination to unjust authority threatened his own voice and dignity. Or Inez,
who no matter how ambitious, visionary, or hard-working *she* might have been and
even if she had a husband home from the war, most likely would not have qualified
for that VA loan guarantee, on account of her race and class location.[13]

My mother's voice was incipient. She seemed to have something of an intuition that would later guide her out. It's funny I pulled this among her papers,
setting it aside, as I prepared this chapter:

But I Still Love You
    Memories of My Life
    ". . . intuition is there . . . a lamp almost extinguished, which only glim-
mers, now and then, for only a moment at most. But it glimmers wherever
a vital interest is at stake, in our personality, in our liberty, on the place
we occupy in the whole of nature, on our origin and perhaps also on our

destiny, it throws a light, feeble and oscillating but, which, none the less, pierces the darkness of the night in which the intellect leaves us." Henri Bergson, Creative Evolution

My mother inhabited an intensely gendered female persona, repeating, enacting, and embodying a social identity through *"habitus"* and *"hexis,"* terms made famous by the French sociologist Pierre Bourdieu. In writing about women who become surgeons and who violate the norms of gendered social identity (thus confusing those around them), anthropologist Joan Cassell describes how *habitus* "constructs the body: internality is externalized. At the same time, the body expresses the *habitus*: externality is internalized."[14] *Hexis* is the embodiment of *habitus*. It articulates and naturalizes social hierarchies and divisions, making it more likely these will be reproduced. Each of us learns to inhabit the set that comprises our social location until it *feels* right and we embody it. It resists change. To overcome "something that one is" takes a coming to consciousness followed by individual or collective action.[15] Maybe consciousness *starts* with intuition.

Cassell's women struggled to make the "fit" as surgeons because they were the "wrong bodies" for their role in the operating room. So some of the women, while performing their surgical duties "took pains to wear lipstick," an act that is itself the "embodied refutation of not-woman status."[16]

Unlike Cassell's "woman in the surgeon's body," my mother looked, felt, and behaved like the proper member of her gender, a "woman in the wife's body." Any hint of transgression was quickly suppressed and silenced, and both she and my father were complicit. Recall that on their wedding night, her transgression had been revealed to him (she was not a virgin), though she begged his forgiveness and promised to be the good wife, the kind he expected. At that moment, the tension was relieved, the breach resolved. For the time being, each retreated to the comfort of *habitus*, he the superordinate and she the subordinate.

I like that I took my mother's lipstick and used it to write on a wall in the beautiful house. There's *habitus*, and transgression, however small, in the gesture. From the moment of my birth (another girl!), I began to enact and embody the gendered social identity and location I shared with my mother. At the same time, she allowed me a tool with which I could find my own voice, writing on a wall *with* lipstick. Was it a vital interest she saw in the glimmer of her intuition?

9

Dictators

It's another year, another Passover. Once again I'm reminded that as a Jew "it is my duty to tell my child not only my story, but also the story of my story, which is also my child's story." I go through the motions of the ritual but wonder, with so many parts and layers to the story, which parts do I tell? There is no road map for that. I have had to make the choice myself, guided by my own internal compass, the one that always seems to direct me to the displaced, the dispossessed, the stigmatized. My father's stories matter to me because he was one among that kind.

My mother had amazing stories of her own, but they didn't pull me in the same way as my father's, although her stories are revealing in their own right. I love the one about my grandmother Marjorie who, in the early 1920s, decided to marry Maxwell Steinberg, a Romanian Jew. Marjorie was the daughter of Joseph Knight and Maude Baker, good Anglos from Mt. Vernon, New York. When Marjorie announced her intention to marry Maxwell, Joseph Knight pulled off his shoe, threw it at his daughter, and sneered, "The least you could have done was marry a white man!" Marjorie not only married him, she *became* a Jew.

My mother had her own experiences of loss and dispossession, but she had a center that my father lacked. His wounds were of a different sort. His losses seemed to penetrate some protective layer that left him raw and vulnerable. Her losses did something else. They seemed to be a starting point that led her to transcend the wounds.

They were two temperaments entangled in a life together, their futures unfolding in a disquieting way.

Louise vowed she would never be the kind of wife  her mother had been nor the kind of mother hers had been, a woman who would abandon her husband and her children just like that.[1] The memory of her own abandonment haunted Louise all the days of her life, though in time she came to understand, even appreciate the courage in her mother's act of survival. For years, Louise erased all thoughts of her father's role in tearing apart the family. What stuck out was the memory of standing on Latham Lane in Queens, herself a 12-year-old girl watching her mother drive away in Jimmy Walsh's truck, with furniture, belongings, and little sister Sylvia in tow. In 1936, mama Marjorie left behind Louise and 9-year-old Maurice at Tessie's house across the street. It was unthinkable. All those nights in the tiny living room, her mama playing Sinding's Rustle of Spring  on the

upright, singing La Habanera or dancing like Carmen while her father Maxwell metamorphized into Don José.[2] The three children sitting cross-legged on
the floor, fully enchanted by their parents. Enchanted when their father recited
Emerson or Whitman, and especially John Burroughs:

> I stay my haste, I make delays
> For what avails this eager pace?
> I stand amid eternal ways
> And what is mine shall know my face

Marjorie destroyed all of this when she picked up and left, leaving Louise and
Maurice to wait and wait until their father Maxwell returned home from work,
late as usual. Louise was strong. She stepped in and replaced her mother, tending her father's sorrows.

All that was past history, and Louise was now living in the present, consumed by
immediate concerns. Maybe she wasn't an attorney like Mrs. Tolkin up the street,
but she was still involved in the world. She hosted meetings in her home to plan the
construction of a new elementary school since, by the mid- to late 1950s, the small
building on Main Street in downtown Tuckahoe could no longer accommodate the
expanding number of the district's school-aged children. Despite the demands of
her own large brood, her husband, and the house, Louise began writing "What's
New in District 2," a weekly column of announcements, accomplishments, and
gossip for the town newspaper, the *Eastchester Record*. With headlines like "'Public
Hearing' Needs the Public," "Volunteers Needed," "Horn-Blowing at the Hard-
arts," and "Juvenile Delinquency," Louise wrote about the annual school-budget
meeting; the need for helpers to catalog 500 new high-school library books; the
birth of Thomas Hardart, Jr. whose father ran the Horn & Hardart's Automat;
and youth in District 2, a place Louise reported as free of "anti-social behavior of
delinquents—juvenile or adult." In one of her last columns titled "The World, The
Nation and District 2," Louise summarized US State Senator Kenneth Keating's
position on "the communist menace on the island of Cuba."

It gave her pleasure to help her husband even if he didn't seem to take notice
or worse, ignored her when she wanted to share with him news about a local
politician or the latest school-board decision. She began helping him with the
business, taking care of invoices in the New York City buying office as needed,
when Michael was away in Havana minding the stores. It bothered her the way
his terms of endearment were so patronizing. "Luisa, cha-cha-cha" he'd call her,
making fun of her late nights staying up after he and the children were asleep.
That was her time. The time she reserved for herself—for reading her father's
old books, writing poetry, and to think. Michael didn't want to grant her that,
and had to demean it, and her. "Luisa is a night-bird," he'd snicker, getting the

expression wrong. She'd never correct him, not wanting him to be embarrassed with his fumbled English phraseology.

It annoyed her the way he constantly harangued her for smoking though he seemed to think it was glamorous when he first took her to nightclubs. Now it was all "look at you, with your *shmucking*," he'd say mockingly, then laugh at his own stupid penis joke about her *smoking*. Still, she hated those months he'd spend in Cuba. "I miss you already—no matter what I said about getting used to having you away—but thanks to you and the kids and the house, I will have enough to do to keep me busy while you are away," she wrote in one of many letters she mailed to Havana.

On a Friday morning in July, 1955, Michael wrote back:

> How are my darling from Meredith Place? How comes that I didn't get any mail yet, Luisa darling? Very busy? Things over here are about the same, if I may say so, very uninterested, all day long at the store and in the evening to someones house for dinner and talk till is time to go to the hotel to sleep . . . I didn't hear from you what you had accomplished in New York last Wednesday. I know that one check for about $2,500.00 is due about the twelveth. I'm sending out two checks for the amount of $2,415.00 direct to the bank to Mr. Sanders today, so this way you won't have to come to New York to make the deposit. Call Monday afternoon Mr. Sanders at the bank Canal 6.4747 and find out if he received it and then mail out that check I mentioned before which is addressed to a factor . . .

Theirs was a full, rich life, its routines punctuated by glorious family trips to Havana and special events at the house. Over the years, Michael clipped the society pages of Cuba's stylish periodicals hoping his family might model the most distinguished of the men, the most elegant of the ladies, and the best mannered of the children. He noticed that people from important families commissioned formal portraitures, and Michael longed to have one too. Luck would have it when he met a young artist from Zaragoza, Spain, the portraitist Ramon Raluy. Michael talked to him and made an arrangement. He'd have Louise hold an exhibition in their home. In exchange for the publicity and the Waterston's connections in Westchester, Raluy would paint an oil of Marsha Linda 🔗.[3] Louise even got a nice article about the artist and the exhibit placed in the *Eastchester Record*.

These were also the years of turmoil, the decade leading up to the overthrow of Batista by the 26th of July movement that got its name in 1953, one year after Batista took the presidency by military coup. Conditions under Batista were intolerable—the massive poverty and starvation, the murders of political enemies, the corruption. Even successful merchants like Michael struggled as gangsters hijacked nearly every package of merchandise shipped from New York and then arrogantly assumed a ransom would be paid. In Cuba there was always political and economic intrigue—a president installed or deposed, intervention by the US government, another power grab, intervention by American mobsters, another *coup d'état*, another financial deal, altogether a clear case of normalized violence if ever there was one. It was always messy but for the most part, the victor would find an ally in Washington, a comforting assurance to a US citizen doing business on these foreign shores.

Michael didn't put much stock in any of that. In spite of himself, he felt more hopeful than he had in a long time with the change everyone knew was coming to Cuba. Louise liked the sound of his new optimism. In a letter postmarked February 28, 1958, Louise wrote:

> But talking to you and hearing your cheerful reports and good spirits has made me so happy! I'm so proud of your courage, and confidence—which is more responsible for your accomplishments than anything . . .

That week the *New York Times* reported from the Sierra Maestra Mountains that the resistance movement's leader, "*Señor* Fidel Castro," was also optimistic. "A rebel leader capable of throwing into battle only 400 riflemen boasts that within a few months he will oust the Batista dictatorship and occupy all of Cuba," Homer Bigart reported on February 27, 1958. Bigart thought it blustering exaggeration but Fidel had courage and confidence. "To see our victory," Fidel is quoted as saying, "it is necessary to have faith."[4]

Before filing his article, Bigart held a briefing with an officer of the US Embassy in Havana. The reporter disclosed what he had learned from spending two weeks with Fidel and his comrades deep in the Sierra Maestra, some five hundred miles from the heart of Havana. Bigart's classified statements were summarized and dispatched to the State Department in Washington, DC.[5]

The Sierra Maestra was no jungle, Bigart shared in the debriefing, but was "covered mainly with scrub growth with many clearings." There was plenty of *malanga*, an edible root, but not much else to fill the bellies of rebels and guests alike, except the intestinal parasites rampant among the men in the mountains. Bigart was not restricted from talking to whomever he wanted, from Fidel to Che, Father Guillermo Sardiñas, attorney Humberto Sori Morin, and physician Dr. Julio Martinez Paez, among others. From them Bigart heard that the rebel platform had not been set in stone beyond the basic goal to liberate the Cuban people from their current suffering condition. Bigart told the Embassy, "the political and economic program of the '26th of July' Movement does not exist yet in other than informal and nebulous form."[6]

The reporter found no "anti-Americanism" among the rebels in the Sierra Maestra although they were very well aware of US support for its man in Havana,

Fulgencio Batista. Bigart told the Embassy: "Castro and his associates complained bitterly of grants and sales by the United States of military equipment to the Batista Government. They said that such aid was the fundamental reason that Batista was able to remain in power."[7]

Castro and his associates were pretty accurate in their assessment. Just a month earlier, William Wieland from the Secretary of State's office recommended that 100,000 rounds of 20 mm. ammunition, 10,000 hand grenades, 3,000 75 mm. howitzer shells, and two aiming devices be sold and shipped to Batista's Cuban government (eleven other requests by Batista to purchase arms had been approved and were shipped in 1957).[8] In March of 1958, however, the US halted shipment of arms to Batista much to the dismay and disappointment of the old ally.[9]

Michael knew nothing of these behind-the-scenes maneuvers, only what he saw when in Havana, and what he read in correspondence his brothers and his employees sent back to him in New York. For the Waterston family, Christmastime at the Hotel Rosita de Hornedo in 1958 was just as it had always been.[10] The children swam in the hotel's two pools, played in the sandlot with their Cuban cousins, and trekked the rocky walkway next door to the Casino Deportivo, a country club where even kids could play the slot machines. To them, there was little outward sign Batista would soon be out, Fidel in.

But it came to pass that there was a revolution. The next time Michael flew to Havana was early May, just a few short months into the post-revolutionary period. On stationery from the Hotel Capri, famed for "sparkling resort luxury with a Champagne flair," Michael sent his own dispatch to Louise. Walking into the hotel, Michael got the surprise of his life. There was not even one slot machine! The New York papers reported Fidel had gotten rid of gambling, but to see it actually gone was something else! The slots were replaced by a set of lounge chairs where Michael sat comfortably and relaxed, smoking his pipe, composing a letter to his wife.

Given the country's state of confusion, Michael was thrilled to find his two stores were intact and even well stocked. Between the two shops, they sold $2800 in one day, one very good day indeed. Michael thought, "If this would only keep up for at least a month, all my troubles will be straightened out."

For Michael, the verdict on Castro was still pending, and like many others, he took a "wait and see" approach though, for the most part, the Wasersteins did not support the new government. From the start of the revolution, they looked to get as much cash out of Cuba as possible and made their way to Miami as quickly as possible. But Michael's old buddy Fito and wife Nivia were among those with great confidence in Fidel. He would make Cuba a great country, they believed. They thought Fidel was "almost like a God." Michael wrote to Louise.[11] "Nivia says that men like Fidel is [sic] born once every hundred years."

He had much more to tell Louise in letters he'd send over the course of his trips to Cuba that year. He wrote about the walk he took one cool and breezy Havana evening before strolling back to the Capri where he stood for hours watching Alec Guinness, Burl Ives, and Ernie Kovacs shooting *Our Man in Havana*. He wrote how Fidel was "making many improvements in every way—schools, roads, housing for poor people"—so many that "Nivia made me a convert again. I'm all confused now!" He wrote how he was worried about the business and getting money out to send to his family in New York. Things were starting to get tough.

With nearly each letter home, Michael sent a postal order for $100 or maybe two, getting Louise some cash to pay household expenses. It's not that sales weren't good. For the most part, El Imperio and Blumin were prosperous. But new rules were being put in place, monitoring and limiting withdrawals, and causing cash-flow problems.

After the revolution, the new Cuban government permitted Michael to continue to buy from garment and textile wholesalers in New York who continued to ship merchandise to Havana. The suppliers did not extend credit to a foreign concern, and knew Michael as an honorable man who had established an excellent credit rating in his own name. As always, purchases for the business were sold to Michael Waterston; in turn, he'd bill Textil Blumin S.A. and get paid according to the invoices for each shipment.

Not long after the revolution, a new system was put into place. Michael no longer had to worry about bribes to get his merchandise into the store but now needed government approval for each transfer of funds to pay suppliers through the bank. Textil Blumin had an account with the Bank of Nova Scotia that on December 16, 1960 sold its Havana branch to the Banco Nacional de Cuba.[12]

Michael and his trusted employees—Sara, the bookkeeper, and Alsinio, the store manager, complied with all regulations, demands, and requests received through the bank, even as these were getting more and more onerous. Proceeds of all sales were deposited in the bank. As a business owner, Michael could no longer draw a salary; all employees except the owner were permitted their salaries. Release of all other funds was put off, and then delayed again. Michael held off his New York creditors promising the bank would soon release the funds. Surely they would be released. In early January, 1960, Nova Scotia Bank posted the Blumin bank balance at $32,189.25; by June of 1961, the bank, renamed the Royal Bank of Canada, showed a Blumin balance of $80,893.21, a financial asset that by some estimates would have the economic power of over two million dollars forty years later.

Louise also helped Michael hold off the creditors, but the couple saw the writing on the wall. The cash-flow problem turned into a cash-flow crisis. Louise borrowed money from relatives and friends. She began sewing dresses in her living room, selling her smart fashions to neighbors, earning a few dollars to buy groceries for her children. Michael had already set his sights on Puerto Rico, a US territory, hoping he had the strength to begin all over again, though he wasn't sure how he could possibly do it, starting out with debt, no income, and no capital whatsoever.

It was difficult to keep up with the contradictions and the changes. On one hand, Fidel was transforming Cuba for the better, intervening in the operations of US companies like the Cuban Telephone Company and the Compañía Cubana de Electricidad, reducing their exorbitant rates and increasing service access of basic utilities to a wider Cuban public. On the other hand, Michael was just a *shmata* salesman, not a big shot like Cuban Telephone, United Fruit, and Standard Oil.

Rumor had it the US was spending more time, energy, and resources undermining the Revolution to protect large interests rather than considering the consequences for little guys like Michael or the needs of the Cuban people. It was hard to tell propaganda from truth since all sides were making claims. In 1960, the new year came with word the US was becoming increasingly committed to overthrowing Castro by covert means. Explosives fell from the sky hitting small cities and the cane fields in the Cuban countryside. By spring of 1960, tensions escalated.

Michael received an alarming letter from Sara 🔎, his trusted bookkeeper, dated June 27, 1960, describing the aftermaths of an explosion that was a stone's throw from the shopping district:[13]

> I am rushing to write you this morning .. .about the scare yesterday, thank God, we have little to lament though not a window or metal door has been left intact in all of Havana, Marianao and Regla. I came to Muralla immediately last night, and Blumin was intact, and El Imperio's windows were miraculously intact . . . Lots of stores are damaged, including Figurin and Tropico.

The explosion blew up a munitions dump that killed two people and injured 200, according to the *New York Times*, just three months after a similar explosion destroyed La Coubre, a French munitions ship in Havana Harbor. "Some [in Havana] expect the United States to be blamed for the blast," the paper reported.[14]

Not three weeks later, a new law, published in the *Gaceta Oficial* (Official Gazette) of July 7, 1960 as *Ley No.* 851, authorized the expropriation of all properties owned by citizens of the United States.

The final days were nearing for the business Textil Blumin S.A. and its shops Blumin and El Imperio. By the following June of 1961, two months after the CIA-orchestrated Bay of Pigs invasion in Playa Girón, the stores had been inspected by the Ministry of Labor. The Inspector asked each employee, one by one: Is this business abandoned? No, they answered. Are you satisfied with its administration? Yes, they responded unanimously. Not long after, a second inspector arrived, looking to give an employee named Samuel the position of "Custodian and Fiscal Agent." Twenty-six employees voted against and three voted in favor of naming Samuel to the new role. Nevertheless, the Ministry authorized Samuel as "Custodian" that meant he was to watch that no merchandise was secretly removed from the store, and as "Fiscal Agent" that required him to observe the store's operations  and to counter-sign all checks the manager and bookkeeper had signed.[15]

And then there came to pass two resolutions: Resolution No. 4983, July 12, 1961, and Resolution No. 396, August 10, 1961 signed by Máximo Berman Berman, Ministro de Comercio Interior (Minister of Interior Commerce). The first resolution authorized "the intervention" of the entity named Compania Textil Blumin, S.A. The second designated a man named Jose L. Concsa as "Delegado Interventor del Ministerio" (Delegate Intervener) to act on behalf of the Ministry. In a letter to Michael, Alsinio described what happened:

Havana, August 16, 1961
Yesterday, when I returned to the store from making the deposit in the bank, I was handed a resolution from the Ministry of Interior Commerce citing the intervention of the store . . . The intervention came about at 6 p.m. They turned over to me a copy of the resolution. I had to surrender the keys to both stores and the corresponding documents.

Surrendering the business, I felt as if I were surrendering something of my own, something I had struggled to maintain and improve . . . it was truly sad for me to see it destroyed in one moment . . .

–Alsinio Espina Fernandez

MURALLA NO. 424   TELF. 6-7598
ESQ. A VILLEGAS   HABANA

Business Card, El Imperio , "Majestic Fabrics"[16]

The Ends of Empires

In July 2000, forty-one years after Resolution 4983 was signed, my brother David and I returned to Cuba with our father. There we found many mementos of his life, not just in Manguito but in Havana too.

One evening, the three of us strolled into La Floridita, the famous restaurant frequented by Hemingway, and known as *cuna de daiquiri*, the birthplace of the daiquiri. The bartender shook our daiquiris by hand, *por mano*, and they were delicious. Before long, a violinist named Omar Gonzalez Alvarez came to our table, with two accompanists— one on bass, one on guitar—to play a beautiful, affecting Besame Mucho 🎻.[17]

My father was lost in the song, and the expression on his face was heart breaking. I didn't know what my father 🎻 was dreaming about, listening to the violinist reach those high notes that sounded as much like a Jewish melody as a Latin love song.[18] He might have been thinking about my mother since Besame Mucho was "their" song, or so she had thought. But many decades before this Havana nocturne, Louise learned otherwise. The couple went out with friends to a Cuban restaurant in Greenwich, Connecticut of all places. The 1950s band began playing Besame Mucho—"Kiss me, Kiss me many times / As if this night were for the last time." Louise looked over at her husband, hoping to catch his eye. Instead, Michael chuckled and said to the group, "Oh this song—it always makes me think of Carmen!" (an old Cuban girlfriend).

Maybe Besame Mucho made him think of the whole of his life, his many losses, the struggles, and the blissful moments in between. After all, he was old now, 87. He had passed through a lot.

My father confessed he had been nervous about taking the journey back to Cuba. "What worries you dad?" I asked him, "Seeing reminders of the past? Re-experiencing painful memories?"

"I was worried we'd have to eat dog," he told me. "I heard it's so poor in Cuba people have to eat dogs."

The three of us saw a lot on that trip. Live music on every corner, wafting from home after home. More people than cars on the streets, and no commercial life. We sat in lovely parks where my father started up conversations—lecturing to one lady why she shouldn't smoke cigarettes, calling over a little *muchachito* (a toddler boy) for a hug, and telling his story to anyone who would listen.

"People seem to be content," he remarked after a few days. "And they've got food," he added as if to convince me.

We took a visit to the Patronato, the Havana synagogue where librarian Adele Dworin gave us a copy of the June, 1953 *Boletin No. 25* that featured news of the Casa de la Comunidad Hebrea de Cuba, and list of synagogue members, including my aunts and uncles Manolo, Jacobo, and Eva, José and Zoila, and Sarah and Herman. Miguel harangued poor Adele, bad-mouthing Fidel while she smiled politely, and David and I begged him to stop. We enjoyed a Kiddush luncheon with the congregation after services, and struck up a conversation with a lovely man named Isaac.

David Waterston

Waserstein & Co "El Figurin" (July 2000)

He helped get us information about where, specifically, my grandfather was buried in the well-tended Jewish cemetery in Guanabacao called United Hebrew Congregation, Centro Macabeo de Cuba.[19] Visiting the cemetery gave Miguel a last chance to recite *Kaddish* at the foot of his father's gravesite, A3 #15.[20]

In what was once the downtown shopping district, a fleeting memory returned to me while I followed my father on the narrow sidewalks. I was a small child, the sidewalks were crowded, and I was terrified of losing him in the throng. That's because he walked so fast and didn't seem to be keeping track whether or not I was behind him. He was scrambling between his two stores, one at 360 and the other at 424 Muralla. Really they were close to one another but seemed a great distance to me, a child on this exotic street.

And there we were, back on those same sidewalks. Michael was talking about the time he stayed at Jacobo and Eva's apartment when their firstborn, Esther, was born more or less the same time Manolo had his first, a boy named Wilfredo. He talked about the jealousies—this one got a boy, that one got a beauty. David was filming when he suddenly gasped and pointed. Above the decaying door were the painted words, now faded and chipped: Waserstein & Co. El Figurin — my uncle Jacobo's old storefront in Havana still there after forty years.[21] Whether deliberate or not, four decades of exclusion from the global market had functioned to preserve Cuba's prized architecture and some very precious memories.[22]

And then we arrived at the corner of Muralla and Villegas, the site of his dream, El Imperio.

"Remember, when you say El Imperio the accent is on the second word. You barely mention "El" You say "l'imperio," so people hear *imperio*, empire, just like in any other language."

It was stunning, literally. In this world unfamiliar to us, there were no stores. There was no Encanta, no Tropico or Figurin, no Imperio. There were also no Starbucks, of course, or The Gap. The only display on the old shop window was a small poster, announcing upcoming festivities. In just a few days, Cubans would be celebrating the 47th anniversary of the 26th of July Movement.

My father stood on that street corner , a dazed look on his face, absorbing what he saw.[23] On the surface, all looked a ruin: run-down buildings and a road of dust, the Paris of the Caribbean a shabby remnant of its former, glorious self. Forty years earlier, the empire on which he pinned his hopes had come to an end. From his contracted view, the end came by proclamation and by a resolution that required Alsinio to hand over the keys. My father never said Castro was the worst president of all, but he felt betrayed by Fidel's *"personalismo,"* personal leadership. "He didn't come out that he was a communist," my father said of the revolutionary, "but then he took businesses away—from ordinary people he took their businesses."

My father had only superficial knowledge of US political and economic hegemony in Cuba since 1898, or later, the brutal impact of Cold War politics on Latin America.[24] Yet he did see the poverty and devastation suffered by the mass of Cuban society, a rural proletariat dependent upon the sugar economy. He may have known the sugar economy was dominated by US corporations but failed to recognize their role in fostering the conditions that gave rise to the revolution, so blinded was he to the cult of *personalismo*, where leadership is believed to begin and end with the person and the personal rather than driven by systemic and structural forces. My father did not know about nor would he have considered anthropologist Eric Wolf's analysis of the kind of conditions that gave rise to the revolution:

> The Cuban sugar industry not only established the regime of a single dominant crop on the island; it also harnessed a large and concentrated labor force to an economic cycle alternating between prolonged periods of hunger and short periods of intense activity. The desire of the Cuban sugar workers to break out of this cycle was to constitute one of the major sources of support for the revolutionary government after its advent to power.[25]

The 26th of July Movement, named for a rebel attack on the Moncada military barracks in Santiago de Cuba, was born in Oriente Province, home to an empire that produced hunger in its midst, sugar for export, and wealth for investors.

In the revolutionary period, my father was not privy to the goings-on within the new government and its major players, including Fidel and Raul Castro, and Che Guevara among others, and within the US State Department, the President's office and the CIA. He was also not privy to the proceedings out of public view, including the political maneuverings between the US, anti-Castro forces, the revolutionary government, its international enemies and allies, the banks, and the corporations. In the years since the revolution, scholars have sought to unravel the complex dynamics involved in the conflict.[26]

Over the past several decades, new information has been released, including but not limited to three volumes produced by the Office of the Historian, the US Department of State that contains over 3000 pages of documents, many of which were once top secret. Tidbits from these documents offer evidence of what Morris H. Morley calls the "US imperial-state . . . [that] interprets, defends and even defines the interest of the US capitalist class in moments of crisis affecting investments abroad."[27] In a discussion at the 432nd meeting of the National Security Council in Washington on January 14, 1960, Livingston T. Merchant, then Under Secretary of State for Political Affairs, and R. Roy Rubottom, Jr., then Assistant Secretary of State for Inter-American Affairs, laid out the set of US interests and policy objectives in Cuba in the first year of the revolution:

> Mr. Merchant: Some of our principal interests in Cuba [are] the strategic importance of the island, our trade and commercial interests, and the safety of U.S. citizens there. The Department of State had been working with CIA on Cuban problems. Our present objective was to adjust all our actions in such a way as to accelerate the development of an opposition in Cuba which would bring about a change in the Cuban Government, resulting in a new government favorable to U.S. interests.
>
> Mr. Rubottom: Our policy objectives toward Cuba include . . . a sound and growing Cuban economy; receptivity to U.S. and Free World capital and increasing trade; the development of democratic government; a maximum limitation on Communist influence; participation in and support of hemisphere defense; access by the U.S. to essential Cuban resources; and Cuban support of regional cooperation.[28]

To protect these interests and accomplish the policy goals, Mr. Rubottom explained, the Department of State realized by June of 1959 that "it was not possible to achieve our objectives with Castro in power . . . In July and August we had been busy drawing up a program to replace Castro." By November of 1959, the Department of State in conjunction with the CIA had pieces of a program in place, approved by President Eisenhower, "to support elements in Cuba opposed to the Castro Government while making Castro's downfall seem to be the result of his own mistakes."[29]

The documents reveal that, starting in January 1960, specific plans for the CIA's ambitious "covert program to overthrow the Castro government" were being put in place, approved by President Eisenhower in March.[30] On the President's orders, the program must not implicate US involvement; instead, "our hand should not show in anything that is done" and "everyone must be prepared to deny its existence."[31]

From the US perspective, the issue was not whether or not the revolutionary government and its policies would help or harm the Cuban population. Had that been the concern, years earlier the US may have supported the reformist agenda of Ramón Grau San Martín who advocated land reform and the nationalization of utilities during his short-lived first presidency (1933–1934), policies that may have advanced more equitable distribution of resources for the people of the island nation.[32] The US opposed Grau San Martín though it long-supported and helped sustain the infamously brutal dictators Machado and Batista.

It is the hypocrisy that stings. My father was naïve. He believed America stood for democracy and righteousness, and that brutes like Batista were aberrations, not really under US dominion. He failed to connect the sickness, hunger, poverty, and inequality he observed in Cuba with the logic of capital and the instrumentality of the imperial state. He accepted the bogeyman that was "communism" in the Cold War period that functioned to locate evil within "it," and goodness with the US position and the economic policies it advocated. The rhetoric was very powerful, creating a protective shield around a more complicated reality.

My father was left out to dry, petty merchant that he was. The merchant class would have no place in the restructured Cuban political economy. In the US context, my father was small fry, and would receive kind words but virtually no support from his own government. Instead, he would rely on his own personal strength, and the cultural and financial capital of family and friends to overcome what was for him a desperate situation.

Cigarettes, Babies, and Change

My father sat on a bench by the ocean, a towel draped over his stooped, slender shoulders. His forearms rested on his open thighs, and his hands were loosely clasped between them. He stared out at the peaceful, endless ocean. He was approaching ninety years old.

I realized there would come a time when I would be missing a piece of information and my father would no longer be alive to give it to me. I'd have a question and he would no longer be there to answer it. Though the stark fact of his advancing age and its implication were obvious, I could not imagine him gone, when the only trace of his voice would be on tapes.

There were already times he could not or would not answer a question. Somehow, I found those blanks comforting. It made me think the project could go on, even with omissions, the silences, and the absence.

"After the revolution, why didn't you move to Miami like the rest of your family?" No answer.

"I don't remember grandma very well, your mother," I observed to him one day. "Did we see her often?" No response.

"You say mom never worked. What about when she made dresses? And worked in the store?" No comment.

So much of my father's life experience occurred before my time, and in places I did not know: his boyhood in Poland or life as a young man in Cuba. I could not accomplish this project without his memories of those places and times.

But as the chapters of his life progressed, I had a place in it, the third of his five children, and one among his four daughters. In those years, I was immersed

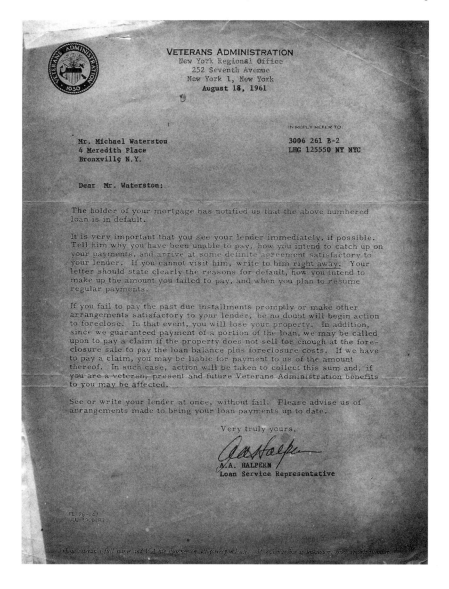

VETERANS ADMINISTRATION
New York Regional Office
252 Seventh Avenue
New York 1, New York
August 18, 1961

IN REPLY REFER TO:

Mr. Michael Waterston   3006 261 B-2
4 Meredith Place   LHG 125550 NY NYC
Bronxville N.Y.

Dear Mr. Waterston:

The holder of your mortgage has notified us that the above numbered
loan is in default.

It is very important that you see your lender immediately, if possible.
Tell him why you have been unable to pay, how you intend to catch up on
your payments, and arrive at some definite agreement satisfactory to
your lender. If you cannot visit him, write to him right away. Your
letter should state clearly the reasons for default, how you intend to
make up the amount you failed to pay, and when you plan to resume
regular payments.

If you fail to pay the past due installments promptly or make other
arrangements satisfactory to your lender, he no doubt will begin action
to foreclose. In that event, you will lose your property. In addition,
since we guaranteed payment of a portion of the loan, we may be called
upon to pay a claim if the property does not sell for enough at the foreclosure sale to pay the loan balance plus foreclosure costs. If we have
to pay a claim, you may be liable for payment to us of the amount
thereof. In such case, action will be taken to collect this sum and, if
you are a veteran, present and future Veterans Administration benefits
to you may be affected.

See or write your lender at once, without fail. Please advise us of
arrangements made to bring your loan payments up to date.

                    Very truly yours,

                    A.A. HALPERN
                    Loan Service Representative

in his cultural milieu, which was also mine, at least in part. That made me an
insider observer, which helped me fill in some of the silences and omissions.
Besides relying on his stories and my mother's, and the letters, notes and documents they saved, there were my own memories I could also tap.

In mid-August, Alsinio's letter arrived at the house, the one from Havana detail-
ing the last hours of El Imperio and Blumin. Two days later, Michael received
another letter. This one was from the New York Regional Office of the Veterans

Administration that just ten years before had guaranteed his mortgage loan for the dream house on Meredith Place. In terms of bearing bad news, some might think Alsinio's letter would be hard to top. For Michael, the VA letter 🖈 was equally disturbing and even more painful. Michael was behind on his mortgage payments.[1] Well, what was to be expected? He didn't have an income. He had no money to buy food for his family. He was trying to set up a new business on another Caribbean island. Louise went to the neighbors to borrow a little cash so she could get some groceries. Frances helped out. Sylvia helped out. Abe and Maria, Phil and Mary, Michael's army buddy Cris, they all helped the Waterston family get back on their feet. The couple borrowed from all of them.

The VA letter, dated August 18, 1961 offered a clear, stern warning:

> If you fail to pay the past due installments promptly or make other arrangements satisfactory to your lender, he no doubt will begin action to foreclosure. In that event, you will lose your property. In addition, since we guaranteed payment of a portion of the loan, we may be called upon to pay a claim if the property does not sell for enough at the foreclosure sale to pay the loan balance plus foreclosure costs. If we have to pay a claim, you may be liable for payment to us of the amount thereof. In such case, action will be taken to collect this sum . . .

It was all he could do to keep his head together, what with the pressure coming from all directions. He was trying his best to start over. Threatening letters from the Veterans Administration didn't give him more courage. It just ate away at his nerve. They made it sound as if he hadn't been talking to the bank. He had. He was talking to everybody, telling the world what was happening, what had happened. Some people were sympathetic. For others, it was business as usual.

Michael felt desperate. "What can you do? What can you do?" he kept asking himself. "I have to accept it," he answered himself. Accept the situation, begin anew, and keep going. It was his burden to bear, he thought. He would take loans but would never abandon his obligation to pay back the debts he accumulated. It was a personal thing. His honor was at stake.

Louise was terrified her husband would commit suicide. Each time he left the house, she worried he might not come back. She feared he'd go to some high rise in New York City and jump off the roof. There were four young children, enormous debt, and besides the little bit she brought in by sewing and selling dresses no steady or sure income.

So yes, Michael had been talking to the bank. In fact he had already been in touch with the Veterans Administration itself. All that time waiting for the Nova Scotia Bank to get approval from the Cuban National Bank to release their funds, and all that time waiting to get a salary from the business, he hadn't been sitting around idle. One year into the revolution, Michael had started scouting his options for a new venture in Puerto Rico. In February 1960, he had Louise compose a letter, copied to President Eisenhower, asking the VA for help. After all, he was a World War II veteran, had a strong track record in business, and had lost everything to circumstances not of his own making. All he needed was a loan. They turned him down.

The rejection got Louise on a letter-writing roll. She contacted Kenneth Keating, the US Senator from New York, who she would also profile in her "What's New in District 2" column. The Senator made some inquiries. The VA wouldn't be any help but she could try for a Small Business Administration (SBA) loan. Louise also enlisted Leon Jick, the family rabbi, to contact officials on her husband's behalf, asking for any kind of assistance whatsoever. "I regret that we can not be more helpful," came the response. The phrase would soon become a familiar, tired refrain.

In the first five years of the revolution, Louise wrote to President Kennedy, and to Eleanor Roosevelt, Milton Eisenhower, and Walter Ruether of the Tractors for Freedom Committee. She wrote to Arturo Morales-Carrión, Assistant Secretary of State for Inter-American Affairs, and to Robert Hurwitch, George W. Spangler, George S. Knight, and Fabian A. Kwiatek, among others from the Department of State. She had ongoing correspondence with Senator Keating and with Congressman Robert Barry of New York.

Her letters went out in waves. Late evenings, with the children quiet in their beds, she'd sit at the table, cigarettes at hand. "February 7, 1961. Dear President Kennedy," she'd type in her machine's cursive font, then give background to the plea, most often composing her story in two pages. The plea changed over time. First it was about getting the money released by the banks, then for help securing a loan, and then for guidance in filing a formal claim with the Foreign Claims Settlement Commission, Cuban Division.

In the first wave, she sought US assistance in getting Blumin's funds released by the Canadian Bank of Nova Scotia, and then the Banco Nacional de Cuba. "I trust you will know of some way to channel this case so that something can be done," she wrote the President, ". . . perhaps the amounts can be deducted from Cuban assets here," she suggested. To Morales-Carrión she wrote:

> I am appealing to you for help or advice on how to get the National Bank of Cuba to approve the transfer of his monies, or can these funds be discounted from Cuban assets here in our country, or can one of our government agencies advance the amounts to my husband until such time as the monies can be removed from the bank in Cuba. Is there any answer to this problem?

She even wrote to the President of the Banco Nacional de Cuba:

Señor Ernesto "Che" Guevara, President
    Dear Sir:
        I am writing to you in desperation to appeal to your sense of fair-
    ness, justice and humanity. The problem that affects me and my family so
    greatly is one that you can solve, and that is why I am taking the liberty of
    approaching you directly . . .

To Robert Hurwitch, Officer in Charge of Cuban Affairs, Louise expressed
her growing frustration and despair. "While we wait for the 'appropriate office'
in our own government and the Cuban government to 'communicate further,'"
she wrote in May of 1961, "the food store, telephone company, mortgage holder,
doctor and dentist will not wait, and we don't know where to turn."

While Louise wrote letters, Michael talked to everyone, especially his creditors.
He owed a thousand dollars to this one, two thousand to that one, and three thousand to the other one. He wanted to open a new business in Puerto Rico, and had
no time to wait. He needed merchandise. He needed his suppliers to wait to get
paid the old debt and still send him new goods. A lot of these guys liked Michael.
He was charming and besides he had always been trustworthy. This problem with
Cuba was a bad break. One guy told him, "Take anything you want, Michael. I
know you're good for it." Another said, "Where should I send the shipment?"
But this one supplier, Abe, he said, "Where's my money you son-of-a-bitch? I'm
going to send someone to beat you up if I don't get my money."

Michael decided to face Abe, go talk to him in person at the fellow's house in
New Jersey. He would never forget that day because it was so beautiful, and it was
springtime. Michael watched out the bus window driving out to Jersey. He passed a
cemetery and thought "Look at those dead people, how calm and comfortable they
are. And I have to go to this bastard who's going to beat me up, so help me God."

He rang the doorbell and Abe came out, grabbing his jacket and taking
Michael in his car for a ride. "Let's park somewhere in a quiet place," Abe suggested. Michael said, "Abe, do you think I don't pay you because I don't want to
pay you?" And he showed him all the papers he'd been collecting—the bank statements, the letters, the official documents, and bills and more bills, the whole
pile. He explained the situation and showed him how the phone company and
the electric company were going to shut off service in his home with four kids.
Abe was shocked, and immediately changed his tune. He told Michael who in the
business to go see and to tell them to call Abe. Abe promised they'd all help out.
They'd wait for their money and send goods to the new store.

And so there was a second coming of the empire, beginning with a little shop
on Calle Fortaleza in Old San Juan. El Imperio, Inc. was incorporated under

the laws of the Commonwealth of Puerto Rico on June 20, 1960, and the new store opened two days later. Only a few months before, Michael had taken the scouting trip.

He had no money to travel. He told Louise he wanted to go to Puerto Rico. He knew Spanish, he heard there were new opportunities on the island, and to get started, it probably wouldn't require as much capital as a place like New York or even Miami. "Yes, go there Michael," Louise told him. "We can go anywhere and live anywhere as long as we are together," she assured him.

Michael's friend Bernie had a shipping company and a lot of connections. Even if he had the money, Michael couldn't get to Puerto Rico because all the flights were booked. The tourists who used to go to Cuba were now flying to Puerto Rico.

"Bernie, can you get me a ticket to Puerto Rico?" Michael asked him. Yes. Bernie got the ticket and had it in hand. Michael would have to pick it up from his office on his way to the airport.

It was raining. Louise put on Michael's old raincoat and drove him to the train station. She asked, "How much money do you have?" He had a train ticket and a dollar in his pocket. She looked in her pocket. She had a quarter. She wanted him to take it. He said, "No. You keep it in case of emergency," as if twenty-five cents would go very far. Bernie didn't know it yet, but Michael would be asking him for cash too, not just the airplane ticket.

At Grand Central, Michael took a taxi to Bernie's office on Canal Street. He told the driver they'd be going to the airport, but first needed to make a quick stop. The cabbie waited while Michael went to see his friend.

"Bernie, you can lend me $200 so I can go to Puerto Rico?" His plea was more a statement than a request.

"Michael, you know I'm giving you the ticket," Bernie answered. "Why don't you borrow it from somebody else?"

"Bernie, don't give me advice. I already borrowed money from my neighbors. If you can't help me, I have to go back home, that's all I can do."

Bernie scrounged up the $200. He didn't have it on him, and had to ask around. It was the dentist down the hall who came through.

In San Juan, Michael stayed at a dilapidated hotel that was dirty, dusty and landed him an asthma attack. But the trip was a success. He met up with Guillermo de Lemos, a textile sales representative from the Dominican Republic who Michael had known for some time. Guillermo showed Miguel the corner store on Fortaleza and Tanca. There was a dying business in the location. Michael could get the merchandise, the fixtures, and the furniture for five thousand dollars.

He bought the store and rented the building, courtesy of many more and larger loans from wealthy acquaintances and friends who dug deep into their pockets to help out. On these borrowed funds, Michael also managed to save the house.

The commuting life of the fifties would not work in the new decade. To get things going, the couple needed to be in the store every day, fixing it up, producing goods, displaying merchandise, attracting customers, and managing the office. Besides, the cost of traveling back and forth was prohibitive. Louise rented out the Bronxville house, the children were prepared, and the family packed up to move in 1964.

El Imperio began small. They started by selling cuts of fabric. Cuts are much cheaper than bolts, allowing you to sell low and offer a greater variety of cloth. "A cut of fabric is two yards, two and a half yards, six yards," Miguel explained. "A bolt is 50 yards or 40 yards or 80 yards."

They sold Simplicity, McCall, and Vogue patterns, and made dresses too, cheap ones created in their own *taller* (workshop) on the second floor, and that they sold on a two-dollar rack on the store's main floor.

Miguel would go outside the arched doorway of the shop and step onto the narrow sidewalk, the second-floor balcony overhead. Cars passed slowly on Fortaleza, navigating the blue cobblestones, and avoiding pedestrians walking on the narrow street. "Come to El Imperio!" he'd call out, handing flyers to the drivers and chatting it up with passersby. Word got around about the Cubano's store with the decorated windows and attractive mannequins.

Before long, Miguel expanded, and opened a second, larger shop on Calle San Francisco on the corner of San Justo 🖉.² Miguel was thrilled to open the second store on Linda's birthday, October 19, 1961, and to greet customers like Olga Guillot 📷, the famous Cuban bolero singer, and her dancer friend Floriana Alba.³ They each bought $250 worth of merchandise and promised to come back!

The crisis subsided though they were always behind on their payments. The family got into a groove. Louise enrolled the three younger children in private school in spite of the fact that she had no money for their tuition or for Linda who stayed in New York for college. Louise paid $100 here, $200 there, and promised to pay up when she could. Same with Michael. If he owed $100, he'd pay $50 or $40. If he owed a thousand, he'd pay $500 until he could get more. One day they'd sell $800, the next $500, and the next $600. It went little by little, *poco a poco*, over the next dozen years.

In between, the last of their babies was born, a girl named Adrienne Adinah in February of 1968. "A baby will bring us luck," Louise claimed, convincing herself and her husband. She was 44 and he 55 years old.

The crisis had subsided, but the stirrings did not. There were movements afoot, and the big assassinations: JFK, Malcolm X, MLK Jr., and RFK. The radio was on in the store, just behind the display of see-through, baby-doll nightgowns that June day in 1968 when news of Bobby's shooting was announced.

It was just three years before that Louise had written to Robert Kennedy about their situation, once he had become US Senator from New York. She was still pleading, this time asking for a loan on her husband's claim against the Government of Cuba. Like the others, Kennedy 🖉 sent his "regret that my reply could not be more favorable."[4]

Kennedy attached a letter from Douglas MacArthur II at the Department of State in response to his own inquiry on the matter. MacArthur explained Louise's options: submit a claim to the Foreign Claims Settlement Commission that on October of 1964 had been authorized by Public law 88-666, 88th Congress, to receive and determine the validity and amount of claims of American nationals against Cuba. MacArthur also noted that the law "does not authorize loans on claims." He explained that bills introduced in the House of Representatives (HR 10327) and in the Senate (S 2625) did authorize loans on such validated claims, but that the Executive Branch opposed the loan provisions of the bill that was ultimately enacted.

She wouldn't get a loan but Louise would get the claim validated. She collected all the documents, testimonies, old letters, and, of course, the pile of bills. She followed the steps outlined by the Commission and corresponded with Marie L. Murphy, attorney in charge of the Cuban Division.[5] Louise succeeded. The validated claim, dated May 12 1971 amounted to $180,738.14 with 6 percent per annum from July 12, 1961 to the date of settlement. Her claim would be among others as part of any future negotiation with the Government of Cuba.

The changes in her life, the revolutions in the world, all this was also beginning to transform Louise. She had done her job, standing by her husband's side through the terrible crisis, and helping protect her children from the worst of it. She could be satisfied knowing what she had accomplished. Without her, there would be no Cuban claim, and she toiled daily at the store, coordinating the *taller* and managing the books when she wasn't on the selling floor.

For the most part, the children were blossoming, and moving on. Linda was back in Puerto Rico, and would not finish college. The times they were a-changin' and Linda would be a part of the era, Puerto Rican style. Her rebellions brought Michael disappointment, and drove Louise further between them as referee. Jessica would be the first in the immediate family to graduate college, and the first of the children to marry. The decade was coming to a close and Louise's third child would soon be off to college on the mainland, with the fourth following suit. She would still have the baby at home, her blessed one and delight.

She found a certain comfort in the new routine of her daily life, considering all the uncertainty leading up to it. Even so, Louise felt it was getting more difficult to ignore the things that had been bothering her, what before had seemed little annoyances. The way her husband talked to her sometimes. The way he assumed she was there to serve his needs like she was his paramour and secretary and caretaker. She wasn't an angry person, but resentment was rising and refused to go away.

Louise saw that Michael had hardened. He was becoming more and more rigid, more and more controlling. He seemed to feel especially sorry for himself, as if he were the only one in the world to experience loss. He made it so the world centered on him. He expected his wife and his children to satisfy his wants, while he neglected to find out what theirs might be. He did not discuss, he lectured. He did not converse, he preached.

For so long, Louise had accommodated Michael's needs and found pleasure in doing so even though it sometimes brought her to silent tears. These days, the couple was getting off track, the marriage so out of tune it grated on her nerves and on her soul.

Working at El Imperio, Louise developed her skills and discovered new capabilities. It felt good. She felt good. She got excited about exploring the possibilities. Working on the Cuban claim, she felt accomplished and recognized her own competency. It also made her aware of her own delusions about the way government operated and on whose behalf. Before this she had blind faith in the United States and its mission. Now she felt foolish and naïve. On one hand, her government would not freeze Cuban government assets in the US to use as leverage in releasing Blumin's deposits held up in the bank in Cuba. It would not advance her husband a loan. And it refused to offer comment on her question regarding the liability of the Royal Bank of Canada for holding up her husband's deposits. On the other hand, large corporations received tax adjustments on their Cuban losses, allowing them to reinvest elsewhere, and still have their claim validated by the Foreign Claims Settlement Commission. A small businessman who lost his business, who lost his income, had nothing against which to claim a tax adjustment. A small businessman with nothing could not afford an attorney to explore the liability issue, or craft and submit the Cuban claim.

Michael had a wife who was his advocate though he was hard pressed to acknowledge her contributions. The more confidence she felt, the more irritable he became. Louise knew he was quick to criticize and slow to praise. In business, he met her suggestions with rejection. "You don't know about business," he'd say, putting her down. More often than not, she'd see her ideas be put in place as if they were his very own. It burned her up.

The scales were falling from her eyes.

The children were coming of age in a different time and Louise wanted to know more about it. She wanted to hear from Linda about her activities organizing a worker union at her job with the Puerto Rican Telephone Company, and about her involvement with La Liga Socialista, the Puerto Rican *independendista* (independence) movement, and her boyfriend Elizam Escobar. She wanted to hear from Jessica about theories on dance and movement, and her young husband's research on the 1968 student uprisings in Paris. She talked with Alisse about Virginia Woolf, Ibsen's *A Doll House*, Betty Friedan's *The Feminine Mystique*, and Kate Chopin's *The Awakening*. With David, she experimented with hashish.

Louise made a decision. She made the decision on her own, and it would be something she would do just for herself. She would go back to school, attend the university as she had always longed to do. She'd study art and literature and history.

Michael was furious. "You need to be in the store. You can be a professor some other time," he'd say, mocking her dream. "You're wasting your energy, Luisa," he'd scoff. "Forget about school," he'd command. His bitterness was intense. It was intimidating but she would not be unnerved.

Possession and Dispossession

It was the first month of the new year of 2012 that I sorted through my mother's documents in a box she labeled "Cuban Claim." She saved each letter and official correspondence, and every piece of evidence, including statements from the bank and from the manufacturers. The documents were not well organized, but they were there. I sifted through them—carefully, for the paper is so very fragile. No matter how gentle I was, tiny pieces flicked off the crisp edges, littering my office floor. There are letters signed by personages now inscribed in history. There are letters from other people—the bookkeeper, the manager, the husband. Their stories also comprise a history. It didn't take long to realize there is enough material in this one box to supply the basis of a rich, scholarly study of that one period alone.

It was all I could do to stay focused on this project, not get pulled away by the quantity and quality of the data in the box. I have been trained in the scholarly arts, a social scientist prepared for the slow, careful examination of data, information, and facts to situate in context, history, and analysis. It is important and exciting to follow the research, to go where it takes you. It is equally important to recognize the place where it can turn into a different project, with different goals. This too is a trained skill.

Despite the temptation, I pulled back from the rich material to concentrate on *My Father's Wars*. For this project, I use the training I've received, the skills I've developed, and I build on my discipline's methodological innovations of the past several decades. Nevertheless, this study is not routine scholarship due in part to the intimate connection between the anthropologist and her subject.

Thus, in my possession are the data, the documents, and my own memories that correspond in time with the happenings since the revolution. For instance, I remember the intense anxiety that permeated our household in the years 1959–1964, much of it centered on money. "Daddy, you didn't pay the electric bill?" I demanded of my father when the lights went out one evening. Turns out it was just a temporary blackout, but I felt the panic of being without.

Even so, those were good times for a child like me. Before we made the grand move to Puerto Rico in 1964, our parents took us to visit the island. While they worked, the children vacationed. The summer of 1962 we rented a house on Calle Manuel Rodriguez Serra in Santurce, right by the beach near Calle Conveniencia. Charlie's Record Shop was just around the corner, Breaking Up is Hard to Do was the hit song, and Marilyn Monroe killed herself. Another time we stayed right on Ashford Avenue in the Gorbea Apartments, a short-stay rental. While our parents prepared our new place to live and worked in the store, we went to Hotel La Concha beach by day, and watched the prostitutes stroll the *Avenida* by night.

We moved a few times before settling into a third floor walkup on Calle Las Marias in Condado, not too far from the St. John's School I attended. In the first years of the move, and with Linda in New York, my sister Jessica and I ran the household while our parents worked. Jessica cleaned and looked after David. I went to the market and prepared dinner. We were worried about our parents who seemed so nervous, overworked, and tired. When they walked in from a long day at the store, the apartment was in perfect shape, and the meal was laid out on the table.

I loved spending time with my mother, sitting with her at the formal, mahogany dining-room table those late evenings after my father had gone to bed. The table had been shipped from the house in New York and didn't fit the small tropical eating area of our new place. Of course that didn't matter. We drank endless cups of coffee and talked. She'd confide in me, and I'd confide in her.

I dreaded spending time with my father. His lectures were unbearable and the constant warnings he delivered were demoralizing. I found his domineering style at once grating and intimidating.

Once in a while, my father planned a dinner out with me, a special time together that I would have preferred to avoid.

"Do you know what happens to a girl who isn't a virgin when she's married?" my father would begin his sermon. I must have been fourteen the first time I got that lecture. "A girl who isn't a virgin, her husband *will* find out on the wedding night. And the next morning, he'll *throw* her back to her father, 'Here, take her! She's nothing but a tramp!'"

By his incongruous logic, my father explained that sex before marriage was disgusting, but afterward it was the most beautiful thing in the world. A man must get as much sexual experience as possible before settling down with a bride to whom he will remain faithful the rest of his days. On the other hand, a good woman, a good girl must stay chaste until she gives herself unto her husband. Only in this way is a woman worthy of a man's love and respect.

As cautionary tale, my father also told me about a "good" family that was forever banished from the island because their son "took marijuana." Always fearful of calamity, he warned me against venturing too far from home, and in grotesque terms, described what boys would do to me, would want from me.

No matter how charming he could be on some occasions, my father was a troubled man. He could be delightful one moment, and a closed-minded bigot the next. With his workers he could be generous and at times incredibly cruel. One time he posted a framed photograph of a large-buttocked woman on a centrally located wall in the store, and wrote the name "Iris" under the fleshy bottom. Iris was an employee. He thought it was funny; it never seemed to dawn on him that she would be thoroughly humiliated.

What am I to make of his behavior and his personality? He could never get beyond his own contradictions. He believed his choices had been righteous, his youthful escapades natural, and his humor at others' expense an acceptable form of entertainment. For him, it was perfectly consistent to encourage the son to fornicate and forbid the daughters their own sexuality. Should his wife intervene (to talk things out with a child, for example), he took it as betrayal. "Parents should have a single voice," he proclaimed. "It is a natural law!" That single voice was the father's prerogative, he assumed.

He met our resistance to his "natural law" by retreating into a mythological past. Family unity, that single voice, he claimed, "it was like that with my parents. It is like that with my brothers' and sisters' families, and most families I know." In my father's fable of his past life, there were no conflicts:

> We were all for one and one for all. We were the envy in Poland as well as in Cuba. We had love and respect for our father and our mother. He was the head of the family because he was the breadwinner. Our mother fed us and cloths [sic] us. They did the best they could and there was devotion.

But in his own family, my father said, there was no unity. His wife didn't listen. His children didn't listen, no matter how many times he repeated the same thing, banging it into their heads. As a result, those of us in his immediate orbit proved to be his greatest disappointment.

My father had his blind spots. I also believe he could never get past the multiple traumas of his life experiences. Sometimes he used the old sad stories to justify his demand for obedience. Sometimes he had glimmers of true insight, though he could only take this so far. I see in the following passage my father's attempt at reflection:

> People ask me why do I work so hard. I couldn't give a straight answer because in my mind I didn't have the answer. I have a goal but did I reach that goal yet? I had my fears and had my hopes. Fear of poverty and hopes for security . . . I feel relieved with acquiring some security. My fear of poverty [is] still there.

For me, the most difficult aspect of this project is grasping the sources and consequences of my father's deep wounds. I have come to recognize it is the whole of my father's story and the multiple contexts within which it was situated that help explain my father's injured self. The chapters of this book illustrate this multiplicity, and illuminate the complexity that resists singular, reductive explanation. As part of that resistance, I know this book will come to a close but will never be complete.

However, I think it is possible to identify certain features of the story that connect to the damage.

The violent, traumatic history of the twentieth century is a major feature of my father's story and is implicated in his damaged self. Writing about Holocaust survivors, Eva Hoffman observes they "are often difficult people, and are found to be so by others."[6] My father was not a Holocaust survivor in the literal sense even as his life touched upon the massacre in Jedwabne. To place my father in the category of Holocaust survivor would be a distortion, exaggerating the role of the Shoah in his saga and shutting out other events of the century that significantly defined his experience. At the same time, my father seemed to share with survivors certain psychological traits often attributed to the Holocaust experience. He was a difficult person: narcissistic, prone to depressions and nightmares, exacting self-sacrifice from close family members, and privileging his own emotional needs over those of others as entitlement for suffering that, in his view, others could never know or experience.[7] Even this is not enough. As Linda Green argues, the "manifestation of a clinical syndrome" does not adequately account for the suffering; to leave it there would serve to "dehistoricize and dehumanize the lived experience."[8]

My father escaped the "Main Event" that was the Holocaust. Still, it is important to acknowledge the significance of his being a Jew in the twentieth century. Writing in the late 1980s, George Steiner notes that collective traumatic memory is shared by Jews throughout the world and is situated in the deep recesses of Jewish identity:

> The Shoah, the remembrance of Auschwitz, the haunting apprehension that, somewhere, somehow, the massacres could begin anew, is today the cement of Jewish identity . . . Above all else, to be a Jew in the second half of [the twentieth] century is to be a survivor, and one who knows that his survival can again be put in question.[9]

The "echoes of persecution" are repeatedly recalled in Jewish liturgy and marked by religious ritual, while diaspora has become the sacred symbol of Zionism, a nationalist, political cause.[10] During this same century, the image of the wandering Jew, ever "unsettled," cast out and exiled from an "original" homeland, became a key motif of Jewish identity and the Jewish national movement, even though the legend itself is polysemic.[11]

My father viewed his life "as if it were always being lived under the sign of extermination."[12] The theme of impending doom was ever present in his lectures, and his fear bordered on paranoia. Victimization was a key motif of his narrative; near misses even come into the funny stories. Always on the edge of ruin, he often described himself in the process of running, suffering, barely surviving, and persecuted. My father never got over the feelings of isolation and loneliness that come from being cast out, from forced absence. In his case, the metanarrative of inevitable destruction and loss played out in his life.

This culture-bound and politics-driven construction of reality is also insufficient to account for my father's suffering.[13] It is not enough to lay blame for my father's wounds on his old Polish neighbors, on antisemitism (historically specific, not timeless), or his sacred belief in Jewish victimization, all of which were in dynamic interaction. There is greater culpability, and it lies in the multiple violences of the century in which he lived. My father was born into war, and, as anthropologist James Quesada notes, "Wars produce a continuum of duress." Like Quesada's little boy described in the article "Suffering Child: An Embodiment of War and Its Aftermath in Post-Sandinista Nicaragua," my father's "lived sense of insecurity [was] sown during a time of war."[14]

My father escaped a massacre, and passed through one revolution and two wars, physically surviving these "spectacular" forms of violence, enduring "the pain of being alive," and even "unmaking the violence" by adapting, rebuilding, and reinventing himself.[15]

The vast majority of my father's days did not pass in or against the spectacular episodes of the century's violence, but in the " 'little' violences produced in the structures . . . of everyday life," as Nancy Scheper-Hughes and Philippe Bourgois label the phenomenon.[16] My father feared poverty because the *structured* arrangements of economic life in the twentieth century did not guarantee freedom from hunger and want. He believed in "do or die," but even that was not necessarily enough. However unfair the burden, he took individual ownership of the debts in his name. He thought that to honor them was to take the moral high ground; he never saw how these debts were systemically produced and the burden of them unfairly distributed. He had dreams, he worked hard, and he was responsible, but no matter where he went, he couldn't hold onto the guarantee.

The "little" violences to which Scheper-Hughes and Bourgois refer encompass the social pathologies of a range of inequalities.[17] These forms of inequity marked the global as well as the local social orders of which my father was a part over the whole of the twentieth century. As such, these social orders were violent and pathological. They required participation from those who lived in them, nurtured their obliviousness to its workings, and demanded their complicity even as these systems meted out deep social suffering to tens of millions of people. Of course individuals and their social groups were variously positioned along the "steep grades of inequality"—some benefited from it, others suffered.[18] And it was at the intersections of the various inequalities—where economics met politics met race met gender, for example—that individuals could find their own "social location," however movable that might have been for some.

Inevitably, the inequalities produced resistance and sometimes revolution, as my father could attest. They also produced victims who could become victimizers, and victimizers who could become victims.

Things Fall Apart

I walked into my father's apartment that I always found so dreary though it was right across the street from the beach in Condado. The glass of the sliding doors to the porch was covered in a film of grit and salt, and the sun beat down hard on it, giving off a muted, dusty glow. I slid the porch doors open.

The noise outside was constant and disturbingly loud with the motorcycles speeding down the street, the sound of jackhammers echoing in the distance, and the car horns blowing. I couldn't stand this place.

I went to the kitchen for a glass from the cabinet that smelled damp, a tropical scent that reminded me of old textiles and aged wood. My father walked in from his bedroom wearing boxer shorts and an undershirt that hung loose on his body. He slid the doors shut, and complained, "Why are these open? Don't you know it's breezy, you'll get a chill?"

The heat was suffocating. Before long, it became unbearable.

It was a tropical winter. Baby Adrienne, born February 13, 1968, was the joy of the family. The local, transient rabbi offered the infant the fitting middle name "Adinah." Rabbi Albert Shulman said it means "cherished one, a delight." Louise and Michael liked the rabbi very much. A fair-minded, gentle man, Rabbi Shulman helped a small group start a reform temple that began with several families coming together for *Shabbat* on Friday evenings. Louise and Michael were among the founding members of the Reform Jewish Congregation, and David was its first Bar Mitzvah in 1967. Rabbi Shulman would lead the congregation those times he was on the island for a visit.

Of course Michael was enchanted by the new baby even if people on the street complimented him on his adorable *grand*child .[1] It really wasn't necessary for Louise to urge him to be glad about the pregnancy, news he heard from her *and* from the children at dinner one evening. "I really feel this is God's will, a gift from heaven to bring happiness to us all," Louise wrote in a short note to her husband.

Louise was thrilled with the new addition, though her sense of discontent and dissatisfaction remained. She wanted something more than babies, though she loved her babies more than anything. She wanted more than to pass the days working to build El Imperio, and she wanted more than to be a loyal wife to a husband she truly loved though she despised how hurtful he could be.

The great joy Louise felt when Adrienne was born was disrupted by news of her own mother's death six months later. Marjorie died in her sleep, a peaceful death at her home in the Adirondacks. That early August day, Marjorie paid the grocers, the druggist, and the landlady before retiring to the garden for tea and pastry. Louise was content her mother had lived a good, eighty-year, unconventional life though the daughter had one deep regret. Looking through old papers, Louise realized that amid the tumult of her own life, she had never acknowledged the death of Marjorie's long-time companion. Marjorie was with Hector for thirty-five years. He died that same June Michael opened the store in Puerto Rico. Of course Louise was busy and distracted then, what with the Cuban losses, the children and a husband finding his way through the troubles. Still, Louise considered her neglect a personal failing. She hadn't visited her mother when Hector died. She hadn't even called.

On the heels of Marjorie's passing came another, more terrible death. Louise's brother Maurice died of a sudden heart attack at the age of 42. Louise found comfort in the embraces of her children. Michael offered her no comfort. He heard the news and her cries but said nothing. He left the room to sit alone.

Michael had other worries since another blow hit the business just three weeks before Maurice's death. It seemed Michael couldn't get away from shenanigans no matter where he went. This time, it was about the building on Fortaleza that housed El Imperio. The owner wanted to sell and Michael wanted to buy, but there was an intermediary between them looking for a payoff. Michael lost out to another buyer but it was sneaky business. The new buyer paid less than Michael's offer. The worst part was facing the marshals with their court order. Or maybe the worst part was Louise. She embarrassed him.

The marshals came in and everyone was in a frenzy to empty the entire contents of the store in one day. Anything left after 5 o'clock would be confiscated. Michael kept things going and upbeat, even chit-chatted with his rival's attorney who was there to monitor the proceedings. Louise was beyond annoyed and she loathed the attorney. How could Michael talk to him in such a friendly way? The day was getting long. There was still much to do, to salvage before the doors were bolted. Louise sipped her coffee and spied the attorney's jacket hanging on a nail in the back of the store. The day ended. Everything was out of the store and the family left. Michael turned to Louise, "You are so childish. The lawyer told me. 'It was your wife poured her coffee in my pocket. My jacket's ruined.' You happy now, Louise?"

Michael couldn't stand the way Louise could be impulsive. He thought she lived in a fantasy as if she were floating on the clouds. She was always "gone with the wind," and he told her so. Often. "Oh, Luisa, cha-cha-cha, you and your gone with the wind," he'd repeat, getting up her ire each time. How could she not know the world is centered on gravity? How could she not know that every person must learn how to balance on this earth, just to walk straight and not plummet?

Rose Shulman, the rabbi's wife, worried how Michael would react to Louise's decision to attend college. "What about the blow to his ego?" Louise recalled her asking. "If his 'ego' cannot take it, he's not the man I thought I married," Louise wrote in her private notes. "My going back to school will have to be a test for both of us."

And so it was. Louise became an undergraduate at the Universidad de Puerto Rico (UPR) in the fall semester of 1972 at the same time David started film school at New York University (NYU). Adrienne was four years old, and Michael was approaching sixty. She thought it was the right time to do something for herself. She was still tending to the business, though not full time. She was still tending to the children; the little one at home, of course, but also the older ones now mostly off carving out their own lives.

The business was doing well, gaining momentum. It had a good name and the old debts were getting paid off, just as Michael had promised his creditors. Everyone knew El Imperio, the most magnificent store in Viejo San Juan. And they knew *Don* Miguel 🖋, the important proprietor.[2]

Michael was dead set against Louise's dream to go to the university, just as Jacobo had been when Miguelito arrived in Manguito. "Doña Luisa," he'd say in mock respect. "Go to bed, it's late now and you have work tomorrow," he'd tell her. With her hands framing her forehead, Louise would form a wall to block him out as she pored over her books. In the first semesters, most of her classes were in Spanish; only later could she take the English literature courses in her major. She wanted to learn and needed to concentrate. So she ignored him. Michael shuffled back to bed.

It went on like this for years, the tension between them escalating with each scornful remark. He became more and more critical, accusing her of neglecting the children from the moment they were born (she didn't cover them in the middle of the night), of being a careless housekeeper (the home was strewn with piles of books and papers), and of failing her husband. He claimed the struggles and losses they had gone through were his own, and his alone. She was a mere bystander—none of it happened to her. In turn, she became hostile, sometimes responding with condescending, sarcastic remarks. More often than not, she responded with steely silence.

The more difficult it became to speak to each other, the more they wrote things down—in personal diaries and notepads, and letters or notes meant for one another.

"Dear Michael," Louise wrote on an undated slip of paper. "I must defend myself when you treat me like an incompetent child. That's my main problem with you—otherwise I love you." In 1978, she began a letter as follows:

> I wrote you the other day that I needed a man with whom I can share my thoughts. So here I am sharing some thoughts. I am doing it this way in writing because they are merely thoughts I want to share—not really talk about, discuss or argue about. I just want to let you see how my mind is working so you can understand me, and I can understand myself better. I'm not asking whether my thoughts are right or wrong, reasonable or illogical, good or evil. They are simply my thoughts which I want to share with you.

By that date, anarchy seemed loosed upon their private world. It was unclear if the center would hold or be enough. They loved each other but there was innocence no more. Too much had happened in the intervening years since Louise enrolled in university.

Louise kept reading Woolf and Faulkner, de Beauvoir and Sartre. She studied Bergson, Frances Yates, and the seventeenth-century mystical poet Abraham Cowley who she called an "apostle in muse's land."[3] Her mind was spinning. She slept little and chain-smoked cigarettes. It was all a fury—the epiphanies, the frustrations, and her sadness.

At the university, Louise was elected to the student council, representing the Department of English, then found herself among twelve students unjustly and illegally suspended for participating in a protest march. She contacted a lawyer, and met with Roger Baldwin of ACLU fame, learning from him that the regulations used against the UPR twelve were found to be unconstitutional in a Puerto Rican court several years prior. The *San Juan Star* depicted the episode in menacing terms. "Student Group Charged with Break-In Try ✐," the headline read.[4]

In her thirty-three-page personal testimony on the matter, Louise noted that of all the Spanish- and English-language newspapers, only *Claridad*, a much-maligned, pro-independence publication, depicted the events as they occurred from her front-seat vantage point. Louise wondered why "independence" seemed to be such a dangerous idea.

Michael avoided talking to Louise about the whole matter except to say she was crazy to get involved with such *mishigas*, and to complain she was neglecting her work at the store.[5] The suspension lasted several weeks until it was lifted on February 13, Adrienne's seventh birthday. Louise started the spring semester with a deeper understanding of the forces that framed her world.

It got so the contradictions became too intense, the opposing pressures too volatile. Louise had always been stoic. When the explosion came, it was internal. Her mind and then her body took the direct blows. But first she passed through a significant rite of passage.

It was the start of summer; and the days were hot. Louise graduated, receiving her Bachelor of Arts degree in the Humanities in June 1976. Michael did not attend the commencement ceremony. All the same, Louise made plans to continue with graduate studies, and offered herself to the Department Chair as a teaching assistant. She approached the Chair at a university event. Louise recalled he had a drink in hand and smiled at her.

"Can you mop floors?" he asked.

At home, Louise went to the piano and played Jalousie , the famous tango by composer Jacob Gade.[6] Afterward, she poured herself a cognac and lit a cigarette.

Louise fell apart before the end of June. The doctors called it a nervous breakdown. She lapsed into a manic episode during which all became clear in a vision she called "the Spirit" that stayed with her for five days. It began, she said, with a snap. She heard the sound, and it was located in her brain. Then it left, she said, with a clapping. She heard the sound, and it moved out from her, and away.

It was the "controlling nerves" that broke, Louise thought. The "snap" was the sound of their breaking down, finally setting her free. It was the life force "the Spirit" left her with, Louise said, all-encompassing love.

The family was alarmed. Louise was beyond agitated: her speech speedy, her movements frenzied, her gaze intense. Linda and Michael hid the kitchen knives. Louise noticed that, and believed it signaled the coming of an age of nonviolence. Michael took her to doctors who had her heavily medicated. Four months later Louise suffered a massive heart attack, barely escaping death. The cigarettes, the tensions, and the Thorazine took their toll. The diagnosis was an acute myocardial infarction of the interior wall, and the damage irreversible.

In the course of her series of physical and mental treatments, Louise made another disclosure. She had had an affair. It was brief, lasting only a few weeks. She hadn't planned for it but it came at a crucial moment in her own awakening. It happened two years into her studies, and exactly one year before her suspension from the university—in February 1974. At the time, she thought this too was spiritual. For Louise, it was also playful and delicious, earthly and carnal.

Michael was devastated by the news of his having been cuckolded, and his rage would not be tamed. It was as if the spark between Louise and her lover discharged and traveled under doors, through the rooms, onto streets, across the terraces, over curbs, and straight into his very being, shocking him.

He searched for explanation, and in his desperation, the venom was unleashed. Things became clear to him too, and Michael put his revelations in spoken words and in writing. Louise was a matriarch, under the spell of feminism, her salvation. She was a wild gypsy who didn't care who she destroyed. She learned it from the feminists, the ones who encouraged women to leave their husbands, murder their children, destroy the family, and demolish capitalism, a refrain Michael apparently copied from evangelist Pat Robertson. Feminists taught women to practice witchcraft and become lesbians. This was a track Michael played and replayed constantly, hounding the children with these charges against their mother.

Michael connected the dots. Sex was a dominating force Louise inherited from her Romanian ancestors. Even *tante* Betty—she wasn't really Louise's aunt but her grandmother, Maxwell's mother, Michael came to believe, though this has never been confirmed. Some *tante* she was, taking a lover. Louise's father was born from an affair with a gypsy. Luisa with her golden earring, Michael once teased her. It was coming full circle and making sense. Louise had gypsy blood, just like Carmen from the opera. "What Carmen wants Carmen gets," Michael recalled the character, likening her to Louise. At least Bizet's Carmen was open and honest, not like this one. Louise was more dangerous, masking the truth, sneaking around. She was the devil herself.

The air was sticky in the tropics; September days were sultry. Two years passed. Louise consulted a lawyer, considered a divorce, and then changed her mind. The couple arranged their own meeting, just the two of them, and audio taped it on September 4, 1978. "Do you want another drink?" Michael asked her. It was a polite request, and startling considering the hurtful words that passed between them before and after the uncomplicated question. Michael and Louise talked past each other, while *coquis*, Puerto Rico's tiny tree frogs, trilled steadily in the background.[7] She wanted acknowledgment. He wanted assurance. Neither one gave it.

Michael had the final word in the taped discussion. He said,

> I guess that's the way people are. You're born with a certain fate. That's the way you're going to die. I build . . . [they] take it away from me. Now I'm building in Puerto Rico . . . Louise [wants] to destroy it. I don't know who the hell next will come to destroy me.

The years passed this way. El Imperio became famous throughout the Caribbean and parts of Latin America. Women came from Venezuela to buy their wedding gowns in El Imperio. Others came from Santo Domingo to buy French lace for the gown they sewed for themselves. In those years, you could ask any woman employed by the Puerto Rican government about El Imperio. She would have told you it is *the* place to get gorgeous, tailored silk blouses and great suits for work. Actresses, the best designers, and social elites bought their gowns, fabrics, accessories, and antique furnishings from El Imperio. Even the Puerto Rican writer Tina Casanova wove El Imperio into her novel *Sambirón*, a family story that also chronicles Puerto Rico's history across two centuries.

By 1990, El Imperio was at its peak, and Michael a wealthy, 77-year-old man. His assets (for he refused Louise's name on these) were valued at over a million and a half dollars. Now Louise begged him to retire—to sell off some assets, or turn the business over to a daughter or two eager to take it on. He refused. He couldn't stop working. Rightly or wrongly, he didn't trust the daughters would be competent to run the business. He wouldn't sell El Imperio after it took so long to build its famous name. He wouldn't sell any of the five properties he had acquired over the years, including the building that housed the store. It seemed safer like this, a way to ward off ruin, destruction, and death.

In Puerto Rico, the sun was brilliant; the days were radiant. Miguel found solace at the beach. Near the Capitol building just short of the old city, he'd scramble down the steep hill to a pool of calm sea carved out by the rocky reef. Or he'd head to Ocean Park near Isla Verde where the ocean was tranquil and wide. He'd swim, breathe deeply, and meditate in a style of his own invention (always keeping one eye out for a thief or, if a daughter was accompanying him, a lecher). The beach was replenishing, giving Miguel the peace of mind he didn't get at work or with his family.

But Louise longed for New York, to be back in her hometown and in her *home* before there were no more days to have. She was getting close to seventy years old herself, and searched for solutions. She sent him a letter:

> Divorce is absurd at this date. Wouldn't it be great if I stayed most of the time in NY, and you here in PR and we could visit each other at certain times and even enjoy each other's company? We have so much between us—so much invested you could say—we have our children and grandchildren and our material possessions—and our memories—and feelings of tenderness towards one another—and we care about one another—maybe this is a different kind of love.

He refused.

She left anyway. It was okay. In place of the devil, Michael found a guardian angel.

Her name was Tanya (a pseudonym). God sent her, Michael had believed. She was incredibly efficient. She practically saved his life, he would claim. Never did he have such a capable person as she to help him in the business. Everything came to her so naturally. Everyday she did something special for him. She told him not to worry about anything. She would take care of it all, now that Doña Luisa wasn't around to interfere. Tanya was just what an eighty-year-old man needed. She offered her understanding, her help, and her respect, giving Don Miguel the uplift he so desperately needed after being knocked down for so long and so many times.

He wondered why he could never find one or two Tanyas in his own family. There are too many evil people in this world, he thought, referring to his own family members. "They just made believe they're angels."

The Sacred and the Secular

My parents were fluent in the language of the sacred. It was not unusual for them to use religious imagery in spoken and written forms. Was it so difficult to convince my father that at age fifty-four he could—he *should*—father a fifth child? Perhaps invoking a power larger than they ("God"), my mother could ease my father's concerns about re-charging the parental, legal, and financial obligations a new child would require. To have this child, in my mother's words, was no longer in their own power, but the result of a force greater than their own: "God's will." More than that, this new child would descend from God's dwelling place—heaven itself.

Perhaps she just wanted to say how very much she wanted to keep this baby, and could find no earthly words to express it. Whether consciously or not, she dipped into the holy to sanctify a choice.

Both parents were schooled from an early age in religious and secular attitudes and the linguistic frames each domain provided. As adults, they were not particularly observant in the religious sphere; Jewish rituals were enacted only on rare, specific occasions. Their participation in starting up a reform temple in San Juan was not rooted in the spiritual per se, but in the social when their son David came to them asking for a Bar Mitzvah (he wanted one like other boys he knew). Their day-to-day lives were much taken up with matters framed by the secular state—how to make a living according to the rules and laws of the nation.[8] The religious domain seemed separate and apart, consistent with prevailing ideas about modern times when spiritual beliefs and practices among individuals were expected to decline.

My father welcomed the so-called "secular modern" to the extent that it ignited his ambitions and dreams of progress.[9] In those moments, he rejected the past, the traditional, the "backward" ways, thinking of these as barriers to his own forward movement. He would be no *shtetl* peasant with a Jewish-sounding name and a style of dress and demeanor that signaled old habits. At the same time—in other domains—he bristled at the coming of the new. As a young man, he fell for my mother because she simultaneously embodied the iconic new (she was a New Yorker, not a Cuban Jewish immigrant from Europe) and the iconic old (she *seemed* sweet, virginal, and respectful). But then she overstepped a line, challenging his authority. The new was good in so far as it didn't cross into his private dominion, the sacred place of the family.

My father located the problem—his problem—in 1970s feminism that he depicted in the most demonizing of terms. He met my mother's desire for self-determination and schooling with a firm, authoritarian "No." She wasn't asking his permission, and according to the law of the land, did not need it. He saw her acts of disobedience as betrayal of her duty to her husband, a violation of the most sacred of oaths. He did not see how his unswerving commitment to those gendered obligations led to his own oppression as much as to hers.

The more he resisted, the more she violated. The battle lines were drawn on the field of their marriage. They injured each other and the war wounded them both. As my mother sought to enlarge her world, my father's grew smaller. He came to see things in increasingly rigid terms, differentiated between "right" and "wrong." From this core distinction, he positioned people in a set of correlated, oppositional pairs: good is to evil as nurturer is to witch as angel is to devil. He never considered the hypocrisy of his gendered stance. It was all very simple. He had fulfilled his duties; the witch had failed at hers.

My mother was a feminist—she believed in women's rights, and in her own way, participated in the movement. For example, she proudly wore her gold-colored ERA (equal rights amendment) pin. Among other publications, she subscribed to *Ms. Magazine* and *SIGNS: Journal of Women in Culture and Society*, a scholarly publication.

The feminist literature that emerged during the period of my parents' personal struggle explored a wide range of issues that included the politics of sexuality, the cultural construction of gender, theories of gender difference, women's location in history, and women's concepts of themselves and their morality, among other topics. Scholars traced the history of the ideological uses of the binary "where two opposed terms mutually define each other"—woman is to man as nature is to culture as private is to public, reason–emotion, mind–body, order–disorder, and so on.[10] These scholars began to uncover the historical, cultural, political, ideological, and philosophical dimensions of Western society's uses of dichotomy to naturalize what are complex sets of social dynamics, a pattern that since the eighteenth century became more fully entrenched in Western culture and thought.

My father had no interest in learning about these things or discussing them with his wife or his children, should any of them also be drawn to this material. It's not that he did not have the intellectual capacity or the linguistic ability to understand it. He simply found it too threatening. It is a sad irony that while my father invoked ever more rigid—and gendered—binaries, second-wave feminist scholars were examining that very practice.

Rather than engage in discussion on the topics, my father took a defensive posture, retreating into nostalgic memories of days long gone when wives obeyed husbands and children were deferential to fathers. Right around this time, the movie version of *Fiddler on the Roof* was released, serving as shorthand for my father's lifelong struggles and sufferings.

He also became more controlling, and his lectures unbearable, augmented with advice columns or newspaper articles that supported his ever-narrowing views. We would often find an "Ann Landers" column on the refrigerator door, or articles like the one with the shrill headline, "Women's Lib Leaders Admit They Were Wrong about Marriage, Men and Beauty." This *National Enquirer* piece featured photographs of three supposed penitents, Betty Friedan, Shirley Chisholm, and Germaine Greer.

In the course of these tumultuous decades, I found it nearly impossible to be in my father's company. It was in this period I transitioned into adulthood, was married and divorced, traveled and worked, had a child of my own, and began graduate school nearly a decade after finishing my undergraduate degree. I raised my son as a single parent in the family home on Meredith Place. If my parents had not provided me that housing, it would have been financially impossible for me to complete my graduate work in anthropology.

I did complete my studies; my dissertation was accepted for publication by a university press. It was my special thrill to send my parents a hot-off-the-press copy. But my father did not say a word about the book. Finally, I asked him directly.

"If you want to know what I think of your book," he answered me, "ask your sister. She knows what I think."

It didn't matter that I said he must tell me himself. He refused. Of course, I called the sister. He had not read the book or even studied the jacket description. He read only one part, the place where I dedicated the volume to my parents. Yet he was insulted because I placed my mother's name before his ("to Louise and Michael"). He took that arrangement of their names to mean I placed her above him in importance.

I was not surprised by this news. It conformed to the pattern: his psychological and emotional needs were to be privileged over all others. Even so, it stung. I now recognize my father was incapable of getting beyond the injuries he had accumulated. He was retreating further and further into a narrowly constructed female world of witches, bitches (and angels), images he may have called up from deep-seated, simplistic stereotypes he held of the Central and East European Romani, those fantasy hyper-sexed trickster-gypsies whose unbridled eroticism was impossible to tame.

"You are born with a certain fate," my father claimed. "That's the way you are going to die." For him, the inevitable, destructive outcome would be the work of those most intimately fastened to his orbit. From this point forward, he would be capable of seeing only through the distorted lens of this worldview.

Consequently, my mother came to see him as a "tragic hero" in the Aristotelian sense of a man in a tragedy who falls by means of *hamartia*. In my mother's eyes, my father refused to acknowledge his own mortality. He would not—he could not—stop working, holding onto El Imperio to keep the inevitable at bay. She saw this as his fatal flaw. His fate was consequent of this hubristic error.

I am not entirely prepared to accept my mother's identification of my father as tragic hero in this book not least because this is a work of nonfiction, not the product of a tragedian. I also wonder about the relationship between the "reversals" (*peripeteia*) my father experienced and "discovery" (*anagnorisis*) in the character of my father, aspects that seem to be significant to the tragic hero. These aspects are not drawn in my mother's analysis.

The discovery aspect is drawn in Arthur Miller's famous discussion "Tragedy and the Common Man," though he does not use the classic terms to describe it.[11] Instead, Miller writes about the tragic feeling, an emotion "evoked in us when we are in the presence of a character who is ready to lay down his life, if need be, to secure one thing—his sense of personal dignity." Not any insult to personal dignity will do. The tragic hero fights for freedom and pushes against that which "suppresses . . . perverts the flowing out of his love and creative instinct." In this way, tragedy illuminates ("it points the heroic finger at the enemy of man's freedom"), and it is optimistic ("its final result . . . the reinforcement of the onlooker's brightest opinions of the human animal").

In certain features of Miller's tragic hero, I recognize my father. He was a common man "as apt a subject for tragedy as kings," and he experienced displacement, loss, and the painful consequences of larger, unjust, and alienating social forces.[12] In this aspect, the figure of my father is tragic, akin to Willy Loman, another salesman. His character and the exterior forces that play into his story evoke pathos.

But Miller also argued against the widespread idea that tragedy entails pessimism rather than an optimistic, hopeful view of humanity. My father's resilience might suggest a hopeful view of humanity. What of my mother's character? She and her story imply optimism. My mother evoked in me the tragic feeling. She came to recognize the value of her personal dignity, and struggled to achieve her humanity. In Miller's terms, the flaw in her character was her unwillingness to remain passive in the face of what she conceived to be a challenge to her dignity, her image of her rightful status. If the passive (those who accept their lot) are flawless, my mother was flawed. Despite the costs, she fought against the forces that would suppress her capacity for love and creativity, choosing instead a life-affirming, inspiring, and tragic course.

12

Te Amamos Siempre, Paisano[1]

For their twelfth anniversary in 1958, Louise sent Michael a poem she had composed:

> To my darling husband Michael,
> The calendar that man has made,
> Is marked each year this day.
> The clock that's ticking, men may say,
> Is marking time away.
> Though mortal, you and I, my love,
> With mortal passions, hopes and fears,
> I suffer not the mortal grief
> For passing mortal years.
> Our love is greater now
> Than ever was before.
> And, what joy to know deep in our hearts,
> That it's forevermore 🖉.[2]

   Louise moved back to their old house on Meredith Place that the couple had managed to maintain all those years. It was a new chapter in her life she greeted with confidence and faith in what she called "the life spirit." She spent her days painting in oils, acrylic, and watercolor, spoke her mind on civil and human rights issues, and supported her children in ways she thought best. She spent her nights reading, having shipped from Puerto Rico the books she had inherited

David Waterston

from her father and the ones she had herself accumulated. And she wrote. She wrote poems and short stories, a memoir, and letters, including keeping a correspondence with the artist and revolutionary Elizam Escobar, Linda's former husband. Elizam was one of the *FALN* 11, imprisoned in 1980 on charges of sedition for his participation in the Fuerzas Armadas de Liberacion Nacional, a resistance group looking to free Puerto Rico of its neo-colonial ties to the US.

February 15, 1992
Dear Elizam,

... I feel freer than at any other time of my life . . . because I have come to terms with the unreality of the term *time*. This creation of man is a convenience and a signifier. It signifies the revolving of the planet earth on its axis or around the sun, the amount of energy needed to house, feed and clothe a family, the changes in a living thing that occur from birth to death. Death puts a period at the end of the sentence of life. As long as we live we are an unfinished life. What does it matter at what point death puts the period? If I am living I have more to

live. If death comes I have nothing to say. Then, a lifetime is as a moment and
at that point—at death—eternity is as the same moment. It is all—the beginning
and the end—out of my control—so why fear or concern myself with it?

She continued to write to Michael, little notes and long letters, begging him
to retire and join her in New York.[3] They had been discussing setting terms
of a divorce. "I don't want an amicable divorce—what I really want is an amicable
marriage," she wrote. She loved him, she missed him, and she felt sorry for him,
a pitiable man who held onto the fear she had let go.

In the meantime, Don Miguel stayed in Puerto Rico where each day at noontime he walked from the store in Viejo San Juan to sit at the same table, at the
same restaurant, at the same time, for the same lunch he had been eating for
thirty years. La Mallorquina had ancient wooden fans hanging from vaulted
ceilings and tables covered with placemats boasting it was the oldest restaurant in
Puerto Rico, a fact most appealing to those tourists who still bothered to wander
the cobblestones of Old San Juan.[4]

Don Miguel's store was just a half block from the restaurant so it was a convenient place to take lunch. It was close and the waiters knew what he wanted—serve
him quickly, and bring a hot *pocillo* when the old man waved his hand. Louise and
his four daughters knew that gesture. Early on, they learned it meant "bring me
something"—water, coffee, salt.

If they did it right—the coffee must be in a cup of a certain size (never a mug),
steaming hot (never lukewarm), and in front of him as soon as the dinner plate
was removed (no wait time)—the waiters would be showered with Don Miguel's
famous charm. Everyone—outside his immediate family—seemed to adore him.

Don Miguel was demanding, but a regular guy, a *paisano*. His sky-blue eyes on
fire, Miguel shared insider anecdotes with waiters (a demeaning story about one
of his women customers? a snippy appraisal of the gringo couple at the table by
the arched window?).

There was good reason for a fast lunch. Don Miguel had to get back to the store.
Nobody else could do the job like he could, and nobody cared about the business
the way he did. So the 82-year-old man continued to run a business he came
to hate. Alone, he worked six days a week, from nine in the morning until the
store closed at six.

That is, until the guardian angel stepped into his life. "Tanya" entered the
scene at a most opportune moment.

Michael's tug of war with Louise had been playing out over the store, the
assets, and some of the children. Close the store or sell it to two of the daughters
who wanted it, Louise had begged. He refused. She took some of their assets anyway, entrusting these to the girls who opened their own version of El Imperio,
which did not succeed.

Michael felt violated—she was spending money on losing propositions. Louise thought he was losing his mind, making irrational business decisions, and neglecting even the most basic of his responsibilities. She felt she had very few options—he was spending money on losing propositions.

He was sealing both their fates, Louise feared. To avert the pending disaster she could see was on the way, Louise brought in the law hoping her husband would be declared legally incompetent. Escorted by the police, Michael was forced to undergo a psychiatric evaluation. The effort backfired. Michael "passed" the evaluation, and his rage took on a violent cast. He hit her; she got an order of protection.

Michael was in a state of exhaustion when Tanya became his confidante. He had complete faith in her, pushing back against Louise and the children who questioned his judgment. He would not hear of it. Why would he trust any of them? Louise most of all; she even had the police enter his home and take him away for a psychiatric evaluation. She tried to take everything away from him, humiliating him like that, and looking to have the officials deem him incompetent. They didn't! They saw he was not some senile old man. They saw he was perfectly capable of taking care of his own affairs.

Louise had one last option. She gave up on the marriage hoping to salvage something of their crumbling possessions. After fifty-one years, Michael lost his wife to divorce. The decree was officially registered on May 1, 1997. She was seventy-three and he eighty-four years old.

Turns out, Tanya was no guardian angel after all. She was a thief. Miguel gave her all the power. He got to the point when he no longer checked the checks he signed. He watched as she became wealthy, purchasing a large house and a fancy car. He lost everything he had accumulated over the years. The condominium he lived in (it was foreclosed), the building that housed the store (in a fire sale), the retirement fund he had saved (Tanya cashed it in), everything.

As El Imperio came to an end, Tanya told him, "Everything is mine. Take your moth-eaten things and go!"

Michael was left with nothing. Not even a place to live.

He may not have known it, but he really did have Louise's love. It was forevermore. His daughter Jessica bought a place for him to live. It was a fourth-floor condominium on Calle Conveniencia, right by the beach where he had once rented a house.

Michael became an old man, managing on Social Security and under the watchful eye of his firstborn, the only one of his children who remained in Puerto Rico. By and by, his short-term memory began to fade like the sun-bleached family photographs that sat on weary display in his apartment, though his memories of Havana, Manguito, and Jedwabne remained deep and clear. He often sat in a favorite, tattered chair and looked out at the ocean, a view that gave him peace of mind.

He kept a single, framed photograph on his bedroom wall. It was of the beautiful Cuban girl, Anita. She was once a very good dancer and a beauty besides. From his bed he could see her simple words of heartfelt affection: "*A Miguel con el sincero afecto de Anita.*"

On another wall, he tacked a bold sign. It was a single line, a rough translation from the nineteenth-century poem "Nuit de Mai" by Alfred de Musset—Chopin's contemporary, and a lover of George Sand: "*Rien ne nous rend si grands qu'une grande douleur*"—nothing makes us greater than a great suffering 🔗.[5]

Michael died on October 17, 2006. By then he was living in Linda's home, no longer able to take care of himself. The doctors could not do much for the 93-year-old with multiple diagnoses. That day he was home with Carlos, Linda's husband. Michael awoke from an afternoon nap, agitated and confused. Carlos calmed him, helped him settle back into the bed, and left him resting quietly. Michael fell back to sleep. And then he died.

Looking back at what was the moment of his death, Linda said she had been very agitated, sitting in the dentist office waiting to get her teeth fixed. Adrienne said she had been in a terrible mood the entire day. David had watched *Our Man in Havana* just the night before, and Jessica, sometime in the minutes of his passing, had finished reading the section in *A Death in the Family* where the mother was struggling to find a way to tell Rufus that his father had died.

The night before Louise dreamt Michael touched her shoulder, assuring her that after all, she was all right. That morning she painted an acrylic and tacked onto its back her poem titled "Pink Waves" 🔗.[6]

> The earth is cold.
> In a trance, I close my eyes
> alone.

The Story of My Story

It seems I was the only one among our narrow family circle who did not have a premonition or meaningful coincidence at the time my father died. For me it was a workday, and I spent it in my college classroom. I arrived home in the evening. It was dark by then, and my husband and daughter were sitting at the kitchen table. As I walked in the door, they gave me funny looks and seemed uncomfortable until they could relieve themselves of the news. I was okay, shocked at the finality but not the reality that my father was dead. I worried about my mother though it turned out she didn't yet know. We'd go to her at Adrienne's place a mile from my house. I would tell them in person, both at the same time. My mother was quiet, managing the news with stoicism though her eyes revealed her grief.

For many years, I knew I would write my father's story. I began this project in 1995 with a short essay I titled "Following Ruth: Towards an Ethnography of Identity." At that time, I had two Ruths in mind. One was the biblical Ruth whose story reveals that the "natural" laws of lineage (tracing a family line through "blood") in point of fact incorporate a set of manmade constructions that determine lineage and shape identity. The story of the biblical Ruth shows there is no one "people" with a common origin and which have permanence, and there is no timeless essence to identity. Ruth did not start out with but became the identity she adopted. "Your people will be my people, and your God will be my God," Ruth said, revealing the reinvention and fluidity of personal and collective identity.[7]

The second one was Ruth Behar, an anthropologist with Cuban Jewish roots who depicted her own multiple identities as well as her fraught relationship with her father in the book *Translated Woman* published in 1993. Each Ruth gave me something significant that led me to start my own project. The biblical Ruth offered the theme of shifting identity over time, a complicated phenomenon I felt needed to be more fully understood and explained. Ruth Behar gave me the courage to consider the deeply personal as an appropriate and legitimate anthropological endeavor.

Ironically, at the same time I began to write about my father, I severed ties with him, not calling or seeing him for a four-year period when he was in his eighties. I could no longer swallow what I perceived to be his assaults on my dignity, or suppress my adult self in the service of his requirements or needs. His assaults were always verbal and the demands trivial but they were constant and overbearing.

When I returned to him (a phone call, without drama), there was a shift in our relationship. He seemed better able to listen when I spoke. He also seemed to acknowledge my autonomy, and even to respect it. I seemed less dependent on his judgment. Of course, the transformation was not complete, but I had not expected that to happen. In the turnaround, my father tended to glorify me, showering me with exaggerated praise at the expense of his other, more loyal and dutiful children.

The shift was very important because I was no longer so enveloped in my father. This opened up the space for my project with him to happen. I felt emotionally brave enough and professionally competent enough to proceed as a daughter and as an anthropologist to gather his life history. I would begin my intimate ethnography.

The project gave us a common ground. It was something we could talk about that was of genuine interest to me and flattering to him. With my father's newfound, albeit limited respect for me as an adult and a professional (not just his daughter), we talked about people and places, and his memories of feelings and thoughts over the long course of his life .[8] In this dialogue, we returned to the various settings of his life. I also literally returned to the main sites—to Cuba with him in the year 2000, then one year later, without him to Poland where I also conducted research in 2008.

In the course of this project, my relationship with my father looked a lot like that of an anthropologist with her informant. When we saw each other, we would sit down together with the purpose of him telling me stories, and of me asking him questions. But I also approached him as a daughter, responding to him in the language of family, with sadness and joy, disgust and sympathy, anger and patience, as these acute emotions surfaced. Sometimes I would get angry, bored, or frustrated: "Oh, come on Dad, why are you saying that?" Other times I was able to keep composure and listen without interrupting. Still other times I would break down under the weight of his sorrows.

This dual daughter--anthropologist role offers a new approach to gathering knowledge that builds on established scholarly practice. Intimate ethnography follows in anthropology's long tradition of writing an individual's biography, the classic life-history method.[9] It grows out of the "reflexive turn" in anthropology, moving beyond autoethnography to situate the personal story in larger history and political economy.[10] It is also informed by and coincides with an emerging genre of scholarly endeavors by "second-generation" scholars engaged in rites of "homeland" return as critical theoretical projects and experiments in memory writing.[11]

In writing about the epistemological, emotional, and methodological challenges of collaborating with a parent in this kind of anthropological project, Rylko-Bauer and I observed:

> The actual practice of interviewing our parents . . . is in some ways no more difficult than conducting research among strangers, some of whom may eventually become intimates . . . We are comfortable in the role of ethnographer, in getting very close to another without losing ourselves in that person, and in standing apart, somewhat detached but with empathy and compassion. With our parents as ethnographic "informants," however, we started our projects with old intimates as research subjects, and with dynamics (of power, duty, and status) in our relationships with them that were determined long before the projects began. We have found the power dynamic to manifest itself most clearly in what we call "narrative management"—the matter of who controls the story . . . The negotiation for control between ethnographer and key informant is exposed in raw form as daughter transacts with parent for more information. This negotiation occurs in every ethnographic exchange. It constitutes the "art" of the method, a kind of dance mediated by social distance, rules of politeness, and the anthropologist's ethical concerns about exploitation and rudeness.[12]

There were certain advantages to gathering "data" from such an intimate. My father tried to manage the narrative by remaining rigidly faithful to the same set of tales , retold again and again, a form of silence.[13] Since I was able to predict my father's responses to questions on particular topics, I was comfortable crossing certain boundaries I might have had trouble doing with more distant informants. I was also comfortable pushing him to enter new territory. As an ethnographer, I knew when I had "pushed" my father to the limit of his ability; with other, less intimate informants, I could never be as sure.

I was also aware of the limitations in "interviewing" my father, knowing full well his compulsion to impart advice may have motivated what he told me and what he left out. I was raised by a father whose stories were also cautionary tales, warning his children to hold onto fear (of death, illness, accident, catastrophe) and conformity (obedience, self-sacrifice, and silence regarding one's own psychological needs). Our negotiation thus entailed aspects of his temperament and his history. As a result, the shift in our relationship was key. It freed us (at least to some degree) from the confines of our intimacy. At the same time, I could listen to what he said as well as to his silences, learning from both aspects.

My father wanted Arthur Miller to author his life history even as he was an eager participant in my project. Although he knew of the book I planned to write and the articles I was already publishing based on this work, he managed to unabashedly ignore all that, privileging his ambitious fantasy over my steadfast efforts. He figured that since his daughter was a researcher she would be able to locate the famous playwright and persuade him to write the book. "Did you look him up?" my father would repeatedly ask me. "Did you find him yet?"

I appreciated my father's determination (some might consider it *chutzpah*), a personality attribute that kept him buoyed when the chips were down. His determination led him to keep his eye on "the best"—for himself and for his children. For this reason, and for his children, there was endless criticism. There were also certain skills he wanted us to develop and specific ambitions he wanted us to attain—goals *he* would identify.

Like becoming Miss America. To his disappointment, I did not seek the crown; instead I studied anthropology. My father's attempt to seduce me with royalty had failed, but the charmer wooed me with the amazing stories he told and retold throughout my life. From my father, I was introduced to key topics in cultural anthropology, although neither one of us gave it that label or would even know to know it when early on I was drawn to his stories. His descriptions of Jedwabne, an East European pastoral community where Jews lived in the town, providing services to the surrounding Polish farmers, became my introduction to peasantry. My domineering father, exacting obedience, service, and "respect" gave me an early, first-hand taste of patriarchy. His vivid anecdotes about brutality under Cuba's Machado and corruption under Batista taught me about dictatorship, while the post-1959 unease and household disruptions taught me something about revolution. I also learned, very powerfully, about diaspora, the presence of loss that penetrated nearly all his stories.

If only this effort were for the purpose of illuminating the events and processes of the past! If only we were beyond the cruelties of modernity, the brutality of empire and nation building, and the violent oppression of difference![14]

It is clear, however, that the present-day world is stained with the blood, destruction, and misery brought on by contemporaneous war, genocide, poverty, economic and resource inequality, economic collapses, power abuses, and other forms of brutality and dehumanization, including the pathologies of xenophobia, racism, and sexism. Contemporary social critics analyze the ways in which the mass of humanity is managed, contained and controlled by means of economic and ideological dominance, and which is or can be enforced by violent means such as war (preemptive or otherwise), imprisonment, and outright displacement of people from their homes.[15] If these observations are true—and I think they are—this is a morally corrupt, inhumane, and unsustainable condition.

Looking back at our dark times from a future vantage point, how many will ask: Where were they amidst the dying? What were they doing? How did they participate, contribute, and collaborate? Who did speak up? What forms of resistance were ignored, suppressed, or effective in creating substantive change? Who resisted? Who did not?

My father's story and my interpretations of it have resonance for contemporary social processes and dynamics. In pursuing this project, I have been guided by the ideas and injunctions of others in this regard. Writing about her Polish-Catholic mother imprisoned in the camps as a slave doctor during the Holocaust, Barbara Rylko-Bauer urges these stories be written to "bring the past into the present."[16] She explains, "If we 'tell the truth' and [connect] personal experience . . . to the political economy of brutality, we may edge closer to understanding how we can remake a world that is less violent and more just."[17] In our collaborative work, Rylko-Bauer and I considered the position taken by genocide scholar Tzvetan Todorov in relation to our respective projects: "Todorov argues that simply retelling past events is not enough. Like Todorov, we believe memory must not simply be a monument to the past but an 'instrument that informs our capacity to analyze the present.'"[18]

The wise words of writer and memoirist Jane Lazarre have also inspired my approach. In her exquisite memoir *Beyond the Whiteness of Whiteness*, Lazarre wrote, "Memory leads to consciousness, recollection to the possibility of meaning which always includes a perception of relation between oneself and the world."[19] Memory with its root in the Latin *memoria*—mindful—is key to my purpose. To be mindful is to be aware, an essential step towards any form of social change. It is my hope that this intimate ethnography is not an exercise in solipsism, but is a means towards mindfulness, awakening.

My father's "wars" come together as embodied history that exposes the interconnections across what Gerald Sider calls the "masks and illusions of culture,

race, nation, society, citizenship (and) civilization."[20] The story reveals that bigotry always has a history and a context, and is intimately tied to power interests. It
shows that scapegoating is a maneuver of deflection that emerges most powerfully
in periods of political and economic crisis. It depicts how prevailing stereotypes
serve to exclude, marginalize, and disvalue a group (and the individuals who
fit into the category), and become constituted as a collective cultural fiction,
an ideology about the group and its purported members. It demonstrates how
the excluded, marginalized, and disvalued can internalize the harsh messages
directed at them, and, as personal identity becomes muddled with dehumanizing
ideologies, the wounds intensify and surface. It points to the way dominant ideologies including beliefs about progress, modernity, and the nation, can mislead
and come back to haunt. It explains how simmering tensions and major conflicts
between groups (ethnic, racial, religious) are shaped by large-scale, often-invisible
forces. It demonstrates that privilege is rooted in inequality, that the image of
limited good is a powerful political and economic tool. It also shows that under
conditions of artificial scarcity, privilege will likely defend privilege, however
limited that advantage may be. It is a cautionary tale about identifying and allying
oneself with power, and the danger in assuming "might is right." It illustrates
that idealization and demonization are two sides of the same distorted coin.
And it illustrates that on the level of the individual, these defensive postures,
identifications, alliances, and distortions are often the frailties of the wounded.

My father offers a case in point. The legacies of history are reflected in his
psychology. He was a sympathetic yet narcissistic character. The upheavals of his
times brought terrible disruptions to the self; my father's subsequent troubles
were rooted in the trauma of loss, his search for respectability, and his yearning
to belong.

There came a day when I began writing this book. I had my fieldnotes, and
interviews with my father on audiotape and on video. I had email correspondence and notes from conversations with my mother. I had her unpublished
memoir, *Cigarettes, Babies and Change*. From both my parents, I had financial papers,
legal documents, claims, scraps, and diaries that I archived into nearly thirty
boxes. I had a forty-page bibliography I developed and categorized by theme and
topic, and archival documents I gathered from brick and mortar institutes and
libraries, and from online sources. While comprehensive in scope, all these are
fragments, offering traces of the past.

I also had photographs. In them, I could see my father metamorphize over
the course of his life. The photographs reflect his transformation, and suggest
meanings both personal and historical. They embody the "truth" and the *fictions*
of the type, of an atmosphere, of cultures, place, and eras.

There was a box of photographs sent to me from my nephew Andres who was
a teenager at the time. For my father's funeral, he had put together a collage of

family photographs using heavy-duty glue. Afterward, Andres took it apart, layered the photographs one atop the other, and sent them to me. I pulled the photographs from the box and held them in my hands—a thick stack, stuck together.
I spent the better part of a day pulling them apart, one from the other. Some
got ruined. One is a photograph 🖋 of my mother from the 1940s.[21] She looks
quite beautiful except for the piece now torn from her face. I felt annoyed. Why
did he glue these precious photographs together? For Andres, the grandchild,
the photographs were glued one atop the other, a single stack. It became my job
to detach them, my task also with this story—to pull apart, rearrange, preserve,
even tear in some places—and tell a story and a history that are at once separate
and together. I would work with what remained.

My parents are now dead. It still comes to me as a shock—even though I antici-
pated it—that they are no longer here to fill in a blank, to answer a question, or
to explain their own version of the world. The beauty is that my father—*and* my
mother—left for me enough detail and vivid description, enough scraps of paper,
notations and documents, enough of what Neni Panourgiá calls "the small, aside,
minor and often obscured remarks," and even enough pain and disappointment
that I could take what remained, and craft this most intimate of ethnographies.[22]

EPILOGUE

My father got some but not all of his requests for when he died. He is buried in the US Veterans' Administration's Puerto Rico National Cemetery because he thought there were too few Jews represented in that place of national recognition. He hadn't wanted any religion or rabbis but he got some of that anyway. The Reform Jewish Congregation's visiting rabbi led the graveside services and the Mourning Kaddish, the Jewish prayer for the dead. Louise, the children and the grandchildren stood by the grave and sang "Sunrise, Sunset." Everybody cried. As if on cue, the tropical skies opened up just as the casket was lowered into the ground. His gravestone is etched with the words, "*Te amamos siempre, paisano* 🔑."[1]

My mother carved out a new life for herself on a shoestring budget and an optimistic spirit those years she lived in New York. She sold the house on Meredith Place and lived in Manhattan for nearly a decade. She lived close to Central Park, which she referred to as her "marvelous backyard." She took classes at the Arts Students League on 57th Street, and marched in anti-war protests in New York and in Washington. She walked down the streets of Manhattan with political buttons lining her front. There was the bright pink "Love the Troops, Hate the War" and the smaller, subtler button with these words attributed to Virginia Woolf: ". . . as a woman I have no country. As a woman I want no country. As a woman my country is the whole world." She gave these away to anyone who admired and promised to wear them.

She was strong-willed but had physical ailments that weakened her. In 1991, she wrote, "I have never felt so peaceful in my entire life. I am glad to be able to get out of my bed each morning and I am prepared never to wake up again each

night." Over the years she had several acute illnesses and many medical interven-
tions: heart attacks, by-pass surgery, defibrillator implant, lymphoma, chemo-
therapy. In these years, I willingly became the primary (not the only) caretaking
child, helped her out financially, and was her legal and medical proxy.

In December 2008, my mother underwent yet another medical procedure.
The surgery was successful, but the patient didn't fare very well. The unpleasant

and time-consuming tasks of caretaking began to take a terrible toll on me, and I grew resentful of my mother's fluctuating condition. For three years, she was near-death on several occasions, and then bounced back. She attributed it to the life force. I found it emotionally and physically exhausting.

In early February of 2009, my mother was hospitalized and requested all her children gather. Ten days earlier I told her I could no longer care for her the way I had been, and that it was time to consider an alternative (live with another child, in assisted living or nursing home). In response, she stood up from the couch and with walker in hand, stepped across the room. "I will think about what I need to do," she said with resolve.

In the hospital, she had us come together. She was no longer a demanding patient, but a dying person. I was grateful. I felt she had taken back the mother-reins, liberating me from that role in relation to her. I had told her I couldn't do it any more; maybe that released her too.

For two days, her daughters draped themselves around her hospital bed, a forty-eight-hour vigil. We were waiting for David to arrive while the morphine dripped. We placed a telephone to her ear. Her sister Sylvia said goodbye. Her best friend Helen said "I love you Louise."

David arrived and leaned over her face now slack in a near-death dream state. "Mother, I'm here," he said. "I love you." Somehow she managed to raise one eyebrow.

We told stories, and dozed off. We cried and checked to see if she were still alive. We touched her, kissed her, said goodbye, maybe helped her feel safe and assured as she took her departure. I sat on the bed by the pillow, my hand on her shoulder the night through. To my left was a window onto the town and I stared out at it. To my right was the door to the room that was left ajar. The room was dark but the light in the hallway reflected as a bold stripe on the long, blank wall outside, almost the same as the view from my childhood bedroom in our home on Meredith Place. My father's old Polish-Jewish lullaby came back to me in this lonely time: "You are my *mamala*, my *shana mamala*, *ay lu lu lu lu*."

We began to time the space between our mother's breaths. They were coming at longer and longer intervals, the opposite of birth contractions. She'd go thirty seconds without a breath, then take one. She'd go forty-three seconds, then fifty-two, then over a minute.

Morning came. It was Adrienne's birthday, February 13. Two of the grand-children walked into the room, bringing us coffee. The doctor listened for a heartbeat, which was very faint. He took a quiet exit, and my mother took one last, small breath.

NOTES

Prologue

1 Barbara Rylko-Bauer, "Lessons About Humanity and Survival from My Mother and from the Holocaust," *Anthropological Quarterly*, Vol. 78, No. 1 (2005): 11–41; Alisse Waterston and Barbara Rylko-Bauer, "Out of the Shadows of History and Memory: Personal Family Narratives in Ethnographies of Rediscovery," *American Ethnologist*, Vol. 330, No. 3 (2006): 397–412; Alisse Waterston and Barbara Rylko-Bauer, "Out of the Shadows of History and Memory: Personal Family Narratives as Intimate Ethnography," in *The Shadow Side of Field Work: Theorizing the Blurred Borders between Ethnography and Life*, ed. Athena McLean and Annette Leibing (Malden, MA and Oxford, UK: Blackwell Publishing, 2007), 31–55.

2 Eva Hoffman, *After Such Knowledge. Memory, History, and the Legacy of the Holocaust*, (New York: Public Affairs, 2004),18; Jonathan Boyarin, *Thinking in Jewish* (Chicago: University of Chicago Press, 1996), 31; Alisse Waterston, "The Story of My Story: An Anthropology of Violence, Dispossession and Diaspora," *Anthropological Quarterly*, e78, No. 1 (2005): 43–61.

3 Bertolt Brecht, and John Willett and Ralph Manheim, eds., *Bertolt Brecht: Poems 1913-1956* (New York: Routledge, 1997), 276; Paul Farmer, *Pathologies of Power: Health, Human Rights, and the New War on the Poor* (Berkeley: University of California Press, 2003), 11.

4 Hoffman, op. cit., 166.

Chapter 1

1 https://maps.google.com/maps?f=q&source=s_q&hl=en&geocode=&q=Podlaskie+Voivodeship,+Poland&aq=1&oq=podlas&sll=42.746632,-75.770041&sspn=3.735097,9.294434&vpsrc=0&t=h&ie=UTF8&hq=&hnear=Podlaskie+Voivodeship,+Poland&z=7.

2 *Purim* is an annual Jewish festival celebrated on the fourteenth day of the Jewish month of Adar (February or March in the Western calendar).

3 *Cheder* (also spelled *heder*) was the traditional Jewish elementary school.

4 www.myfatherswars.com/ch1-01.

5 www.myfatherswars.com/ch1-02.

6 www.youtube.com/watch?v=nLLEBAQLZ3Q.

7 www.myfatherswars.com/ch1-03.

8 Seth L. Wolitz, "The Americanization of Tevye or Boarding the Jewish 'Mayflower,'" *American Quarterly*, Vol. 40, No. 4 (1988): 514–536.

9 www.jewishgen.org/yizkor/jedwabne/Yedwabne.html.

10 Moshe Tzinovitz, "Rabbi Meyer Eliyahu Winer," *Yedwabne: History and Memorial Book* (Jerusalem–New York: Yedwabne Societies in Israel and the United States of America, 1980): 17 Accessed July 7, 2005. www.jewishgen.org/yizkor/jedwabne/yed001.html#17.

11 Julius L. Baker and Moshe Tzinovitz, "My Hometown Yedwabne, Province of Łomża, Poland," in *Yedwabne: History and Memorial Book* (Jerusalem–New York: Yedwabne Societies in Israel and the United States of America, 1980). www.jewishgen.org/yizkor/jedwabne/Yedwabne.html (accessed July 7, 2005).

12 Alisse Waterston, "Sacred Memory and the Secular World: The Poland Narratives," in *War and Peace: Essays on Religion, Violence, and Space*, ed. Bryan S. Turner (London: Anthem Press, 2013): 19–36.

13 Dirk Hoerder, *Cultures in Contact: World Migrations in the Second Millennium* (Durham, NC and London: Duke University Press, 2002), 8, 23.

14 Norman Davies, *God's Playground: A History of Poland. Volume 1: The Origins to 1795* (New York: Columbia University Press, 1982), 3.

15 Ibid., 3–4.

16 Eva Hoffman, *Shtetl: The Life and Death of a Small Town and the World of Polish Jews* (Boston: Mariner/Houghton Mifflin Company, 1997), 43; Antony Polonsky, *The Jews in Poland and Russia, Volume I, 1350–1881* (Oxford: Littman Library of Jewish Civilization, 2010).

17 Carolyn Nordstrom, Global Fractures, in *An Anthropology of War: Views from the Frontline*, ed. Alisse Waterston (New York and Oxford: Berghahn Books, 2009), 72.

18 Hoffman 1997, op. cit., 61; Polonsky op. cit.

19 Immanuel Wallerstein, *The Modern World System II: Mercantilism and the Consolidation of the European World-Economy, 1600–1750* (Berkeley: University of California Press, 2011 [1980]).

20 Davies, op. cit., 280.

21 Hoffman 1997, op. cit., 60.

22 Anthony D. Smith, *Nationalism: Theory, Ideology, History* (Cambridge: Polity Press, 2010 [2001]), 42.

23 Benedict Anderson, *Imagined Communities* (London and New York: Verso, 1991 [1983]); Ernst Gellner, *Nations and Nationalism* (Malden, MA: Blackwell Publishing, 2006 [1983]); Eric J. Hobsbawm, *Nations and Nationalism since 1780: Programme, Myth, Reality* (New York: Cambridge University Press, 2004 [1990]); Eric J. Hobsbawm and Terence Ranger, eds., *The Invention of Tradition* (New York: Cambridge University Press, 1989); Anthony D. Smith, 2010 (2001). *Nationalism: Theory, Ideology, History* (Cambridge: Polity Press, 2010 [2001]).

24 www.youtube.com/watch?v=KZGi49Bnghs.

25 Joanna Beata Michlic, *Poland's Threatening Other: The Image of the Jew from 1880 to the Present* (Lincoln: University of Nebraska Press, 2006), 41–42; Antony Polonsky, *The Jews in Poland and Russia, Volume II, 1881–1914* (Oxford: Littman Library of Jewish Civilization, 2010).

26 Ibid., Michlic 60–61.

Chapter 2

1 *Matzah* (also spelled *matzo*) is unleavened bread significant to the eight-day Passover holiday.

2 http://www.sztetl.org.pl/en/article/bialystok/11,synagogues-prayer-houses-and-others/397, dawid-druskin-gymnasium-11-4-pilsudskiego-alley-/

3 www.myfatherswars.com/ch2-01.

4 www.myfatherswars.com/ch2-02.

5 www.myfatherswars.com/ch2-03.

6 www.myfatherswars.com/ch2-04.

7 Paul Ricoeur, *Time and Narrative*, Vol. 1 (Chicago: University of Chicago Press, 1990), 245; Paul Ricoeur, *Memory, History, Forgetting* (Chicago: University of Chicago Press, 2006).

8 www.myfatherswars.com/ch2-05.

9 Antony Polonsky, ed., 2004. *The Shtetl: Myth and Reality*. Polin: Studies in Polish Jewry, Vol. 17 (Oxford: Littman Library of Jewish Civilization, 2004).

10 Dina Abramowicz and Jeffrey Shandler, eds., trans. Eva Zeitlin Dobkin, *Profiles of a Lost World: Memoirs of East European Jewish Life before World War II* (Detroit: Wayne State University Press, 1999); Lucjan Dobroszycki and Barbara Kirshenblatt-Gimblett, *Image Before My Eyes: A Photographic History of Jewish Life in Poland, 1864–1939* (New York: Schocken Books, 1977); Simon M. Dubnow, *History of the Jews in Russia and Poland* (Philadelphia: Jewish Publication Society of America 1916); Yaffah Eliach, *There Once Was a World: A 900 Year Chronicle of the Shtetl of Eishyshok* (Boston: Little, Brown &

Co., 1998); Toby Knobel Fluek, *Memories of My Life in a Polish Village, 1930–1949.* New York: Alfred A. Knopf, 1990); David Gershon Hundert, *Jews in Early Modern Poland.* Polin: Studies in Polish Jewry, Vol. 10 (London: Littman Library of Jewish Civilization, 1997); Alter Kacyzne, *Poyln: Jewish Life in the Old Country* (New York: Henry Holt &Company, 1999); Jack Kugelmass and Jonathan Boyarin, with Zachary M. Baker, *From a Ruined Garden: The Memorial Books of Polish Jewry,* second edition (Bloomington: Indiana University Press, 1988 [1983]); Dan Miron, *The Image of the Shtetl and Other Studies of Modern Jewish Literary Imagination* (Syracuse, NY: Syracuse University Press, 2000); Alisa Solomon, "How 'Fiddler' Became Folklore," *Jewish Daily Forward,* September 1, 2006. www.forward.com/articles/1710/#ixzz1Rd5bEoY9 (accessed July 6, 2011); Alisa Solomon, "Tevye, Today and Beyond," *Jewish Daily Forward,* September 8, 2006. www.forward. com/articles/2422/#ixzz1Rd8isEIV (accessed July 6, 2011); Roman Vishniac, *Polish Jews* (New York: Schocken, 1947); Roman Vishniac, *A Vanished World* (New York: Farrar, Straus & Giroux, 1983); Mark Zborowski and Elizabeth Herzog, *Life Is with People: The Culture of the Shtetl* (New York: Schocken, 1995 [1952]); Arnold Zweig, *The Face of East European Jewry* (Berkeley: University of California Press, 1004 [1920]).

11 Barbara Kirshenblatt-Gimblett, "Introduction," *Life is with People: The Culture of the Shtetl,* by Mark Zborowski and Elizabeth Herzog (New York: Schocken, 1995), xi.; Barbara Kirshenblatt-Gimblett, "Imagining Europe: The Popular Arts of American Jewish Ethnography." In *Divergent Centers: Shaping Jewish Cultures in Israel and America,* ed. Deborah Dash Moore and Ilan Troen (New Haven, CT: Yale University Press, 2001): 155–191.

12 Wolitz, op. cit., 516.

13 Kirshenblatt-Gimblett, op. cit., xii; Antony Polonsky. *The Jews in Poland and Russia, Volume III, 1914–2008* (Oxford: Littman Library of Jewish Civilization, 2012).

14 Polonsky 2004, introduction, op. cit., 3–23.

15 Kirshenblatt-Gimblett, op. cit., x.

16 David Biale, "Eros and Enlightenment: Love against Marriage in East European Jewish Enlightenment," in *From Shtetl to Socialism,* ed. Antony Polonsky. Polin: Studies in Polish Jewry (Oxford: Littman Library of Jewish Civilization, 1993), 168–186.

Chapter 3

1 *Baalabus* is a Yiddish word for a man whose home is well-managed, clean, and neat. Of course, the *baalabus* needs a *baalabuste*—the good, homemaker wife.

2 www.myfatherswars.com/ch3-01.

3 *Tchotchkes* is a Yiddish word that refers to miscellany, generally items of little monetary value.

4 https://maps.google.com/maps?f=q&source=s_q&hl=en&geocode=&q=Manguito,+Matanzas,+Cuba&aq=&sll=23.051111,-81.575278&sspn=0.292532,0.580902&vpsrc=6&t=h&g=Matanzas+Cuba&ie=UTF8&hq=&hnear=Manguito,+Calimete,+Cienfuegos,+Cuba&ll=22.596262,-80.914307&spn=1.17402,2.323608&z=9.

5 Jenny B. Wahl, "Slavery in the United States," *EH.Net Encyclopedia,* ed. Robert Whaples. March 26, 2008. http://eh.net/encyclopedia/article/wahl.slavery.us (accessed October 1, 2011); Jenny B. Wahl, *The Bondsman's Burden: An Economic Analysis of the Common Law of Southern Slavery* (New York: Cambridge University Press, 1998).

6 Steven T. Newcomb, "The Evidence of Christian Nationalism in Federal Indian Law: The Doctrine of Discovery, Johnson v. McIntosh, and Plenary Power," *N.Y.U. Review of Law and Social Change,* Vol. 20 (1992–1994): 304–305.

7 Immigration Act of 1924. H.R. 7995; Pub.L. 68–139; 43 Stat. 153. 68th Congress; May 26, 1924; www.myfatherswars.com/ch3-02.

8 The Immigration Act of 1924 (The Johnson–Reed Act). Office of the Historian. US Department of State. http://history.state.gov/milestones/1921-1936/ImmigrationAct (accessed October 3, 2011).

9 David A. Reed, "America of the Melting Pot Comes to an End: Effects of New Immigration Described by Senate Sponsor of Bill—Chief Aim, He States, Is to Preserve Racial Type as It Exists Today," *New York Times,* April 27, 1924, XX3. ProQuest Historical Newspapers: *New York Times* (1851–2009).

10 Ellison DuRant Smith, Speech on April 9, 1924, *Congressional Record,* 68th Congress, 1st Session (Washington, DC: Government Printing Office, 1924), Vol. 65, 5961–5962.

11 Frederick C. Croxton, *Statistical Review of Immigration, 1820–1910. Distribution of Immigrants, 1850–1900* (Washington: G.P.O., 1911). http://nrs.harvard.edu/urn-3:FHCL:679756 (accessed October

3, 2011). Collection Development Department, Widener Library, Harvard University; Lee D. Baker, *From Savage to Negro: Anthropology and the Construction of Race, 1896–1954* (Berkeley: University of California Press, 1998).

12 Henry Fairfield Osborn, "Lo! The Poor Nordic! Professor Osborn's Position on the Immigrant Question," *New York Times*, April 8, 1924, 18. ProQuest Historical Newspapers: *New York Times* (185–-2009).

13 Franz Boas, "Serious Flaws Are Suspected in Professor Osborn's Theories—Views as To Nordic Italians—Pre-War Ethnology as 'Made in Germany,'" *New York Times*, April 13, 1924, XXI9. ProQuest Historical Newspapers: *New York Times* (1851–2009).

14 Paul A. Lombardo, "Medicine, Eugenics, and the Supreme Court: From Coercive Sterilization to Reproductive Freedom," *Journal of Contemporary Health Law and Policy*, Vol. 13 (1996): 1–25; Paul A. Lombardo, ed. *A Century of Eugenics in America: From the Indiana Experiment to the Human Genome Era* (Bloomington: Indiana University Press, 2011).

15 Jonathan Peter Spiro, *Defending the Master Race: Conservation, Eugenics, and the Legacy of Madison Grant,* (Lebanon, NH: University of Vermont Press, 2009), xi.

16 Ibid., 391; Immigration Restriction League. (U.S.) Records (MS Am 2245). Houghton Library, Harvard University. http://ocp.hul.harvard.edu/immigration/restrictionleague.html#arc (accessed September 30, 2011).

Chapter 4

1 www.myfatherswars.com/ch4-01.

2 In the Puerto Rican context, *jíbaro* refers to a person from the rural countryside.

3 www.myfatherswars.com/ch4-02.

4 www.myfatherswars.com/ch4-03.

5 www.myfatherswars.com/ch4-04.

6 www.myfatherswars.com/ch4-05.

7 www.myfatherswars.com/ch4-06.

8 www.myfatherswars.com/ch4-07.

9 www.myfatherswars.com/ch4-08.

10 www.myfatherswars.com/ch4-09.

11 www.myfatherswars.com/ch4-10.

12 Fernando Ortiz, *Cuban Counterpoint: Tobacco and Sugar* (Durham, NC and London: Duke University Press, 1995); Sidney Mintz, *Sweetness and Power: The Place of Sugar in Modern History* (New York: Penguin Books, 1986).

13 Ibid., Ortiz, 6–7.

14 Ibid., 29–30.

15 Ibid., 33.

16 Eric R. Wolf, *Europe and the People Without History* (Berkeley: University of California Press, 1982), 315–317.

17 Verena Martinez-Alier, *Marriage, Class and Colour in Nineteenth-Century Cuba: A Study of Racial Attitudes and Sexual Values in a Slave Society* (Ann Arbor: University of Michigan Press, 1989), 2.

18 Wolf, op. cit., 196.

19 Ibid., 196, 201, 315.

20 Paul Farmer, "Never Again? Reflections on Human Values and Human Rights," in *The Tanner Lectures on Human Values*, Vol. 25, ed. G.B. Petersen (Salt Lake City: University of Utah Press, 2006), 184.

21 Martinez-Alier, op. cit., 5.

22 Ortiz, op. cit., 64.

23 Wolf, op. cit., 335; Laird W. Bergad, "The Economic Viability of Sugar Production Based on Slave Labor in Cuba, 1859–1878," *Latin American Research Review*, Vol. 24, No. 1 (1989): 95–113.

24 Cesar J. Ayala, "Social and Economic Aspects of Sugar Production in Cuba, 1880–1930," *Latin American Research Review*, Vol. 30, No. 1 (1995): 95–124; Louis A. Pérez, "Toward Dependency and Revolution: The Political Economy of Cuba between Wars, 1878–1895," *Latin American Research Review*, Vol. 18, No. 1 (1983): 127–142.

25 Ayala, op. cit., 210.

Chapter 5

1 www.myfatherswars.com/ch5-01.

2 http://libimages.wolfsonian.org/XC2002.11.4.232_000.jpg.

3 www.myfatherswars.com/ch5-02.
4 www.myfatherswars.com/ch5-03.
5 www.myfatherswars.com/ch5-04.
6 www.myfatherswars.com/ch5-05.
7 www.myfatherswars.com/ch5-06.
8 http://merrick.library.miami.edu/cdm/singleitem/collection/cubanphotos/id/1364/rec/21; www.myfatherswars.com/ch5-07.
9 www.myfatherswars.com/ch5-08.
10 *Shmata* is a Yiddish word for a rag or cheap clothing.
11 www.myfatherswars.com/ch5-09.
12 www.myfatherswars.com/ch5-10.
13 Martinez-Alier, op. cit., 5–6.
14 Jonathan Curry-Machado, "'Sin azúcar no hay país': The Transnational Counterpoint of Sugar and Nation in Nineteenth-Century Cuba," *Bulletin of Hispanic Studies*, Vol. 84, No. 1 (2007): 35.
15 Aline Helg, *Our Rightful Share: The Afro-Cuban Struggle for Equality, 1886–1912* (Chapel Hill: University of North Carolina Press, 1995), 3, 9, 56–67.
16 Alejandro de la Fuente, "Race, National Discourse, and Politics in Cuba: An Overview," *Latin American Perspectives*, Vol. 25, No. 3 (1998): 47.
17 "Heard that Boynton Blew Up the Maine," *New York Times*, May 29, 1911, 9. ProQuest Historical Newspapers: *New York Times* (1851–2009).
18 Howard Zinn, *A People's History of the United States* (New York: HarperCollins, 2005), 312.
19 Theodore Roosevelt, *Presidential Addresses and State Papers: April 14, 1906 to January 14, 1907*, Vol. 5 (New York: Kessinger Publishing, 2006), 822; "The Revolution in Cuba," *Cuba Review and Bulletin*, Vol. IV, No. 10 (September, 1906): 21. http://books.google.com/books?id=yx0TAAAAYAAJ&printsec=frontcover&source=gbs_ge_summary_r&cad=0#v=onepage&q=Roosevelt&f=false (accessed January 5, 2013).
20 de la Fuente, op. cit., 56; Marial Iglesias Utset, trans. Russ Davidson, *A Cultural History of Cuba during the U.S. Occupation, 1898–1902* (Chapel Hill: University of North Carolina Press, 2011).
21 Philip Brenner, Marguerite Rose Jiménez, John M. Kirk, and William M. LeoGrande, *Reinventing the Revolution: A Contemporary Cuban Reader* (Lanham, MD: Rowman & Littlefield, 2008), 21.
22 David F. Schmitz, *Thank God They're on Our Side: The United States and Right-Wing Dictatorships, 1921–1965* (Chapel Hill: University of North Carolina Press, 1999).
23 de la Fuente, op. cit., 51.
24 Ibid.
25 Terence Hopkins and Immanuel Maurice Wallerstein, *World Systems Analysis: Theory and Methodology* (Beverly Hills, CA: Sage Publications, 1982).

Chapter 6

1 Jane Lazarre, *Beyond the Whiteness of Whiteness* (Durham, NC: Duke University Press, 1996), 22.
2 www.myfatherswars.com/ch6-01.
3 www.myfatherswars.com/ch6-02; www.myfatherswars.com/ch6-03.
4 http://life.time.com/history/jimmy-stewart-world-war-ii-hero-comes-home-1945/#10; www.myfatherswars.com/ch6-04.
5 www.myfatherswars.com/ch6-05.
6 www.myfatherswars.com/ch6-06.
7 Milton Leitenberg, "Deaths in Wars and Conflicts in the 20th Century, third edition," Occasional Paper #29 (Ithaca, NY: Cornell University Peace Studies Program, 2006), 1.
8 Carolyn Nordstrom, *A Different Kind of War Story* (Philadelphia: University of Pennsylvania Press, 1997), 16–17.
9 Ibid., 17–18.
10 Virginia Woolf, *Three Guineas* (New York: Harcourt Brace & Company, 1966 [1938]), 11.
11 Paul Fussell, *The Great War and Modern Memory* (Oxford: Oxford University Press, 2000 [1975]), 288.
12 Ibid., 7.
13 Jeffrey C. Alexander, "Between Progress and Apocalypse: Social Theory and the Dream of Reason in the Twentieth Century," in *Rethinking Progress*, ed. Jeffrey C. Alexander and Piotr Sztompka (London: Unwin Hyman Limited, 1990), 15.
14 Margaret Drabble, "A Beastly Century," *American Scholar*, Vol. 70, No. 1 (Winter 2001): 160.
15 Zinn, op. cit., 17.

16 Alexander Laban Hinton, "The Dark Side of Modernity: Toward an Anthropology of Genocide," in *Annihilating Difference: The Anthropology of Genocide*, ed. Alexander Laban Hinton (Berkeley:
University of California Press, 2002), 1, 8.

17 Zygmunt Baumann, *Modernity and the Holocaust* (Cambridge: Polity, 1989), 87.

18 R. Brian Ferguson, "A Paradigm for the Study of War and Society," in *War and Society in the Ancient
and Medieval Worlds: Asia, the Mediterranean, Europe, and Mesoamerica*, ed. Kurt Raaflaub and Nathan
Rosenstein (Cambridge, MA: Harvard University Press, 1999), 390; R. Brian Ferguson, "Ten
Points on War," in *An Anthropology of War: Views from the Frontline*, ed. Alisse Waterston (New York and
Oxford: Berghahn Books, 2009), 36–38.

19 Leitenberg, op. cit., 9.

20 Edward W. Said, "Reflections on Exile," in *Reflections on Exile and Other Essays* (Cambridge, MA:
Harvard University Press, 2002), 173–186.

21 Hannah Arendt, *Men in Dark Times* (San Diego, CA: Harcourt, Brace & Company, 1983), ix.

22 Hannah Arendt, "Beyond Personal Frustration: The Poetry of Bertolt Brecht," *Kenyon Review*,
Vol. 10, No. 2 (Spring, 1948): 304.

23 Ibid., 306; Barbara Rylko-Bauer, Linda Whiteford, and Paul Farmer, prologue to *Global Health
in Times of Violence*, ed. Barbara Rylko-Bauer, Linda Whiteford, and Paul Farmer (Santa Fe, CA:
School for Advanced Research Press, 2009), 3.

24 Zinn, op. cit., 10.

25 Howard Zinn, *On War* (New York: Seven Stories Press, 2001), 176.

26 Ibid., 178.

27 Ibid., 178–181, 185, 197, 203.

Chapter 7

1 www.myfatherswars.com/ch7-01.

2 www.myfatherswars.com/ch7-02.

3 www.myfatherswars.com/ch7-03.

4 www.myfatherswars.com/ch7-04.

5 www.myfatherswars.com/ch7-05.

6 www.myfatherswars.com/ch7-06.

7 http://brooklynheightsblog.com/archives/497.

8 www.myfatherswars.com/ch7-07.

9 Samuel Waserstein Kahn and Yehudi Monestel Arce. *La Denuncia. 10 de Julio de 1941* (San José,
Costa Rica: Editorial Guayacán Centroamericana, S.A., 2001).

10 Eva Hoffman, *After Such Knowledge: Memory, History, and the Legacy of the Holocaust* (New York: Public
Affairs, 2004), 137.

11 www.myfatherswars.com/ch7-08.

12 www.jhi.pl/en.

13 Jan T. Gross, *Neighbors: The Destruction of the Jewish Community in Jedwabne, Poland* (Princeton, NJ: Princeton University Press, 2002 [2001]), 7.

14 Waterston 2013, op. cit.; Alisse Waterston, "Sacred Memory and the Secular World: The Poland
Narratives," *Anthropology News*, Vol. 52, No. 6 (September, 2012): 11–12.

15 www.myfatherswars.com/ch7-09.

16 Joanna Beata Michlic, "Coming to Terms with the 'Dark Past': The Polish Debate about the Jedwabne
Massacre," *ACTA 21* (Jerusalem: Hebrew University of Jerusalem, 2002): 7–9. http://sicsa.huji.ac.il/
actatxt1.html (accessed September 11, 2010).

17 William Brand, ed., *Thou Shalt Not Kill: Poles on Jedwabne* (Warsaw: Towarzystwo "Wiez," 2001);
Marek Jan Chodakiewicz, *The Massacre in Jedwabne, July 10, 1941*. East European Monographs, 655
(2005); Marta Kurkowska, "Jedwabne and Wizna: Monuments and Memory in the Łomża
Region," in *Making Holocaust Memory*, ed. Gabriel N. Finder, Natlaia Aleksiun, Antony Polonsky,
and Jan Schwarz. Polin: Studies in Polish Jewry, Vol. 20 (2008): 244–270; Antony Polonsky
and Joanna B. Michlic, eds. *The Neighbors Respond: The Controversy over the Jedwabne Massacre in Poland*
(Princeton, NJ: Princeton University Press, 2004).

18 Michlic, op. cit., 12; www.myfatherswars.com/ch7-10.

19 John T. Matteson, "Grave Discussions: The Image of the Sepulchre in Webster, Emerson and
Melville," *New England Quarterly*, Vol. 74, No. 3 (2001): 419–446.

20 Institute for National Remembrance, *Beginning of the Search in the Jedwabne Site*, November 18,
2003. www.ipn.gov.pl/portal/en/19/192/Beginning_of_the_Search_in_the_Jedwabne_Site.html
(accessed August 15, 2010).

21 "Polish Mass Grave Dig Ends," CNN, June 4, 2001. http://articles.cnn.com/2001-06-04/
    world/poland.grave_1_witold-kulesza-search-for-more-graves-exhumation?_s=PM:WORLD
    (Accessed August 16, 2010); Gross, op. cit., 122.

22 Kurkowska, op. cit; Joanna Tokarska-Bakir, "You from Jedwabne," in *Making Holocaust Memory*,
    ed. Gabriel N. Finder, Natlaia Aleksiun, Antony Polonsky, and Jan Schwarz. Polin: Studies in
    Polish Jewry, Vol. 20 (2008), 413–428.

23 Shlomo Sand, *The Invention of the Jewish People*, trans. Yael Lotan (London and New York: Verso,
    2009), 14; Joanna Tokarska-Bakir, "Jedwabne: History as Fetish," in *Imaginary Neighbors: Mediating
    Polish–Jewish Relations after the Holocaust*, ed Dorota Glowacka and Joanna Zylinska (Lincoln: Univer-
    sity of Nebraska Press, 2007).

24 Samuel P. Huntington, *The Clash of Civilizations and the Remaking of the World Order* (New York: Simon &
    Schuster, 2011 [1996]); Robert D. Kaplan, *Balkan Ghosts: A Journey Through History* (New York: Vintage
    Books, 1996 [1993]); Bernard Lewis, "The Roots of Muslim Rage," *Atlantic Magazine*. September,
    1990. www.theatlantic.com/magazine/archive/1990/09/the-roots-of-muslim-rage/4643 (accessed
    June 10, 2011); cf. John Bowen, "The Myth of Global Ethnic Conflict," *Journal of Democracy*, Vol. 7,
    No. 4 (October 1996): 3–14.

25 Joanna Beata Michlic, *Poland's Threatening Other: The Image of the Jew from 1880 to the Present* (Lincoln:
    University of Nebraska Press, 2006).

26 Douglas Rushkoff, *Nothing Sacred: The Truth About Judaism* (New York: Three Rivers Press, 2004), 53.

Chapter 8

 1 www.myfatherswars.com/ch8-01.
 2 www.myfatherswars.com/ch8-02.
 3 www.myfatherswars.com/ch8-03.
 4 www.youtube.com/watch?v=Ojytcx7cabQ.
 5 www.myfatherswars.com/ch8-04.
 6 www.youtube.com/watch?v=UUF-jHyEuNg.
 7 www.myfatherswars.com/ch8-05.
 8 www.myfatherswars.com/ch8-06.
 9 www.myfatherswars.com/ch8-07.
10 www.myfatherswars.com/ch8-08.
11 www.youtube.com/watch?v=k4Ii-RZDj2c; www.youtube.com/watch?v=vOQ4Wx8jzsE; www.
    youtube.com/watch?v=VOhr9DHoL3M.
12 Bronislaw Malinowski, *Argonauts of the Western Pacific* (New York: E.P. Dutton, 1966), 18.
13 Karen Brodkin, *How Jews Became White Folks and What That Says About Race in America* (New Brunswick,
    NJ: Rutgers University Press, 1998), 42–54; Charles Abrams, *Forbidden Neighbors: A Study of Prejudice
    in Housing* (New York: Harper & Brothers, 1955); Jack Foner, *Blacks and the Military in American History:
    A New Perspective* (New York: Praeger Publishers, 1974); Mark I. Gelfand, *A Nation of Cities: The Federal
    Government and Urban America, 1933–1965* (New York: Oxford University Press, 1975); Manning
    Marable, *How Capitalism Underdeveloped Black America* (Boston, MA: South End Press, 1983); Alex F.
    Schwartz, *Housing Policy in the United States*, second edition (New York: Routledge, 2012); Neil A.
    Wynn, *The Afro-American and the Second World War* (Teaneck, NJ: Holmes & Meier, 1993).
14 Joan Cassell, "The Woman in the Surgeon's Body: Understanding Difference," *American Anthro-
    pologist*, Vol. 98, No. 1 (1996): 43; Joan Cassell, *The Woman in the Surgeon's Body* (Cambridge, MA:
    Harvard University Press, 2000).
15 Ibid., 1996, 45; Pierre Bourdieu, *Outline of a Theory of Practice*, trans. Richard Nice (Cambridge:
    Cambridge University Press, 1992); Pierre Bourdieu, *The Logic of Practice*, trans. Richard Nice
    (Stanford, CA: Stanford University Press, 1977); Pierre Bourdieu and Loïc J. D. Wacquant,
    "Language, Gender, and Symbolic Violence," in *An Invitation to Reflective Sociology* (Chicago: Univer-
    sity of Chicago Press, 1992), 140–216.
16 Ibid., Cassell 1996, 44.

Chapter 9

 1 www.myfatherswars.com/ch9-01.
 2 www.youtube.com/watch?v=ga_sMIankFM; www.youtube.com/watch?v=3rjOrOt6wFw.
 3 www.myfatherswars.com/ch9-02.
 4 Homer Bigart, "Castro Declares He Will Win Soon—In Interview, Rebel Leader with Battle
    Force of 400 Is Certain of Victory, *New York Times*, February 27, 1958, 10. ProQuest Historical
    Newspapers: *New York Times* (1851–2009).

5 John P. Glennon and Ronald D. Landa, *Foreign Relations of the United States 1958–1960, Volume VI: Cuba* (Washington, DC: US Government Printing Office, 1991): 38–42. http://history.state.gov/historicaldocuments/frus1958-60v06 (accessed January 5, 2012).

6 Ibid., 38–39.

7 Ibid., 40.

8 Ibid., 5–6.

9 Ibid., 60–65.

10 www.myfatherswars.com/ch9-03.

11 www.myfatherswars.com/ch9-04.

12 John G. Harding, "The Nationalization of Canadian Property in Cuba under International Law," *Western Law Review*, Vol. 2, No. 50 (1962–1963): 50–65.

13 www.myfatherswars.com/ch9-05.

14 "Arms Dump Blast Shakes Havana-Two Killed, 200 Reported Hurt-Castro Hints at Sabotage Charges," *New York Times*, June 27, 1960, 1. ProQuest Historical Newspapers: *New York Times* (1851–2009).

15 www.myfatherswars.com/ch9-06.

16 www.myfatherswars.com/ch9-07.

17 www.myfatherswars.com/ch9-08.

18 www.myfatherswars.com/ch9-09.

19 www.myfatherswars.com/ch9-10.

20 www.myfatherswars.com/ch9-11.

21 www.myfatherswars.com/ch9-12.

22 www.myfatherswars.com/ch9-13.

23 www.myfatherswars.com/ch9-14.

24 Lesley Gill, "War and Peace in Colombia," in *An Anthropology of War: Views from the Frontline*, ed. Alisse Waterston (New York and Oxford: Berghahn Books, 2009), 131–132; Alfred W. McCoy, *A Question of Torture: CIA Interrogation, from the Cold War to the War on Terror* (New York: Metropolitan Books, 2006); J. Patrice McSherry, *Predatory States: Operation Condor and Covert War in Latin America* (Lanham, MD: Rowan & Littlefield, 2005).

25 Eric R. Wolf, *Peasant Wars of the Twentieth Century* (New York: Harper Torchbooks, 1973), 258; Leland Johnson, "U.S. Business Interests in Cuba and the Rise of Castro," *World Politics*, Vol. 17, No. 3 (1965): 440–459.

26 Morris H. Morley, *Imperial State and Revolution: The United States and Cuba, 1952–1986*, (Cambridge: Cambridge University Press, 1987); Morris H. Morley and Chris McGillion, *Cuba, the United States, and the Post-Cold War World: The International Dimensions of the Washington-Havana Relationship* (Gainesville: University Press of Florida, 2005); Robin Blackburn, "Prologue to the Cuban Revolution," *New Left Review*, Vol. 1, No. 21 (1963): 52–91; Jorge I. Domínguez, "U.S. –Cuban Relations: From the Cold War to the Colder War," *Journal of Interamerican Studies and World Affairs*, Vol. 39, No. 3 (1997): 49–75; Jorge I. Domínguez, "Revolution and Its Aftermath in Cuba: A Review Essay," *Latin American Research Review*, Vol. 43, No. 2 (2008): 225–240; Marifeli Pérez-Stable, *The Cuban Revolution: Origins, Course, and Legacy* (Oxford: Oxford University Press, 1999); James Petras, *Class, State, and Power in the Third World, with Case Studies on Class Conflict in Latin America* (Lanham, MD: Rowman & Littlefield, 1981).

27 Morris H. Morley, "Reinterpreting the State–Class Relationship: American Corporations and U.S. Policy toward Cuba, 1959–1960," *Comparative Politics*, Vol. 16, No. 1 (1983): 67–83.

28 Glennon and Landa, op. cit., 742.

29 Ibid., 743, 656–658.

30 Ibid., 747, 850; National Security Archive, "Bay of Pigs: Forty Years After," www.gwu.edu/~nsarchiv/bayofpigs/chron.html (accessed January 5, 2012), Gelman Library, George Washington University; Piero Gleijeses, "Ships in the Night: The CIA, the White House and the Bay of Pigs," *Journal of Latin American Studies*, Vol. 27, No. 1 (Feb., 1995): 1–42; Jack B. Pfeiffer, "Taylor Committee Investigation of the Bay of Pigs," November 8, 1984. www.foia.cia.gov/bay-of-pigs/bop-vol4.pdf (accessed January 5, 2012); Peter Wyden, *Bay of Pigs: The Untold Story* (New York: Simon & Schuster, 1979).

31 Ibid., National Security Archive.

32 Wolf 1973, op. cit., 263; Federico G. Gil, "Cuban Politics and Political Parties: 1933–1953," in *Background to Revolution: The Development of Modern Cuba*," ed. Robert F. Smith (New York: Knopf, 1966), 149–156.

Chapter 10

1 www.myfatherswars.com/ch10-01.
2 www.myfatherswars.com/ch10-02.
3 www.youtube.com/watch?v=Hu95ECRMie8.
4 www.myfatherswars.com/ch10-03.
5 Marie L. Murphy, "Claims Against the Republic of Cuba," *University of Miami Law Review*, Vol. 27 (1972–1973): 372–394.
6 Hoffman 2004, op. cit., 54.
7 Robert Krell, Marc I. Sherman and Elie Wiesel, *Medical and Psychological Effects of Concentration Camps on Holocaust Survivors; Genocide – A Critical Bibliographic Review*, Vol. 4 (New Brunswick, NJ: Transaction Publishers, 1997); Paul Marcus and Alan Rosenberg, eds., *Healing Their Wounds: Psychotherapy with Holocaust Survivors and Their Families* (New York: Praeger Publishers, 1989); Art Spiegelman, *The Complete Maus. A Survivor's Tale* (New York: Pantheon Books, 1997).
8 Linda Green, "Lived Lives and Social Suffering: Problems and Concerns in Medical Anthropology," *Medical Anthropology Quarterly*, Vol. 12, No. 1 (1998): 5.
9 George Steiner, "The Long Life of Metaphor," in *Writing and the Holocaust*, ed. Berel Lang (New York: Holmes & Meier Publishers, 1988), 154–171.
10 Jeremy Cohen, *Sanctifying the Name of God: Jewish Martyrs and Jewish Memories of the First Crusade* (Philadelphia: University of Pennsylvania Press, 2004), 160.
11 George K. Anderson, *The Legend of the Wandering Jew* (Lebanon, NH: Brown University Press, 1965); Melvin Konner, *Unsettled: An Anthropology of the Jews* (New York: Viking Compass, Penguin Group, 2003).
12 Alan Mintz, *Popular Culture and the Shaping of Holocaust Memory in America* (Seattle: University of Washington Press, 2001).
13 Green, op. cit.
14 James Quesada, "Suffering Child: An Embodiment of War and Its Aftermath in Post-Sandinista Nicaragua," *Medical Anthropology Quarterly*, Vol. 12, No. 1 (1998): 64; James Quesada, "The Vicissitudes of Structural Violence: Nicaragua at the Turn of the Twenty-first Century," in *Global Health in Times of Violence*, ed. Barbara Rylko-Bauer, Linda Whiteford, and Paul Farmer (Santa Fe, NM: School for Advanced Research Press, 2009), 157–180.
15 Quesada 1998, op. cit., 51; Carolyn Nordstrom, "Terror Warfare and the Medicine of Peace," *Medical Anthropology Quarterly*, Vol. 12, No. 1 (1998): 115–118; Veena Das, Arthur Kleinman, Margaret Lock, Mamphela Ramphele and Pamela Reynolds, eds., *Remaking a World: Violence, Social Suffering and Recovery* (Berkeley: University of California Press, 2001).
16 Nancy Scheper-Hughes and Philippe Bourgois, eds., "Introduction: Making Sense of Violence," in *Violence in War and Peace. An Anthology*, ed. Nancy Scheper-Hughes and Philippe Bourgois (Malden, MA: Blackwell Publishing, 2004), 19.
17 Ibid.
18 Paul Farmer, "An Anthropology of Structural Violence," *Current Anthropology*, Vol. 45, No. 3 (2004): 307.

Chapter 11

1 www.myfatherswars.com/ch11-01.
2 www.myfatherswars.com/ch11-02.
3 Louise Waterston, "Abraham Cowley: Apostle in Muse's Land" (MA thesis, University of Puerto Rico, 1980).
4 www.myfatherswars.com/ch11-03.
5 *Mishigas* (also spelled *mishegas*) is a Yiddish word that refers to craziness.
6 www.youtube.com/watch?v=ZUW_DKlM8Og.
7 www.myfatherswars.com/ch11-04.
8 Veena Das, "Secularism and the Argument from Nature," in *Powers of the Secular Modern: Talal Asad and His Interlocuters*, ed. David Scott and Charles Hirschkind (Stanford, CA: Stanford University Press, 2006), 93.
9 Talal Asad, *Formations of the Secular: Christianity, Islam, Modernity* (Stanford, CA: Stanford University Press, 2003); David Scott and Charles Hirschkind, eds., *Powers of the Secular Modern: Talal Asad and His Interlocuters* (Stanford, CA: Stanford University Press, 2006).

10 L.J. Jordanova, "Natural Facts: A Historical Perspective on Science and Sexuality," in *Nature, Culture and Gender*, ed. Carol MacCormack and Marilyn Strathern (Cambridge: Cambridge University Press, 1980), 42; Michelle Zimbalist Rosaldo and Louise Lamphere, eds., *Woman, Culture, and Society* (Stanford, CA: Stanford University Press, 1974); Spike V. Peterson, "Feminist Theories Within, Invisible To, and Beyond IR," *Brown Journal of World Affairs*, Vol. X, No. 2 (2004): 35–46.

11 Arthur Miller, "Tragedy and the Common Man," *New York Times Books*, February 27, 1949. www. nytimes.com/books/00/11/12/specials/miller-common.html?_r=1&scp=1&sq=Arthur%20 Miller,%20Tragedy%20and%20the%20Common%20Man&st=cse (accessed February 9, 2012).

12 Ibid.

Chapter 12

1   *"We love you always, friend/fellow countryman."*

2   www.myfatherswars.com/ch12-01.

3   www.myfatherswars.com/ch12-02.

4   http://newsismybusiness.com/historic-la-mallorquina-restaurant-in-osj-closes-after-86-years/.

5   www.myfatherswars.com/ch12-03.

6   www.myfatherswars.com/ch12-04.

7   F.E. Peters, *The Monotheists: Jews, Christians, and Muslims in Conflict and Competition, Volume I, The Peoples of God* (Princeton, NJ: Princeton University Press, 2003), 125.

8   www.myfatherswars.com/ch12-05.

9   Vincent Crapanzano, "Life History in Anthropological Fieldwork," *Anthropology and Humanism Quarterly*, Vol. 2, Nos. 2–3 (1977): 3–7; Vincent Crapanzano, *Tuhami: Portrait of a Moroccan* (Chicago: University of Chicago Press, 1980); L.L.Langness and Gelya Frank, *Lives: An Anthropological Approach to Biography* (Novato, CA: Chandler and Sharp, 1981); Sidney W. Mintz, *Worker in the Cane: A Puerto Rican Life History* (New York: W.W. Norton & Company, 1974 [1960]); Marjorie Shostak, *Nisa: The Life and Words of a !Kung Woman* (New York: Vintage Books, 1981); Lawrence C. Watson and Maria-Barbara Watson-Franke, *Interpreting Life Histories: An Anthropological Inquiry* (New Brunswick, NJ: Rutgers University Press, 1985).

10 Lila Abu-Lughod, *Writing Women's Worlds: Bedouin Stories* (Berkeley: University of California Press, 1993); Gloria Anzaldúa, *Borderlands/La Frontera: The New Mestiza* (San Francisco: Aunt Lute, 1987); Ruth Behar, *Translated Woman: Crossing the Border with Esperanza's Story* (Boston: Beacon Press, 1993); Ruth Behar, *The Vulnerable Observer: Anthropology That Breaks Your Heart* (Boston: Beacon Press, 1996); Carolyn Ellis and Arthur P. Bochner, "Autoethnography, Personal Narrative, Reflexivity: Researcher as Subject," in *Handbook of Qualitative Research*, second edition, ed. Norman K. Denzin and Yvonna S. Lincoln (Thousand Oaks, CA: Sage, 2000), 733–768; Mary Patrice Erdmans, "The Personal is Political, but Is It Academic?" *Journal of American Ethnic History*, Vol. 26, No. 4 (2007): 7–23; Marc Kaminsky, "Meyerhoff's 'Third Voice': Ideology and Genre in Ethnographic Narrative," *Social Text*, No. 33 (1992): 124–144; Athena McLean and Annette Leibing, eds. *The Shadow Side of Field Work: Theorizing the Blurred Borders between Ethnography and Life* (Malden, MA and Oxford, UK: Blackwell Publishing, 2007); Barbara Myerhoff, *Number Our Days* (New York: Simon & Schuster, 1978); Deborah Reed Danahay, *Auto/ethnography: Rewriting the Self and the Social* (Oxford: Berg, 1997); Carolyn Steedman, *Landscape for a Good Woman: A Story of Two Lives* (New Brunswick, NJ: Rutgers University Press, 2003).

11 Lila Abu-Lughod, "Return to Half-Ruins: Fathers and Daughters, Memory and History in Palestine," in *Rites of Return: Diaspora Poetics and the Politics of Memory*, ed. Marianne Hirsch and Nancy K. Miller (New York: Columbia University Press, 2011), 124–136; Andrew Beatty, "How Did It Feel for You? Emotion, Narrative, and the Limits of Ethnography," *American Anthropologist*, Vol. 112, No. 3 (2010): 430–443; Marta Bladek, *Pilgrimages to the Past: Place, Memory, and Return in Contemporary Life Writing* (Ph.D. dissertation, City University of New York, 2009); Marta Bladek, "Jewish American Postgenerational Returns to Eastern and Central Europe," in *Cultural Memory: Reformations of the Past in the Present, and Present in the Past*, ed. Malcolm Miles and Vardan Azatyan (Plymouth, UK: Plymouth University Press, 2010); Erika Bourguignon, "Vienna and Memory: Anthropology and Experiences," *Ethos*, Vol. 24, No. 2 (1996): 374–387; Erika Bourguignon and Barbara Hill Rigney, eds. *Exile: A Memoir of 1939, by Bronka Schneider* (Columbus: Ohio State University, 1998); Ellen Cassedy, *We Are Here: Memories of the Lithuanian Holocaust* (Nebraska: University of Nebraska Press, 2012); Helen Epstein, *Where She Came From: A Daughter's Search for Her Mother's History* (New York: Plume, 1998); Mary Patrice Erdmans, *Grasinski Girls: Choices They Had and Choices They Made* (Athens: Ohio University Press,

2004); Marianne Hirsch, *The Generation of Postmemory: Writing and Visual Culture After the Holocaust* (New York: Columbia University Press, 2012); Marianne Hirsch and Nancy K. Miller, eds. *Rites of Return: Diaspora Poetics and the Politics of Memory* (New York: Columbia University Press, 2011); Marianne Hirsch and Leo Spitzer, *Ghosts of Home: The Afterlife of Czernowitz in Jewish History* (Berkeley: University of California Press, 2011); Marlene Kadar, Linda Warley, Jeanne Perreault, and Susanna Egan, eds. *Tracing the Autobiographical* (Waterloo, ON: Wilfrid Laurier University Press, 2005); Barbara Kirshenblatt-Gimblett, "A Daughter's Afterword," in *They Called Me Mayer July: Painted Memories of a Jewish Childhood in Poland Before the Holocaust*, Mayer Kirshenblatt and Barbara Kirshenblatt-Gimblett (Berkeley: University of California Press, 2007), 359–385; Annette Kuhn, *Family Secrets: Acts of Memory and Imagination* (London: Verso, 2002); Daniel Mendelsohn, *The Lost: A Search for Six of Six Million* (New York: HarperCollins Publishers, 2006); Nancy K. Miller, *Bequest and Betrayal: Memoirs of a Parent's Death* (Bloomington: Indiana University Press, 1996); Nancy K. Miller, *What They Saved: Pieces of a Jewish Past* (Lincoln: University of Nebraska Press, 2011); Ben Orlove, *In My Father's Study* (Iowa City: University of Iowa Press, 1995); Neni Panourgiá, *Dangerous Citizens: The Greek Left and the Terror of the State* (New York: Fordham University Press, 2009); Gabriele Schwab, "Writing against Memory and Forgetting," *Literature and Medicine*, Vol. 25, No. 1 (2006): 95–121.

12 Waterston and Rylko-Bauer 2006, op. cit., 405.

13 www.myfatherswars.com/ch12-06.

14 Ibid., 409.

15 Jane L. Collins, Micaela di Leonardo, and Brett Williams, eds., *New Landscapes of Inequality: Neoliberalism and the Erosion of Democracy in America* (Santa Fe, NM: School for Advanced Research, 2008); Judith Butler, "Remarks to Brooklyn College on BDS," *The Nation*, February 7, 2013. www.thenation.com/article/172752/judith-butlers-remarks-brooklyn-college-bds# (accessed February 9, 2013); Farmer 2003, op. cit.; David Graeber, *Direct Action, An Ethnography* (Oakland, CA: AK Press, 2009); Jeff Halper, *An Israeli In Palestine: Resisting Dispossession, Redeeming Israel*, second edition (London: Pluto Press, 2010); Barbara Rose Johnston, ed. *Life and Death Matters: Human Rights, Environment, and Social Justice*, second edition (Walnut Creek, CA: Left Coast Press, 2011); Catherine Lutz, *The Bases of Empire: The Global Struggle Against U.S. Military Posts* (New York: NYU Press, 2009); Catherine Lutz, "The Military Normal," in *The Counter-Counterinsurgency Manual*, ed. Network of Concerned Anthropologists (Chicago: Prickly Paradigm Press, 2009), 23–37; Carolyn Nordstrom, *Global Outlaws: Crime, Money, and Power in the Contemporary World* (Berkeley: University of California Press, 2007); Stephen P. Reyna and R.E. Downs, eds., *Deadly Developments: Capitalism, States, and War* (New York: Taylor & Francis, 1999); Barbara Rylko-Bauer, Linda Whiteford, and Paul Farmer, eds., *Global Health in Times of Violence* (Santa Fe, NM: School for Advanced Research Press, 2009); Gino Strada *Green Parrots: A War Surgeon's Diary* (Milan: Edizioni Charta, 2004); Alisse Waterston, ed., *An Anthropology of War: Views from the Frontline* (New York and Oxford: Berghahn Books, 2009).

16 Barbara Rylko-Bauer, "Introduction: Bringing the Past into the Present: Family Narratives of Holocaust, Exile, and Diaspora," *Anthropological Quarterly*, Vol. 78, No. 1 (2005): 7–10.

17 Ibid., 10; Barbara Rylko-Bauer *A Polish Doctor in the Nazi Camps: My Mother's Memories of Imprisonment, Immigration and a Life Reclaimed* (Norman: Oklahoma University Press, forthcoming, 2014).

18 Waterston and Rylko-Bauer, op. cit., 398.

19 Lazarre, op. cit., 23.

20 Gerald Sider, "Between Silences and Culture: A Partisan Anthropology," in *Silence: The Currency of Power*, ed Maria-Luisa Achino-Loeb (New York and Oxford: Berghahn Books, 2006), 151.

21 www.myfatherswars.com/ch12-07.

22 Neni Panourgiá, "'. . . for three days and three nights . . .' Women, political persecution, and radical kinship" (paper presented at the annual meeting of the American Anthropological Association, New Orleans, November 18, 2010): 8.

Epilogue

1 www.myfatherswars.com/ch-ep-01.

REFERENCES

Abramowicz, Dina and Jeffrey Shandler, eds. *Profiles of a Lost World: Memoirs of East European Jewish Life before World War II*. Translated by Eva Zeitlin Dobkin. Detroit: Wayne State University Press, 1999.

Abrams, Charles. *Forbidden Neighbors: A Study of Prejudice in Housing*. New York: Harper & Brothers, 1955.

Abu-Lughod, Lila. *Writing Women's Worlds: Bedouin Stories*. Berkeley: University of California Press, 1993.

Abu-Lughod, Lila. "Return to Half-Ruins: Fathers and Daughters, Memory and History in Palestine." In *Rites of Return: Diaspora Poetics and the Politics of Memory*, edited by Marianne Hirsch and Nancy K. Miller, 124–135. New York: Columbia University Press, 2011.

Alexander, Jeffrey C. "Between Progress and Apocalypse: Social Theory and the Dream of Reason in the Twentieth Century." In *Rethinking Progress*, edited by Jeffrey C. Alexander and Piotr Sztompka, 15–39. London: Unwin Hyman Limited.

Anderson, Benedict. *Imagined Communities*. London and New York: Verso, 1991 (1983).

Anderson, George K. *The Legend of the Wandering Jew*. Lebanon, NH: Brown University Press, 1965.

Anzaldúa, Gloria. *Borderlands/La Frontera: The New Mestiza*. San Francisco: Aunt Lute, 1987.

Arendt, Hannah. "Beyond Personal Frustration: The Poetry of Bertolt Brecht," *The Kenyon Review*, Vol. 10, No. 2 (Spring, 1948): 304–312.

Arendt, Hannah. *Men in Dark Times*. San Diego, CA: Harcourt, Brace & Company, 1983.

"Arms Dump Blast Shakes Havana-Two Killed, 200 Reported Hurt-Castro Hints at Sabotage Charges," *New York Times*, June 27, 1960: 1. ProQuest Historical Newspapers: *New York Times* (1851–2009).

Asad, Talal, *Formations of the Secular: Christianity, Islam, Modernity*. Stanford, CA: Stanford University Press, 2003.

Ayala, Cesar J. "Social and Economic Aspects of Sugar Production in Cuba, 1880–1930," *Latin American Research Review*, Vol. 30, No. 1 (1995): 95–124.

Baker, Julius L. and Moshe Tzinovitz, "My Hometown Yedwabne, Province of Łomża, Poland." In *Yedwabne: History and Memorial Book* (Jerusalem–New York: The Yedwabne

Societies in Israel and the United States of America), 1980. www.jewishgen.org/ yizkor/jedwabne/Yedwabne.html (accessed July 7, 2005).

Baker, Lee D. *From Savage to Negro: Anthropology and the Construction of Race, 1896–1954.* Berkeley: University of California Press, 1998.

Baumann, Zygmunt. *Modernity and the Holocaust.* Cambridge: Polity, 1989.

Beatty, Andrew. 2010. "How Did It Feel for You? Emotion, Narrative, and the Limits of Ethnography," *American Anthropologist*, Vol. 112, No. 3 (2010): 430–443.

Behar, Ruth. *Translated Woman: Crossing the Border with Esperanza's Story.* Boston: Beacon Press, 1993.

Behar, Ruth. *The Vulnerable Observer: Anthropology That Breaks Your Heart.* Boston: Beacon Press, 1996.

Bergad, Laird W. "The Economic Viability of Sugar Production Based on Slave Labor in Cuba, 1859–1878," *Latin American Research Review*, Vol. 24, No. 1 (1989): 95–113.

Biale, David. "Eros and Enlightenment: Love against Marriage in East European Jewish Enlightenment." In *From Shtetl to Socialism*, edited by Antony Polonsky, Polin: Studies in Polish Jewry, 168–186. Oxford: Littman Library of Jewish Civilization.

Bigart, Homer. "Castro Declares He Will Win Soon—In Interview, Rebel Leader with Battle Force of 400 Is Certain of Victory, *New York Times*, February 27, 1958: 10. ProQuest Historical Newspapers: *New York Times* (1851–2009).

Blackburn, Robin. "Prologue to the Cuban Revolution." *New Left Review*, Vol. 1, No. 21 (1963): 52–91.

Bladek, Marta. "Jewish American Postgenerational Returns to Eastern and Central Europe." In *Cultural Memory: Reformations of the Past in the Present, and Present in the Past*, edited by Malcolm Miles and Vardan Azatyan. Plymouth, UK: Plymouth University Press, 2010.

Bladek, Marta. *Pilgrimages to the Past: Place, Memory, and Return in Contemporary Life Writing.* Ph.D. dissertation, City University of New York, 2009.

Boas, Franz. "Serious Flaws Are Suspected in Professor Osborn's Theories—Views as to Nordic Italians—Pre-War Ethnology as 'Made in Germany,'" *New York Times*, April 13, 1924: XX19 ProQuest Historical Newspapers: *New York Times* (1851–2009).

Bourdieu, Pierre. *The Logic of Practice*, translated by Richard Nice. Stanford, CA: Stanford University Press, 1977.

Bourdieu, Pierre. *Outline of a Theory of Practice*, translated by Richard Nice. Cambridge: Cambridge University Press, 1992.

Bourdieu, Pierre and Loïc J. D. Wacquant. "Language, Gender, and Symbolic Violence." In *An Invitation to Reflective Sociology*, 140–216. Chicago: University of Chicago Press, 1992.

Bourguignon, Erika. "Vienna and Memory: Anthropology and Experiences." *Ethos*, Vol. 24, No. 3 (1996): 374–387.

Bourguignon, Erika and Barbara Hill Rigney, eds. *Exile: A Memoir of 1939, by Bronka Schneider.* Columbus: Ohio State University, 1998.

Bowen, John. "The Myth of Global Ethnic Conflict." *Journal of Democracy.* Vol. 7, No. 4 (October, 1996): 3–14.

Boyarin, Jonathan. *Thinking in Jewish.* Chicago: University of Chicago Press, 1996.

Brand, William, ed. *Thou Shalt Not Kill: Poles on Jedwabne.* Warsaw: Towarzystwo "Wiez", 2001.

Brecht, Bertolt, John Willett and Ralph Manheim, eds, *Bertolt Brecht: Poems 1913–1956.* New York: Routledge, 1997.

Brenner, Philip, Marguerite Rose Jiménez, John M. Kirk, and William M. LeoGrande, eds. *Reinventing the Revolution: A Contemporary Cuban Reader.* Lanham, MD: Rowman & Littlefield, 2008.

Brodkin, Karen. *How Jews Became White Folks and What that Says about Race in America.* New Brunswick, NJ: Rutgers University Press, 1998.

Butler, Judith "Remarks to Brooklyn College on BDS," *The Nation*, February 7, 2013. www.thenation.com/article/172752/judith-butlers-remarks-brooklyn-college-bds# (accessed February 9, 2013).

Cassedy, Ellen. *We Are Here: Memories of the Lithuanian Holocaust*. Lincoln: University of Nebraska Press, 2012.

Cassell, Joan. "The Woman in the Surgeon's Body: Understanding Difference." *American Anthropologist*, Vol. 98, No. 1 (1996): 41–53.

Cassell, Joan. *The Woman in the Surgeon's Body*. Cambridge, MA: Harvard University Press, 2000.

Chodakiewicz, Marek Jan. *The Massacre in Jedwabne, July 10, 1941*. East European Monographs, 655, 2005.

CNN. 2001. Polish Mass Grave Dig Ends. http://articles.cnn.com/2001-06-04/world/poland.grave_1_witold-kulesza-search-for-more-graves-exhumation?_s=PM:WORLD (accessed August 16, 2010).

Cohen, Jeremy. *Sanctifying the Name of God. Jewish Martyrs and Jewish Memories of the First Crusade*. Philadelphia: University of Pennsylvania Press, 2004.

Collins, Jane L., Micaela di Leonardo, and Brett Williams, eds. *New Landscapes of Inequality: Neoliberalism and the Erosion of Democracy in America*. Santa Fe, NM: School for Advanced Research, 2008.

Crapanzano, Vincent. "The Life History in Anthropological Fieldwork." *Anthropology and Humanism Quarterly*, Nos. 2–3 (1977): 3–7.

Crapanzano, Vincent. *Tuhami: Portrait of a Moroccan*. Chicago: University of Chicago Press, 1980.

Croxton, Frederick C. *Statistical Review of Immigration, 1820–1910. Distribution of Immigrants, 1850–1900*. Washington: G.P.O., 1911. Collection Development Department, Widener Library, Harvard University. http://nrs.harvard.edu/urn-3:FHCL:679756 (accessed October 3, 2011).

Curry-Machado, Jonathan "'*Sin azúcar no hay país*': The Transnational Counterpoint of Sugar and Nation in Nineteenth-Century Cuba," *Bulletin of Hispanic Studies*, Vol. 84, No. 1 (2007): 25–42.

Das, Veena. "Secularism and the Argument from Nature." In *Powers of the Secular Modern: Talal Asad and His Interlocuters*, edited by David Scott and Charles Hirschkind, 93–112. Stanford, CA: Stanford University Press, 2006.

Das, Veena, Arthur Kleinman, Margaret Lock, Mamphela Ramphele, and Pamela Reynolds, eds. *Remaking a World: Violence, Social Suffering and Recovery*. Berkeley: University of California Press, 2001.

Davies, Norman. *God's Playground: A History of Poland. Volume 1: The Origins to 1795*. New York: Columbia University Press, 1982.

de la Fuente, Alejandro. "Race, National Discourse, and Politics in Cuba: An Overview," *Latin American Perspectives*, Vol. 25, No. 3 (1998): 43–69.

Dobroszycki, Lucjan and Barbara Kirshenblatt-Gimblett. *Image Before My Eyes: A Photographic History of Jewish Life in Poland, 1864–1939*. New York: Schocken Books, 1977.

Domínguez, Jorge I. "U.S. –Cuban Relations: From the Cold War to the Colder War." *Journal of Interamerican Studies and World Affairs*, Vol. 39, No. 3 (1997): 49–75.

Domínguez, Jorge I. "Revolution and Its Aftermath in Cuba: A Review Essay." *Latin American Research Review*, Vol. 43, No. 2 (2008): 225–240.

Drabble, Margaret. "A Beastly Century," *American Scholar*, Vol. 70, No. 1 (Winter 2001): 160.

Dubnow, Simon M. *History of the Jews in Russia and Poland*. Philadelphia: The Jewish Publication Society of America, 1916.

Eliach, Yaffa. *There Once Was a World: A 900 Year Chronicle of the Shtetl of Eishyshok*. Boston: Little, Brown & Co., 1998.

Eliot, T.S. "Little Gidding." In *Four Quartets*. London: Houghton Mifflin Harcourt Publishing Company, 1942.

Ellis, Carolyn and Arthur P. Bochner. "Autoethnography, Personal Narrative, Reflexivity: Researcher as Subject." In *Handbook of Qualitative Research*, second edition, edited by Norman K. Denzin and Yvonna S. Lincoln, 733–768. Thousand Oaks, CA: Sage, 2000.

Epstein, Helen. *Where She Came From: A Daughter's Search for Her Mother's History*. New York: Plume, 1998.

Erdmans, Mary Patrice. *Grasinski Girls: Choices They Had and Choices They Made*. Athens: Ohio University Press, 2004.

Erdmans, Mary Patrice. "The Personal is Political, But Is It Academic?" *Journal of American Ethnic History*, Vol. 26, No. 4 (2007): 7–23.

Farmer, Paul. *Pathologies of Power: Health, Human Rights, and the New War on the Poor*. Berkeley: University of California Press, 2003.

Farmer, Paul. "An Anthropology of Structural Violence." *Current Anthropology*, Vol. 45, No. 3 (2004): 305–317.

Farmer, Paul. "Never again? Reflections on Human Values and Human Rights." In *The Tanner Lectures on Human Values*, Vol. 25, edited by G.B. Petersen, 137–188. Salt Lake City: University of Utah Press, 2006.

Ferguson, R. Brian. "A Paradigm for the Study of War and Society." In *War and Society in the Ancient and Medieval Worlds: Asia, the Mediterranean, Europe, and Mesoamerica*, edited by Kurt Raaflaub and Nathan Rosenstein, 389–437. Cambridge, MA: Harvard University Press, 1999.

Ferguson, R. Brian. "Ten Points on War." In *An Anthropology of War: Views from the Frontline*, edited by Alisse Waterston, 32–49. New York and Oxford: Berghahn Books, 2009.

Fluek, Toby Knobel. *Memories of My Life in a Polish Village, 1930–1949*. New York: Alfred A. Knopf, 1990.

Foner, Jack. *Blacks and the Military in American History: A New Perspective*. New York: Praeger Publishers, 1974.

Fussell, Paul. *The Great War and Modern Memory*. Oxford: Oxford University, 2000 (1975).

Gelfand, Mark I. *A Nation of Cities: The Federal Government and Urban America, 1933–1965*. New York: Oxford University Press, 1975.

Gellner, Ernst. *Nations and Nationalism*. Malden, MA: Blackwell Publishing, 2006 (1983).

Gil, Federico G., "Cuban Politics and Political Parties: 1933–1953." In *Background to Revolution: The Development of Modern Cuba*," edited by Robert F. Smith, 149–156. New York: Knopf, 1966.

Gill, Lesley. "War and Peace in Colombia." In *An Anthropology of War: Views from the Frontline*, edited by Alisse Waterston, 131–150. New York & Oxford: Berghahn Books, 2009.

Gleijeses, Piero. "Ships in the Night: The CIA, the White House and the Bay of Pigs." *Journal of Latin American Studies*, Vol. 27, No. 1 (Feb., 1995):1–42.

Glennon, John P. and Ronald D. Landa. *Foreign Relations of the United States 1958–1960, Volume VI: Cuba*. Washington, DC: US Government Printing Office, 1991): 38–42. http://history.state.gov/historicaldocuments/frus1958-60v06 (accessed January 5, 2012).

Graeber, David. *Direct Action, An Ethnography*. Oakland, CA: AK Press, 2009.

Green, Linda. "Lived Lives and Social Suffering: Problems and Concerns in Medical Anthropology," *Medical Anthropology Quarterly*, Vol. 12, No. 1 (1998): 3–7.

Gross, Jan T. *Neighbors: The Destruction of the Jewish Community in Jedwabne, Poland*. Princeton, NJ: Princeton University Press, 2002 (2001).

Halper, Jeff. *An Israeli In Palestine: Resisting Dispossession, Redeeming Israel*, second edition. London: Pluto Press, 2010.

Harding, John G. "The Nationalization of Canadian Property in Cuba under International Law." *Western Law Review*, Vol. 2, No. 50 (1962–1963): 50–65.

"Heard That Boynton Blew Up The Maine," *New York Times*, May 29, 1911: 9. ProQuest Historical Newspapers: *New York Times* (1851–2009).

Helg, Aline. *Our Rightful Share: The Afro-Cuban Struggle for Equality, 1886–1912*. Chapel Hill: University of North Carolina Press, 1995.

Hinton, Alexander Laban. "The Dark Side of Modernity: Toward an Anthropology of Genocide," in *Annihilating Difference: The Anthropology of Genocide*, edited by Alexander Laban Hinton, 1–40. Berkeley: University of California Press, 2002.

Hirsch, Marianne. *The Generation of Postmemory: Writing and Visual Culture After the Holocaust*. New York: Columbia University Press, 2012.

Hirsch, Marianne Hirsch and Nancy K. Miller, eds. *Rites of Return: Diaspora Poetics and the Politics of Memory*. New York: Columbia University Press, 2011.

Hirsch, Marianne and Leo Spitzer. *Ghosts of Home: The Afterlife of Czernowitz in Jewish History*. Berkeley: University of California Press, 2011.

Hobsbawm, Eric and Terence Ranger, eds. *The Invention of Tradition*. New York: Cambridge University Press, 1989 (1983).

Hobsbawm, Eric J. *Nations and Nationalism since 1780: Programme, Myth, Reality*. New York: Cambridge University Press, 2004 (1990).

Hoerder, Dirk. *Cultures in Contact: World Migrations in the Second Millennium*. Durham, NC and London: Duke University Press, 2002.

Hoffman, Eva. *Shtetl: The Life and Death of a Small Town and the World of Polish Jews*. Boston: Mariner/Houghton Mifflin Company, 1997.

Hoffman, Eva. *After Such Knowledge: Memory, History, and the Legacy of the Holocaust*. New York: Public Affairs, 2004.

Hopkins, Terence and Immanuel Maurice Wallerstein. *World Systems Analysis: Theory and Methodology*. Beverly Hills, CA: Sage Publications, 1982.

Hundert, Gershon David, ed. *Jews in Early Modern Poland*. Polin: Studies in Polish Jewry, Volume 10. London: Littman Library of Jewish Civilization, 1997.

Huntington, Samuel P. *The Clash of Civilizations and the Remaking of the World Order*. New York: Simon & Schuster, 2011 (1996).

Immigration Act of 1924. H.R. 7995; Pub.L. 68–139; 43 Stat. 153. 68th Congress; May 26, 1924.

Immigration Restriction League. (U.S.) Records (MS Am 2245). Houghton Library, Harvard University. http://ocp.hul.harvard.edu/immigration/restrictionleague.html#arc (accessed September 30, 2011).

Institute for National Remembrance. *Beginning of the Search in the Jedwabne Site*, November 18, 2003. www.ipn.gov.pl/portal/en/19/192/Beginning_of_the_Search_in_the_Jedwabne_Site.html (accessed August 15, 2010).

Johnson, Leland. "U.S. Business Interests in Cuba and the Rise of Castro." *World Politics*, Vol. 17, No. 3 (1965): 440–459.

Johnston, Barbara Rose, ed. *Life and Death Matters: Human Rights, Environment, and Social Justice*, second edition. Walnut Creek, CA: Left Coast Press, 2011.

Jordanova, L.J. "Natural Facts: A Historical Perspective on Science and Sexuality." On *Nature, Culture and Gender*, edited by Carol MacCormack and Marilyn Strathern, 42–69. Cambridge: Cambridge University Press, 1980.

Kacyzne, Alter. *Poyln: Jewish Life in the Old Country*. New York: Henry Holt & Company, 1999.

Kadar, Marlene, Linda Warley, Jeanne Perreault, and Susanna Egan, eds. *Tracing the Autobiographical*. Waterloo, ON: Wilfrid Laurier University Press, 2005.

Kaminsky, Marc. "Meyerhoff's 'Third Voice': Ideology and Genre in Ethnographic Narrative." *Social Text*, No. 33 (1992): 124–144.

Kaplan, Robert D. *Balkan Ghosts: A Journey Through History*. New York: Vintage Books, 1996 (1993).

Kirshenblatt-Gimblett, Barbara. Introduction to *Life is with People: The Culture of the Shtetl*, by Mark Zborowski and Elizabeth Herzog, ix–xlviii. New York: Schocken, 1995.

Kirshenblatt-Gimblett, Barbara. "Imagining Europe: The Popular Arts of American Jewish Ethnography." In *Divergent Centers: Shaping Jewish Cultures in Israel and America*, edited by Deborah Dash Moore and Ilan Troen, 155–191. New Haven, CT: Yale University Press, 2001.

Kirshenblatt-Gimblett, Barbara. "A Daughter's Afterword." In *They Called Me Mayer July: Painted Memories of a Jewish Childhood in Poland Before the Holocaust*, Mayer Kirshenblatt and Barbara Kirshenblatt-Gimblett, 359–385. Berkeley: University of California Press, 2007.

Konner, Melvin. *Unsettled: An Anthropology of the Jews*. New York: Viking Compass, Penguin Group, 2003.

Krell, Robert, Marc I. Sherman, and Elie Wiesel. *Medical and Psychological Effects of Concentration Camps on Holocaust Survivors; Genocide — A Critical Bibliographic Review*, Vol. 4. New Brunswick, NJ: Transaction Publishers, 1997.

Kugelmass, Jack and Jonathan Boyarin, with Zachary M. Baker. *From a Ruined Garden: The Memorial Books of Polish Jewry*, second edition. Bloomington: Indiana University Press, 1998 (1983).

Kuhn, Annette. *Family Secrets: Acts of Memory and Imagination*. London: Verso, 2002.

Kurkowska, Marta. "Jedwabne and Wizna: Monuments and Memory in the Łomża Region." In *Making Holocaust Memory*, edited by Gabriel N. Finder, Natlaia Aleksiun, Antony Polonsky, and Jan Schwarz. Polin: Studies in Polish Jewry, Vol. 20, 244–70. Oxford: Littman Library of Jewish Civilization, 2008.

Langness, L.L., and Gelya Frank. *Lives: An Anthropological Approach to Biography*. Novato, CA: Chandler & Sharp, 1981.

Lazarre, Jane. *Beyond the Whiteness of Whiteness*. Durham, NC: Duke University Press, 1996.

Leitenberg, Milton. "Deaths in Wars and Conflicts in the 20th Century, third edition." *Occasional Paper #29*. Ithaca, NY: Cornell University Peace Studies Program (2006): 1–86.

Lewis, Bernard. 1990. "The Roots of Muslim Rage." *Atlantic Magazine*, September, 1990. www.theatlantic.com/magazine/archive/1990/09/the-roots-of-muslim-rage/4643/ (accessed June 10, 2011).

Lombardo, Paul A. "Medicine, Eugenics, and the Supreme Court: From Coercive Sterilization to Reproductive Freedom." *Journal of Contemporary Health Law and Policy*, Vol. 13 (1996): 1–25.

Lombardo, Paul A. ed. *A Century of Eugenics in America: From the Indiana Experiment to the Human Genome Era*. Bloomington: Indiana University Press, 2011.

Lutz, Catherine. *The Bases of Empire: The Global Struggle Against U.S. Military Posts*. New York: New York University Press, 2009.

Lutz, Catherine. "The Military Normal." In *The Counter-Counterinsurgency Manual*, edited by Network of Concerned Anthropologists, 23–37. Chicago: Prickly Paradigm Press, 2009.

Malinowski, Bronislaw. *Argonauts of the Western Pacific*. New York: E.P. Dutton, 1966.

Marable, Manning. *How Capitalism Underdeveloped Black America*. Boston: South End Press, 1983.

Marcus, Paul and Alan Rosenberg, eds. *Healing Their Wounds: Psychotherapy with Holocaust Survivors and Their Families*. New York: Praeger Publishers, 1989.

Martinez-Alier, Verena. *Marriage, Class and Colour in Nineteenth-Century Cuba: A Study of Racial Attitudes and Sexual Values in a Slave Society*. Ann Arbor: University of Michigan Press, 1989.

Matteson, John T. "Grave Discussions: The Image of the Sepulchre in Webster, Emerson and Melville." *New England Quarterly*, Vol. 74. No. 3 (2001): 419–446.

Matteson, John. *The Lives of Margaret Fuller: A Biography*. New York: W.W. Norton & Company, 2012.

McCoy, Alfred W. *A Question of Torture: CIA Interrogation, from the Cold War to the War on Terror*. New York: Metropolitan Books, 2006.

McLean, Athena and Annette Leibing, eds. *The Shadow Side of Field Work: Theorizing the Blurred Borders between Ethnography and Life*. Malden, MA and Oxford, UK: Blackwell Publishing, 2007.

McSherry, J. Patrice. *Predatory States: Operation Condor and Covert War in Latin America*. Lanham, MD: Rowan & Littlefield, 2005.

Mendelsohn, Daniel. *The Lost: A Search for Six of Six Million*. New York: HarperCollins Publishers, 2006.

Michlic, Joanna Beata. "Coming to Terms with the 'Dark Past': The Polish Debate About the Jedwabne Massacre. *ACTA 21*. Jerusalem: Hebrew University of Jerusalem (2002): 1–43. http://sicsa.huji.ac.il/actatxt1.html (accessed September 11, 2010).

Michlic, Joanna Beata. *Poland's Threatening Other: The Image of the Jew from 1880 to the Present*. Lincoln: University of Nebraska Press, 2006.

Miller, Arthur. "Tragedy and the Common Man," *New York Times Books*, February 27, 1949. www.nytimes.com/books/00/11/12/specials/miller-common.html?_r=1&scp=1&sq=Arthur%20Miller,%20Tragedy%20and%20the%20Common%20Man&st=cse (accessed February 9, 2012).

Miller, Nancy K. *Bequest and Betrayal: Memoirs of a Parent's Death*. Bloomington: Indiana University Press, 1996.

Miller, Nancy K. *What They Saved: Pieces of a Jewish Past*. Lincoln: University of Nebraska Press, 2011.

Mintz, Alan. *Popular Culture and the Shaping of Holocaust Memory in America*. Seattle: University of Washington Press, 2001.

Mintz, Sidney W. *Worker in the Cane: A Puerto Rican Life History*. New York: W.W. Norton & Company, 1974 (1960).

Mintz, Sidney. *Sweetness and Power: The Place of Sugar in Modern History*. New York: Penguin Books, 1986.

Miron, Dan. 2000. *The Image of the Shtetl and Other Studies of Modern Jewish Literary Imagination*. Syracuse, NY: Syracuse University Press, 2000.

Morley, Morris H., "Reinterpreting the State–Class Relationship: American Corporations and U.S. Policy toward Cuba, 1959–1960." *Comparative Politics*, Vol. 16, No. 1 (1983): 67–83.

Morley, Morris H., *Imperial State and Revolution: The United States and Cuba, 1952–1986*. Cambridge: Cambridge University Press, 1987.

Morley, Morris H. and Chris McGillion. *Cuba, the United States, and the Post-Cold War World: The International Dimensions of the Washington–Havana Relationship*. Gainesville: University Press of Florida, 2005.

Murphy, Marie L. "Claims Against The Republic of Cuba." *University of Miami Law Review*, Vol. 27 (1972–1973): 372–394.

Myerhoff, Barbara. *Number Our Days*. New York: Simon & Schuster, 1978.

National Security Archive. "Bay of Pigs: Forty Years After." Gelman Library, George Washington University. www.gwu.edu/~nsarchiv/bayofpigs/chron.html (accessed January 5, 2012).

Newcomb, Steven T. "The Evidence of Christian Nationalism in Federal Indian Law: The Doctrine of Discovery, Johnson v. McIntosh, and Plenary Power," *N.Y.U. Review of Law and Social Change*, Vol. 20 (1992–1994): 303–341.

Nordstrom, Carolyn. *A Different Kind of War Story*. Philadelphia: University of Pennsylvania, 1997.

Nordstrom, Carolyn, "Terror Warfare and the Medicine of Peace." *Medical Anthropology Quarterly*, Vol. 12, No. 1 (1998): 103–121.

Nordstrom, Carolyn. *Global Outlaws: Crime, Money, and Power in the Contemporary World*. Berkeley: University of California Press, 2007.

Nordstrom, Carolyn. "Global Fractures." In *An Anthropology of War: Views from the Frontline*, edited by Alisse Waterston, 71–86. New York and Oxford: Berghahn Books, 2009.

Orlove, Ben. *In My Father's Study*. Iowa City: University of Iowa Press, 1995.

Ortiz, Fernando. *Cuban Counterpoint: Tobacco and Sugar*. Durham, NC and London: Duke University Press, 1995.

Osborn, Henry Fairfield. "Lo! The Poor Nordic! Professor Osborn's Position on the Immigrant Question," *New York Times*, April 8, 1924: 18. ProQuest Historical Newspapers: *New York Times* (1851–2009).

Panourgiá, Neni. *Dangerous Citizens: The Greek Left and the Terror of the State*. New York: Fordham University Press, 2009.

Panourgiá, Neni. "'...for three days and three nights...' Women, Political Persecution, and Radical Kinship." Paper presented at the annual meeting of the American Anthropological Association, New Orleans, November 18, 2010, 1–8.

Pérez, Louis A. "Toward Dependency and Revolution: The Political Economy of Cuba between Wars, 1878–1895," *Latin American Research Review*, Vol. 18, No. 1 (1983): 127–142.

Pérez-Stable, Marifeli. *The Cuban Revolution: Origins, Course, and Legacy*. Oxford: Oxford University Press, 1999.

Peters, F.E., *The Monotheists: Jews, Christians, and Muslims in Conflict and Competition, Volume I, The Peoples of God*. Princeton, NJ: Princeton University Press, 2003.

Peterson, Spike V., "Feminist Theories Within, Invisible To, and Beyond IR," *Brown Journal of World Affairs*, Vol. X, No. 2 (2004): 35–46.

Petras, James. *Class, State, and Power in the Third World, with Case Studies on Class Conflict in Latin America*. Lanham, MD: Rowman & Littlefield, 1981.

Pfeiffer, Jack B. "Taylor Committee Investigation of the Bay of Pigs, November 8, 1984." www.foia.cia.gov/bay-of-pigs/bop-vol4.pdf (accessed January 5, 2012).

Polonsky, Antony. Introduction to *The Shtetl: Myth and Reality*, edited by Antony Polonsky Polin: Studies in Polish Jewry, Volume 17, 3–23. Oxford: Littman Library of Jewish Civilization, 2004.

Polonsky, Antony, ed. *The Shtetl: Myth and Reality*. Polin: Studies in Polish Jewry, Vol. 17. Oxford: Littman Library of Jewish Civilization, 2004.

Polonsky, Antony. *The Jews in Poland and Russia, Volume I, 1350–1881*. Oxford: Littman Library of Jewish Civilization, 2010.

Polonsky, Antony. *The Jews in Poland and Russia, Volume II, 1881–1914*. Oxford: Littman Library of Jewish Civilization, 2010.

Polonsky, Antony. *The Jews in Poland and Russia, Volume III, 1914–2008*. Oxford: Littman Library of Jewish Civilization, 2012.

Polonsky, Antony, and Joanna B. Michlic, eds. *The Neighbors Respond: The Controversy over the Jedwabne Massacre in Poland*. Princeton, NJ: Princeton University Press, 2004.

Quesada, James. "Suffering Child: An Embodiment of War and Its Aftermath in Post-Sandinista Nicaragua." *Medical Anthropology Quarterly*, Vol. 12, No. 1 (1998): 51–73.

Quesada, James. "The Vicissitudes of Structural Violence: Nicaragua at the Turn of the Twenty-first Century." In *Global Health in Times of Violence*, edited by Barbara Rylko-Bauer, Linda Whiteford, and Paul Farmer, 157–180. Santa Fe, NM: School for Advanced Research Press, 2009.

Reed Danahay, Deborah. *Auto/ethnography: Rewriting the Self and the Social*. Oxford: Berg, 1997.

Reed, David A., "America of the Melting Pot Comes to an End: Effects of New Immigration Described by Senate Sponsor of Bill—Chief Aim, He States, Is To Preserve Racial Type as It Exists Today," *New York Times*, April 27, 1924: XX3. ProQuest Historical Newspapers: *New York Times* (1851–2000).

Reyna, Stephen P. and R.E. Downs, eds. *Deadly Developments: Capitalism, States, and War*. New York: Taylor & Francis, 1999.

Ricoeur, Paul, *Time and Narrative*, Vol. 1. Chicago: University of Chicago Press, 1990.

Ricoeur, Paul. *Memory, History, Forgetting*. Chicago: University of Chicago Press, 2006.

Roosevelt, Theodore. *Presidential Addresses and State Papers: April 14, 1906 to January 14, 1907*, Vol. 5. New York: Kessinger Publishing, 2006.

Rosaldo, Michelle Zimbalist and Louise Lamphere, eds. *Woman, Culture, and Society*. Stanford, CA: Stanford University Press, 1974.

Rushkoff, Douglas. *Nothing Sacred: The Truth about Judaism*. New York: Three Rivers Press, 2004.

Rylko-Bauer, Barbara. "Introduction: Bringing the Past into the Present: Family Narratives of Holocaust, Exile, and Diaspora," *Anthropological Quarterly*, Vol. 78, No. 1 (2005): 7–10.

Rylko-Bauer, Barbara. "Lessons about Humanity and Survival from My Mother and from the Holocaust," *Anthropological Quarterly*, Vol. 78, No. 1 (2005): 11–41.

Rylko-Bauer, Barbara. *A Polish Doctor in the Nazi Camps: My Mother's Memories of Imprisonment, Immigration and a Life Reclaimed*. Norman, OK: Oklahoma University Press, forthcoming, 2014.

Rylko-Bauer, Barbara, Linda Whiteford, and Paul Farmer, eds. Prologue to *Global Health in Times of Violence*, edited by Barbara Rylko-Bauer, Linda Whiteford, and Paul Farmer, 3–16. Santa Fe, NM: School for Advanced Research Press, 2009.

Rylko-Bauer, Barbara, Linda Whiteford, and Paul Farmer, eds. *Global Health in Times of Violence*. Santa Fe, NM: School for Advanced Research Press, 2009.

Said, Edward W. "Reflections on Exile." In *Reflections on Exile and Other Essays*, 173–186. Cambridge: Harvard University Press, 2002.

Sand, Shlomo. *The Invention of the Jewish People*, translated by Yael Lotan. London and New York: Verso, 2009.

Scheper-Hughes, Nancy and Philippe Bourgois, eds. "Introduction: Making Sense of Violence." In *Violence in War and Peace: An Anthology*, edited by Nancy Scheper-Hughes and Philippe Bourgois, 1–31. Malden, MA: Blackwell Publishing, 2004.

Schmitz, David F. *Thank God They're on Our Side: The United States and Right-Wing Dictatorships, 1921–1965*. Chapel Hill: University of North Carolina Press, 1999.

Schwab, Gabriele. "Writing against Memory and Forgetting." *Literature and Medicine*, Vol. 25, No. 1 (2006): 95–121.

Schwartz, Alex F. *Housing Policy in the United States*, second edition. New York: Routledge, 2012.

Scott, David and Charles Hirschkind, eds. *Powers of the Secular Modern: Talal Asad and His Interlocuters*. Stanford, CA: Stanford University Press, 2006.

Shostak, Marjorie. *Nisa: The Life and Words of a !Kung Woman*. New York: Vintage Books, 1981.

Sider, Gerald. "Between Silences and Culture: A Partisan Anthropology." In *Silence: The Currency of Power*, edited by Maria-Luisa Achino-Loeb, 141–157. New York and Oxford: Berghahn Books, 2006.

Smith, Anthony D. *Nationalism: Theory, Ideology, History*. Cambridge: Polity Press, 2010 (2001).

Smith, Ellison DuRant. "Speech on April 9, 1924." *Congressional Record*, 68th Congress, 1st Session, Washington, DC: Government Printing Office, 1924, Vol. 65, 5961–5962.

Solomon, Alisa. "How 'Fiddler' Became Folklore." *Jewish Daily Forward*, September 1, 2006. www.forward.com/articles/1710/#ixzz1Rd5bEoY9 (accessed July 6, 2011).

Solomon, Alisa. "Tevye, Today and Beyond." *Jewish Daily Forward*, September 8, 2006. http://www.forward.com/articles/2422/#ixzz1Rd8isEIV (accessed July 6, 2011).

Spiegelman, Art. *The Complete Maus. A Survivor's Tale*. New York: Pantheon Books, 1997.

Spiro, Jonathan Peter. *Defending the Master Race: Conservation, Eugenics, and the Legacy of Madison Grant*. Lebanon, NH: University of Vermont Press, 2009.

Steedman, Carolyn. *Landscape for a Good Woman: A Story of Two Lives*, New Brunswick, NJ: Rutgers University Press, 2003.

Steiner, George. "The Long Life of Metaphor." In *Writing and the Holocaust*, edited by Berel Lang, 154–171. New York: Holmes & Meier Publishers, 1988.

Strada, Gino. *Green Parrots: A War Surgeon's Diary*. Milan: Edizioni Charta, 2004.

The Immigration Act of 1924 (The Johnson–Reed Act). Office of the Historian. US Department of State. http://history.state.gov/milestones/1921-1936/ImmigrationAct (accessed October 3, 2011).

"The Revolution in Cuba," *Cuba Review and Bulletin*, Vol. IV, No. 10 (September, 1906): 20–22. http://books.google.com/books?id=yx0TAAAAYAAJ&printsec=frontcover&source=gbs_ge_summary_r&cad=0#v=onepage&q=Roosevelt&f=false (accessed January 5, 2013).

Todorov, Tzvetan. *Facing the Extreme: Moral Life in the Concentration Camps*, translated by Arthur Denner and Abigail Pollak. New York: Henry Holt, 1996.

Tokarska-Bakir, Joanna. "Jedwabne: History as Fetish." In *Imaginary Neighbors: Mediating Polish-Jewish Relations after the Holocaust*, edited by Dorota Glowacka and Joanna Zylinska, 40–63. Lincoln: University of Nebraska Press, 2007.

Tokarska-Bakir, Joanna. "You from Jedwabne," in *Making Holocaust Memory*, edited by Gabriel N. Finder, Natlaia Aleksiun, Antony Polonsky, and Jan Schwarz. Studies in Polish Jewry, Vol. 20: 413–428. Oxford: Littman Library of Jewish Civilization, 2008. .

Tzinovitz, Moshe. "Rabbi Meyer Eliyahu Winer," *Yedwabne: History and Memorial Book*. Jerusalem–New York: The Yedwabne Societies in Israel and the United States of America, 1980, 17. www.jewishgen.org/yizkor/jedwabne/yed001.html#17 (accessed July 7, 2005).

Utset, Marial Iglesias. *A Cultural History of Cuba during the U.S. Occupation, 1898–1902/* Translated by Russ Davidson. Chapel Hill: University of North Carolina Press, 2011.

Vishniac, Roman. *Polish Jews*. New York: Schocken, 1947.

Vishniac, Roman. *A Vanished World*. New York: Farrar, Straus & Giroux, 1983.

Wahl, Jenny B. *The Bondsman's Burden: An Economic Analysis of the Common Law of Southern Slavery*. New York: Cambridge University Press, 1998.

Wahl, Jenny. "Slavery in the United States." EH.Net Encyclopedia, edited by Robert Whaples. March 26, 2008. http://eh.net/encyclopedia/article/wahl.slavery.us (accessed October 1, 2011).

Wallerstein, Immanuel. *The Modern World System II: Mercantilism and the Consolidation of the European World-Economy, 1600–1750*. Berkeley: University of California Press, 2011 (1980).

Waserstein Kahn, Samuel and Yehudi Monestel Arce. *La Denuncia. 10 de Julio de 1941*. San José, Costa Rica: Editorial Guayacán Centroamericana, S.A., 2001.

Waterston, Alisse. "The Story of My Story: An Anthropology of Violence, Dispossession and Diaspora." *Anthropological Quarterly* 78, No. 2 (2005): 43–61.

Waterston, Alisse, ed., *An Anthropology of War: Views from the Frontline*. New York and Oxford: Berghahn Books, 2009.

Waterston, Alisse. "Sacred Memory and the Secular World: The Poland Narratives," *Anthropology News*, Vol. 52, No. 6 (September, 2012): 11–12.

Waterston, Alisse. "Sacred Memory and the Secular World: The Poland Narratives." In *War and Peace: Essays on Religion, Violence, and Space*, edited by Bryan S. Turner. London: Anthem Press, 2013: 19–36.

Waterston, Alisse and Barbara Rylko-Bauer. "Out of the Shadows of History and Memory: Personal Family Narratives in Ethnographies of Rediscovery," *American Ethnologist*, Vol. 330, No. 3 (2006): 397–412.

Waterston, Alisse and Barbara Rylko-Bauer. "Out of the Shadows of History and Memory: Personal Family Narratives as Intimate Ethnography." In *The Shadow Side of Field Work: Theorizing the Blurred Borders between Ethnography and Life*, edited by Athena McLean and Annette Leibing, 31–55. Malden, MA and Oxford, UK: Blackwell Publishing, 2010.

Waterston, Louise. "Abraham Cowley: Apostle in Muse's Land." M.A. thesis, University of Puerto Rico, 1980.

Watson, Lawrence C. and Maria-Barbara Watson-Franke. *Interpreting Life Histories: An Anthropological Inquiry*. New Brunswick, NJ: Rutgers University Press, 1985.

Wolf, Eric R. *Peasant Wars of the Twentieth Century*. New York: Harper Torchbooks, 1973.

Wolf, Eric R. *Europe and the People Without History*. Berkeley: University of California Press, 1982.

Wolitz, Seth L. "The Americanization of Tevye or Boarding the Jewish 'Mayflower'." *American Quarterly*, Vol. 40, No. 4 (1988): 514–536.

Woolf, Virginia. *Three Guineas*. New York: Harcourt Brace & Company, 1966 (1938).

Wyden, Peter. *Bay of Pigs: The Untold Story*. New York: Simon & Schuster, 1979.

Wynn, Neil A. *The Afro-American and the Second World War*. Teaneck, NJ: Holmes & Meier, 1993.

Zborowski, Mark and Elizabeth Herzog. *Life Is with People: The Culture of the Shtetl*. New York: Schocken, 1995 (1952).

Zinn, Howard. *On War*. New York: Seven Stories Press, 2001.

Zinn, Howard. *A People's History of the United States*. New York: HarperCollins, 2005.

Zweig, Arnold. *The Face of East European Jewry*. Berkeley: University of California Press, 2004 (1920).

INDEX

Page numbers in **bold** refer to illustrations

 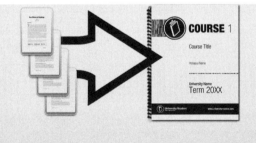